Mometrix
TEST PREPARATION

TExES

Special Education Supplemental (163) Secrets Study Guide

I0880285

Dear Future Exam Success Story

First of all, **THANK YOU** for purchasing Mometrix study materials!

Second, congratulations! You are one of the few determined test-takers who are committed to doing whatever it takes to excel on your exam. **You have come to the right place.** We developed these study materials with one goal in mind: to deliver you the information you need in a format that's concise and easy to use.

In addition to optimizing your guide for the content of the test, we've outlined our recommended steps for breaking down the preparation process into small, attainable goals so you can make sure you stay on track.

We've also analyzed the entire test-taking process, identifying the most common pitfalls and showing how you can overcome them and be ready for any curveball the test throws you.

Standardized testing is one of the biggest obstacles on your road to success, which only increases the importance of doing well in the high-pressure, high-stakes environment of test day. Your results on this test could have a significant impact on your future, and this guide provides the information and practical advice to help you achieve your full potential on test day.

Your success is our success

We would love to hear from you! If you would like to share the story of your exam success or if you have any questions or comments in regard to our products, please contact us at **800-673-8175** or **support@mometrix.com**.

Thanks again for your business and we wish you continued success!

Sincerely,
The Mometrix Test Preparation Team

Need more help? Check out our flashcards at:
http://MometrixFlashcards.com/TExES

TABLE OF CONTENTS

Introduction

Thank you for purchasing this resource! You have made the choice to prepare yourself for a test that could have a huge impact on your future, and this guide is designed to help you be fully ready for test day. Obviously, it's important to have a solid understanding of the test material, but you also need to be prepared for the unique environment and stressors of the test, so that you can perform to the best of your abilities.

For this purpose, the first section that appears in this guide is the **Secret Keys**. We've devoted countless hours to meticulously researching what works and what doesn't, and we've boiled down our findings to the five most impactful steps you can take to improve your performance on the test. We start at the beginning with study planning and move through the preparation process, all the way to the testing strategies that will help you get the most out of what you know when you're finally sitting in front of the test.

We recommend that you start preparing for your test as far in advance as possible. However, if you've bought this guide as a last-minute study resource and only have a few days before your test, we recommend that you skip over the first two Secret Keys since they address a long-term study plan.

If you struggle with **test anxiety**, we strongly encourage you to check out our recommendations for how you can overcome it. Test anxiety is a formidable foe, but it can be beaten, and we want to make sure you have the tools you need to defeat it.

Secret Key #1 – Plan Big, Study Small

There's a lot riding on your performance. If you want to ace this test, you're going to need to keep your skills sharp and the material fresh in your mind. You need a plan that lets you review everything you need to know while still fitting in your schedule. We'll break this strategy down into three categories.

Information Organization

Start with the information you already have: the official test outline. From this, you can make a complete list of all the concepts you need to cover before the test. Organize these concepts into groups that can be studied together, and create a list of any related vocabulary you need to learn so you can brush up on any difficult terms. You'll want to keep this vocabulary list handy once you actually start studying since you may need to add to it along the way.

Time Management

Once you have your set of study concepts, decide how to spread them out over the time you have left before the test. Break your study plan into small, clear goals so you have a manageable task for each day and know exactly what you're doing. Then just focus on one small step at a time. When you manage your time this way, you don't need to spend hours at a time studying. Studying a small block of content for a short period each day helps you retain information better and avoid stressing over how much you have left to do. You can relax knowing that you have a plan to cover everything in time. In order for this strategy to be effective though, you have to start studying early and stick to your schedule. Avoid the exhaustion and futility that comes from last-minute cramming!

Study Environment

The environment you study in has a big impact on your learning. Studying in a coffee shop, while probably more enjoyable, is not likely to be as fruitful as studying in a quiet room. It's important to keep distractions to a minimum. You're only planning to study for a short block of time, so make the most of it. Don't pause to check your phone or get up to find a snack. It's also important to **avoid multitasking**. Research has consistently shown that multitasking will make your studying dramatically less effective. Your study area should also be comfortable and well-lit so you don't have the distraction of straining your eyes or sitting on an uncomfortable chair.

The time of day you study is also important. You want to be rested and alert. Don't wait until just before bedtime. Study when you'll be most likely to comprehend and remember. Even better, if you know what time of day your test will be, set that time aside for study. That way your brain will be used to working on that subject at that specific time and you'll have a better chance of recalling information.

Finally, it can be helpful to team up with others who are studying for the same test. Your actual studying should be done in as isolated an environment as possible, but the work of organizing the information and setting up the study plan can be divided up. In between study sessions, you can discuss with your teammates the concepts that you're all studying and quiz each other on the details. Just be sure that your teammates are as serious about the test as you are. If you find that your study time is being replaced with social time, you might need to find a new team.

Secret Key #2 – Make Your Studying Count

You're devoting a lot of time and effort to preparing for this test, so you want to be absolutely certain it will pay off. This means doing more than just reading the content and hoping you can remember it on test day. It's important to make every minute of study count. There are two main areas you can focus on to make your studying count.

Retention

It doesn't matter how much time you study if you can't remember the material. You need to make sure you are retaining the concepts. To check your retention of the information you're learning, try recalling it at later times with minimal prompting. Try carrying around flashcards and glance at one or two from time to time or ask a friend who's also studying for the test to quiz you.

To enhance your retention, look for ways to put the information into practice so that you can apply it rather than simply recalling it. If you're using the information in practical ways, it will be much easier to remember. Similarly, it helps to solidify a concept in your mind if you're not only reading it to yourself but also explaining it to someone else. Ask a friend to let you teach them about a concept you're a little shaky on (or speak aloud to an imaginary audience if necessary). As you try to summarize, define, give examples, and answer your friend's questions, you'll understand the concepts better and they will stay with you longer. Finally, step back for a big picture view and ask yourself how each piece of information fits with the whole subject. When you link the different concepts together and see them working together as a whole, it's easier to remember the individual components.

Finally, practice showing your work on any multi-step problems, even if you're just studying. Writing out each step you take to solve a problem will help solidify the process in your mind, and you'll be more likely to remember it during the test.

Modality

Modality simply refers to the means or method by which you study. Choosing a study modality that fits your own individual learning style is crucial. No two people learn best in exactly the same way, so it's important to know your strengths and use them to your advantage.

For example, if you learn best by visualization, focus on visualizing a concept in your mind and draw an image or a diagram. Try color-coding your notes, illustrating them, or creating symbols that will trigger your mind to recall a learned concept. If you learn best by hearing or discussing information, find a study partner who learns the same way or read aloud to yourself. Think about how to put the information in your own words. Imagine that you are giving a lecture on the topic and record yourself so you can listen to it later.

For any learning style, flashcards can be helpful. Organize the information so you can take advantage of spare moments to review. Underline key words or phrases. Use different colors for different categories. Mnemonic devices (such as creating a short list in which every item starts with the same letter) can also help with retention. Find what works best for you and use it to store the information in your mind most effectively and easily.

Secret Key #3 – Practice the Right Way

Your success on test day depends not only on how many hours you put into preparing, but also on whether you prepared the right way. It's good to check along the way to see if your studying is paying off. One of the most effective ways to do this is by taking practice tests to evaluate your progress. Practice tests are useful because they show exactly where you need to improve. Every time you take a practice test, pay special attention to these three groups of questions:

- The questions you got wrong
- The questions you had to guess on, even if you guessed right
- The questions you found difficult or slow to work through

This will show you exactly what your weak areas are, and where you need to devote more study time. Ask yourself why each of these questions gave you trouble. Was it because you didn't understand the material? Was it because you didn't remember the vocabulary? Do you need more repetitions on this type of question to build speed and confidence? Dig into those questions and figure out how you can strengthen your weak areas as you go back to review the material.

Additionally, many practice tests have a section explaining the answer choices. It can be tempting to read the explanation and think that you now have a good understanding of the concept. However, an explanation likely only covers part of the question's broader context. Even if the explanation makes perfect sense, **go back and investigate** every concept related to the question until you're positive you have a thorough understanding.

As you go along, keep in mind that the practice test is just that: practice. Memorizing these questions and answers will not be very helpful on the actual test because it is unlikely to have any of the same exact questions. If you only know the right answers to the sample questions, you won't be prepared for the real thing. **Study the concepts** until you understand them fully, and then you'll be able to answer any question that shows up on the test.

It's important to wait on the practice tests until you're ready. If you take a test on your first day of study, you may be overwhelmed by the amount of material covered and how much you need to learn. Work up to it gradually.

On test day, you'll need to be prepared for answering questions, managing your time, and using the test-taking strategies you've learned. It's a lot to balance, like a mental marathon that will have a big impact on your future. Like training for a marathon, you'll need to start slowly and work your way up. When test day arrives, you'll be ready.

Start with the strategies you've read in the first two Secret Keys—plan your course and study in the way that works best for you. If you have time, consider using multiple study resources to get different approaches to the same concepts. It can be helpful to see difficult concepts from more than one angle. Then find a good source for practice tests. Many times, the test website will suggest potential study resources or provide sample tests.

Practice Test Strategy

If you're able to find at least three practice tests, we recommend this strategy:

Untimed and Open-Book Practice

Take the first test with no time constraints and with your notes and study guide handy. Take your time and focus on applying the strategies you've learned.

Timed and Open-Book Practice

Take the second practice test open-book as well, but set a timer and practice pacing yourself to finish in time.

Timed and Closed-Book Practice

Take any other practice tests as if it were test day. Set a timer and put away your study materials. Sit at a table or desk in a quiet room, imagine yourself at the testing center, and answer questions as quickly and accurately as possible.

Keep repeating timed and closed-book tests on a regular basis until you run out of practice tests or it's time for the actual test. Your mind will be ready for the schedule and stress of test day, and you'll be able to focus on recalling the material you've learned.

Secret Key #4 – Pace Yourself

Once you're fully prepared for the material on the test, your biggest challenge on test day will be managing your time. Just knowing that the clock is ticking can make you panic even if you have plenty of time left. Work on pacing yourself so you can build confidence against the time constraints of the exam. Pacing is a difficult skill to master, especially in a high-pressure environment, so **practice is vital**.

Set time expectations for your pace based on how much time is available. For example, if a section has 60 questions and the time limit is 30 minutes, you know you have to average 30 seconds or less per question in order to answer them all. Although 30 seconds is the hard limit, set 25 seconds per question as your goal, so you reserve extra time to spend on harder questions. When you budget extra time for the harder questions, you no longer have any reason to stress when those questions take longer to answer.

Don't let this time expectation distract you from working through the test at a calm, steady pace, but keep it in mind so you don't spend too much time on any one question. Recognize that taking extra time on one question you don't understand may keep you from answering two that you do understand later in the test. If your time limit for a question is up and you're still not sure of the answer, mark it and move on, and come back to it later if the time and the test format allow. If the testing format doesn't allow you to return to earlier questions, just make an educated guess; then put it out of your mind and move on.

On the easier questions, be careful not to rush. It may seem wise to hurry through them so you have more time for the challenging ones, but it's not worth missing one if you know the concept and just didn't take the time to read the question fully. Work efficiently but make sure you understand the question and have looked at all of the answer choices, since more than one may seem right at first.

Even if you're paying attention to the time, you may find yourself a little behind at some point. You should speed up to get back on track, but do so wisely. Don't panic; just take a few seconds less on each question until you're caught up. Don't guess without thinking, but do look through the answer choices and eliminate any you know are wrong. If you can get down to two choices, it is often worthwhile to guess from those. Once you've chosen an answer, move on and don't dwell on any that you skipped or had to hurry through. If a question was taking too long, chances are it was one of the harder ones, so you weren't as likely to get it right anyway.

On the other hand, if you find yourself getting ahead of schedule, it may be beneficial to slow down a little. The more quickly you work, the more likely you are to make a careless mistake that will affect your score. You've budgeted time for each question, so don't be afraid to spend that time. Practice an efficient but careful pace to get the most out of the time you have.

Secret Key #5 – Have a Plan for Guessing

When you're taking the test, you may find yourself stuck on a question. Some of the answer choices seem better than others, but you don't see the one answer choice that is obviously correct. What do you do?

The scenario described above is very common, yet most test takers have not effectively prepared for it. Developing and practicing a plan for guessing may be one of the single most effective uses of your time as you get ready for the exam.

In developing your plan for guessing, there are three questions to address:

- When should you start the guessing process?
- How should you narrow down the choices?
- Which answer should you choose?

When to Start the Guessing Process

Unless your plan for guessing is to select C every time (which, despite its merits, is not what we recommend), you need to leave yourself enough time to apply your answer elimination strategies. Since you have a limited amount of time for each question, that means that if you're going to give yourself the best shot at guessing correctly, you have to decide quickly whether or not you will guess.

Of course, the best-case scenario is that you don't have to guess at all, so first, see if you can answer the question based on your knowledge of the subject and basic reasoning skills. Focus on the key words in the question and try to jog your memory of related topics. Give yourself a chance to bring the knowledge to mind, but once you realize that you don't have (or you can't access) the knowledge you need to answer the question, it's time to start the guessing process.

It's almost always better to start the guessing process too early than too late. It only takes a few seconds to remember something and answer the question from knowledge. Carefully eliminating wrong answer choices takes longer. Plus, going through the process of eliminating answer choices can actually help jog your memory.

Summary: Start the guessing process as soon as you decide that you can't answer the question based on your knowledge.

How to Narrow Down the Choices

The next chapter in this book (**Test-Taking Strategies**) includes a wide range of strategies for how to approach questions and how to look for answer choices to eliminate. You will definitely want to read those carefully, practice them, and figure out which ones work best for you. Here though, we're going to address a mindset rather than a particular strategy.

Your odds of guessing an answer correctly depend on how many options you are choosing from.

Number of options left	5	4	3	2	1
Odds of guessing correctly	20%	25%	33%	50%	100%

You can see from this chart just how valuable it is to be able to eliminate incorrect answers and make an educated guess, but there are two things that many test takers do that cause them to miss out on the benefits of guessing:

- Accidentally eliminating the correct answer
- Selecting an answer based on an impression

We'll look at the first one here, and the second one in the next section.

To avoid accidentally eliminating the correct answer, we recommend a thought exercise called **the $5 challenge**. In this challenge, you only eliminate an answer choice from contention if you are willing to bet $5 on it being wrong. Why $5? Five dollars is a small but not insignificant amount of money. It's an amount you could afford to lose but wouldn't want to throw away. And while losing $5 once might not hurt too much, doing it twenty times will set you back $100. In the same way, each small decision you make—eliminating a choice here, guessing on a question there—won't by itself impact your score very much, but when you put them all together, they can make a big difference. By holding each answer choice elimination decision to a higher standard, you can reduce the risk of accidentally eliminating the correct answer.

The $5 challenge can also be applied in a positive sense: If you are willing to bet $5 that an answer choice *is* correct, go ahead and mark it as correct.

Summary: Only eliminate an answer choice if you are willing to bet $5 that it is wrong.

Which Answer to Choose

You're taking the test. You've run into a hard question and decided you'll have to guess. You've eliminated all the answer choices you're willing to bet $5 on. Now you have to pick an answer. Why do we even need to talk about this? Why can't you just pick whichever one you feel like when the time comes?

The answer to these questions is that if you don't come into the test with a plan, you'll rely on your impression to select an answer choice, and if you do that, you risk falling into a trap. The test writers know that everyone who takes their test will be guessing on some of the questions, so they intentionally write wrong answer choices to seem plausible. You still have to pick an answer though, and if the wrong answer choices are designed to look right, how can you ever be sure that you're not falling for their trap? The best solution we've found to this dilemma is to take the decision out of your hands entirely. Here is the process we recommend:

Once you've eliminated any choices that you are confident (willing to bet $5) are wrong, select the first remaining choice as your answer.

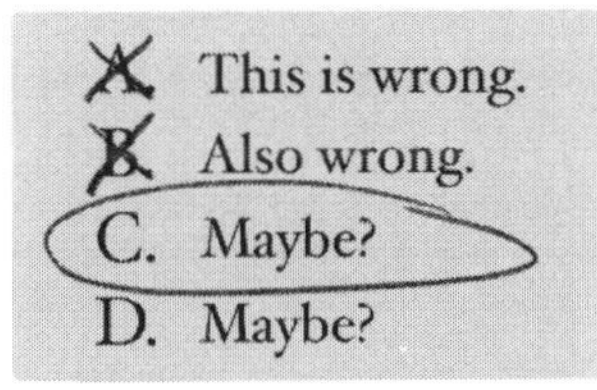

Whether you choose to select the first remaining choice, the second, or the last, the important thing is that you use some preselected standard. Using this approach guarantees that you will not be enticed into selecting an answer choice that looks right, because you are not basing your decision on how the answer choices look.

This is not meant to make you question your knowledge. Instead, it is to help you recognize the difference between your knowledge and your impressions. There's a huge difference between thinking an answer is right because of what you know, and thinking an answer is right because it looks or sounds like it should be right.

Summary: To ensure that your selection is appropriately random, make a predetermined selection from among all answer choices you have not eliminated.

Test-Taking Strategies

This section contains a list of test-taking strategies that you may find helpful as you work through the test. By taking what you know and applying logical thought, you can maximize your chances of answering any question correctly!

It is very important to realize that every question is different and every person is different: no single strategy will work on every question, and no single strategy will work for every person. That's why we've included all of them here, so you can try them out and determine which ones work best for different types of questions and which ones work best for you.

Question Strategies

READ CAREFULLY

Read the question and the answer choices carefully. Don't miss the question because you misread the terms. You have plenty of time to read each question thoroughly and make sure you understand what is being asked. Yet a happy medium must be attained, so don't waste too much time. You must read carefully and efficiently.

CONTEXTUAL CLUES

Look for contextual clues. If the question includes a word you are not familiar with, look at the immediate context for some indication of what the word might mean. Contextual clues can often give you all the information you need to decipher the meaning of an unfamiliar word. Even if you can't determine the meaning, you may be able to narrow down the possibilities enough to make a solid guess at the answer to the question.

PREFIXES

If you're having trouble with a word in the question or answer choices, try dissecting it. Take advantage of every clue that the word might include. Prefixes can be a huge help. Usually, they allow you to determine a basic meaning. *Pre-* means before, *post-* means after, *pro-* is positive, *de-* is negative. From prefixes, you can get an idea of the general meaning of the word and try to put it into context.

HEDGE WORDS

Watch out for critical hedge words, such as *likely, may, can, often, almost, mostly, usually, generally, rarely,* and *sometimes.* Question writers insert these hedge phrases to cover every possibility. Often an answer choice will be wrong simply because it leaves no room for exception. Be on guard for answer choices that have definitive words such as *exactly* and *always.*

SWITCHBACK WORDS

Stay alert for *switchbacks.* These are the words and phrases frequently used to alert you to shifts in thought. The most common switchback words are *but, although,* and *however.* Others include *nevertheless, on the other hand, even though, while, in spite of, despite,* and *regardless of.* Switchback words are important to catch because they can change the direction of the question or an answer choice.

⊘ FACE VALUE

When in doubt, use common sense. Accept the situation in the problem at face value. Don't read too much into it. These problems will not require you to make wild assumptions. If you have to go beyond creativity and warp time or space in order to have an answer choice fit the question, then you should move on and consider the other answer choices. These are normal problems rooted in reality. The applicable relationship or explanation may not be readily apparent, but it is there for you to figure out. Use your common sense to interpret anything that isn't clear.

Answer Choice Strategies

⊘ ANSWER SELECTION

The most thorough way to pick an answer choice is to identify and eliminate wrong answers until only one is left, then confirm it is the correct answer. Sometimes an answer choice may immediately seem right, but be careful. The test writers will usually put more than one reasonable answer choice on each question, so take a second to read all of them and make sure that the other choices are not equally obvious. As long as you have time left, it is better to read every answer choice than to pick the first one that looks right without checking the others.

⊘ ANSWER CHOICE FAMILIES

An answer choice family consists of two (in rare cases, three) answer choices that are very similar in construction and cannot all be true at the same time. If you see two answer choices that are direct opposites or parallels, one of them is usually the correct answer. For instance, if one answer choice says that quantity *x* increases and another either says that quantity *x* decreases (opposite) or says that quantity *y* increases (parallel), then those answer choices would fall into the same family. An answer choice that doesn't match the construction of the answer choice family is more likely to be incorrect. Most questions will not have answer choice families, but when they do appear, you should be prepared to recognize them.

⊘ ELIMINATE ANSWERS

Eliminate answer choices as soon as you realize they are wrong, but make sure you consider all possibilities. If you are eliminating answer choices and realize that the last one you are left with is also wrong, don't panic. Start over and consider each choice again. There may be something you missed the first time that you will realize on the second pass.

⊘ AVOID FACT TRAPS

Don't be distracted by an answer choice that is factually true but doesn't answer the question. You are looking for the choice that answers the question. Stay focused on what the question is asking for so you don't accidentally pick an answer that is true but incorrect. Always go back to the question and make sure the answer choice you've selected actually answers the question and is not merely a true statement.

⊘ EXTREME STATEMENTS

In general, you should avoid answers that put forth extreme actions as standard practice or proclaim controversial ideas as established fact. An answer choice that states the "process should be used in certain situations, if..." is much more likely to be correct than one that states the "process should be discontinued completely." The first is a calm rational statement and doesn't even make a definitive, uncompromising stance, using a hedge word *if* to provide wiggle room, whereas the second choice is far more extreme.

✓ BENCHMARK

As you read through the answer choices and you come across one that seems to answer the question well, mentally select that answer choice. This is not your final answer, but it's the one that will help you evaluate the other answer choices. The one that you selected is your benchmark or standard for judging each of the other answer choices. Every other answer choice must be compared to your benchmark. That choice is correct until proven otherwise by another answer choice beating it. If you find a better answer, then that one becomes your new benchmark. Once you've decided that no other choice answers the question as well as your benchmark, you have your final answer.

✓ PREDICT THE ANSWER

Before you even start looking at the answer choices, it is often best to try to predict the answer. When you come up with the answer on your own, it is easier to avoid distractions and traps because you will know exactly what to look for. The right answer choice is unlikely to be word-for-word what you came up with, but it should be a close match. Even if you are confident that you have the right answer, you should still take the time to read each option before moving on.

General Strategies

✓ TOUGH QUESTIONS

If you are stumped on a problem or it appears too hard or too difficult, don't waste time. Move on! Remember though, if you can quickly check for obviously incorrect answer choices, your chances of guessing correctly are greatly improved. Before you completely give up, at least try to knock out a couple of possible answers. Eliminate what you can and then guess at the remaining answer choices before moving on.

✓ CHECK YOUR WORK

Since you will probably not know every term listed and the answer to every question, it is important that you get credit for the ones that you do know. Don't miss any questions through careless mistakes. If at all possible, try to take a second to look back over your answer selection and make sure you've selected the correct answer choice and haven't made a costly careless mistake (such as marking an answer choice that you didn't mean to mark). This quick double check should more than pay for itself in caught mistakes for the time it costs.

✓ PACE YOURSELF

It's easy to be overwhelmed when you're looking at a page full of questions; your mind is confused and full of random thoughts, and the clock is ticking down faster than you would like. Calm down and maintain the pace that you have set for yourself. Especially as you get down to the last few minutes of the test, don't let the small numbers on the clock make you panic. As long as you are on track by monitoring your pace, you are guaranteed to have time for each question.

✓ DON'T RUSH

It is very easy to make errors when you are in a hurry. Maintaining a fast pace in answering questions is pointless if it makes you miss questions that you would have gotten right otherwise. Test writers like to include distracting information and wrong answers that seem right. Taking a little extra time to avoid careless mistakes can make all the difference in your test score. Find a pace that allows you to be confident in the answers that you select.

⊘ KEEP MOVING

Panicking will not help you pass the test, so do your best to stay calm and keep moving. Taking deep breaths and going through the answer elimination steps you practiced can help to break through a stress barrier and keep your pace.

Final Notes

The combination of a solid foundation of content knowledge and the confidence that comes from practicing your plan for applying that knowledge is the key to maximizing your performance on test day. As your foundation of content knowledge is built up and strengthened, you'll find that the strategies included in this chapter become more and more effective in helping you quickly sift through the distractions and traps of the test to isolate the correct answer.

Now that you're preparing to move forward into the test content chapters of this book, be sure to keep your goal in mind. As you read, think about how you will be able to apply this information on the test. If you've already seen sample questions for the test and you have an idea of the question format and style, try to come up with questions of your own that you can answer based on what you're reading. This will give you valuable practice applying your knowledge in the same ways you can expect to on test day.

Good luck and good studying!

Understanding Individuals with Disabilities and Evaluating Their Needs

Transform passive reading into active learning! After immersing yourself in this chapter, put your comprehension to the test by taking a quiz. The insights you gained will stay with you longer this way. Scan the QR code to go directly to the chapter quiz interface for this study guide. If you're using a computer, simply visit the online resources page at **mometrix.com/resources719/texesspedsupp** and click the Chapter Quizzes link.

Overview of Human Developmental Theories

Issues of Human Development

Historically, there have been a number of arguments that theories of human development seek to address. These ideas generally lie on a spectrum but are often essential concepts involved in developmental theories. For instance, the nature vs. nurture debate is a key concept involved in behaviorist camps of development, insisting that a substantial portion of a child's development may be attributed to his or her social environment.

- **Universality vs. context specificity**: Universality implies that all individuals will develop in the same way, no matter what culture they live in. Context specificity implies that development will be influenced by the culture in which the individual lives.
- **Assumptions about human nature** (three doctrines: original sin, innate purity, and tabula rasa):
  - Original sin says that children are inherently bad and must be taught to be good.
  - Innate purity says that children are inherently good.
  - Tabula rasa says that children are born as "blank slates" without good or bad tendencies and can be taught right and wrong.
- **Behavioral consistency**: Children either behave in the same manner no matter what the situation or setting or they change their behavior depending on the setting and who is interacting with them.
- **Nature vs. nurture**: Nature refers to the genetic influences on development. Nurture refers to the environmental and social influences on development.
- **Continuity vs. discontinuity**: Continuity states that development progresses at a steady rate and that the effects of change are cumulative. Discontinuity states that development progresses in a stair-step fashion and that the effects of early development have no bearing on later development.
- **Passivity vs. activity**: Passivity refers to development being influenced by outside forces. Activity refers to development influenced by the child him or herself and how he or she responds to external forces.
- **Critical vs. sensitive period**: The critical period is the window of time when the child will be able to acquire new skills and behaviors. The sensitive period refers to a flexible time period when a child will be receptive to learning new skills, even if it is later than the norm.

Theoretical Schools of Thought on Human Development

- **Behaviorist Theory** – This philosophy discusses development in terms of conditioning. As children interact with their environments, they learn what behaviors result in rewards or punishments and develop patterns of behaviors as a result. This school of thought lies heavily within the nurture side of the nature/nurture debate, arguing that children's personalities and behaviors are a product of their environments.
- **Constructivist Theory** – This philosophy describes the process of learning as one in which individuals build or construct their understanding from their prior knowledge and experiences in an environment. In constructivist thought, individuals can synthesize their old information to generate new ideas. This school of thought is similar to behaviorism in that the social environment plays a large role in learning. Constructivism, however, places greater emphasis on the individual's active role in the learning process, such as the ability to generate ideas about something an individual has not experienced directly.
- **Ecological Systems Theory** – This philosophy focuses on the social environments in and throughout a person's life. Ecological systems theorists attempt to account for all of the complexities of various aspects of a person's life, starting with close relationships, such as family and friends, and zooming out into broader social contexts, including interactions with school, communities, and media. Alongside these various social levels, ecological systems discuss the roles of ethnicity, geography, and socioeconomic status in development across a person's lifespan.
- **Maturationist Theory** – This philosophy largely focuses on the natural disposition of a child to learn. Maturationists lean heavily into the nature side of the nature/nurture argument and say that humans are predisposed to learning and development. As a result, maturationists propose that early development should only be passively supported.
- **Psychoanalytic Theory** – Psychoanalytic theorists generally argue that beneath the conscious interaction with the world, individuals have underlying, subconscious thoughts that affect their active emotions and behaviors. These subconscious thoughts are built from previous experiences, including developmental milestones and past traumas. These subconscious thoughts interact with conscious thoughts to form a person's desires, personality, attitudes, and habits.

Freud's Psychosexual Developmental Theory

Sigmund Freud was a neurologist who founded the psychoanalytic school of thought. He described the distinction between the conscious and unconscious mind and the effects of the unconscious mind on personality and behavior. He also developed a concept of stages of development, in which an individual encounters various conflicts or crises, called psychosexual stages of development. The way in which an individual handles these crises were thought to shape the individual's personality over the course of life. This general formula heavily influenced other psychoanalytic theories.

Erikson's Psychosocial Developmental Theory

Eric Erikson's psychosocial development theory was an expansion and revision of Freud's psychosexual stages. Erikson describes eight stages in which an individual is presented with a crisis, such as an infant learning to trust or mistrust his or her parents to provide. The choice to trust or mistrust is not binary, but is on a spectrum. According to the theory, the individual's resolution of the crisis largely carries through the rest of his or her life. Handling each of the eight conflicts well theoretically leads to a healthy development of personality. The conflicts are spaced out throughout life, beginning at infancy and ending at death.

Kohlberg's Stages of Moral Development

Kohlberg's stages of moral development are heavily influenced by Erikson's stages. He describes three larger levels of moral development with substages. In the first level, the **preconventional level**, morality is fully externally controlled by authorities and is motivated by the avoidance of punishment and pursuit of rewards. In the second level, the **conventional level**, the focus shifts to laws, social factors, and the pursuit of being seen by others as good or nice. In the third and final level, the **postconventional** or **principled level**, the individual looks beyond laws and social obligations to more complex situational considerations. A person in this stage might consider that a law may not always be the best for individuals or society and that a particular situation may warrant breaking the rule for the true good.

George Herbert Mead's Play and Game Stage Development Theory

George Herbert Mead was a sociologist and psychologist who described learning by stepping into **social roles**. According to his theory, children first interact with the world by imitating and playing by themselves. While engaged in this play, a child can experiment with concepts. Mead describes this development in terms of three stages characterized by increasing complexity of play. A child in the **preparatory stage** can **play** pretend and learn cooking concepts by pretending to cook. As a child develops socially, he or she learns to step in and out of increasingly abstract and complex **roles** and includes more interaction. This is known as the **play stage**, including early interactive roles. For instance, children may play "cops and robbers," which are more symbolically significant roles because they are not natural roles for children to play in society. As social understanding develops, children enter the **game stage**, in which the child can understand his or her own role and the roles of others in a game. In this stage, children can participate in more complex activities with highly structured rules. An example of a complex game is baseball, in which each individual playing has a unique and complex role to play. These stages are thought to contribute to an individual's ability to understand complex social roles in adulthood.

Ivan Pavlov

Ivan Pavlov was a predecessor to the behaviorist school and is credited with being the first to observe the process of classical conditioning, also known as Pavlovian conditioning. Pavlov observed that dogs would begin salivating at the sound of a bell because they were conditioned to expect food when they heard a bell ring. According to classical conditioning, by introducing a neutral stimulus (such as a bell) to a naturally significant stimulus (such as the sight of food), the neutral stimulus will begin to create a conditioned response on its own.

John B. Watson

Watson is credited as the founder of behaviorism and worked to expand the knowledge base of conditioning. He is famous for his experiments, including highly unethical experiments such as the "Little Albert" experiment in which he used classical conditioning to cause an infant to fear animals that he was unfamiliar with. Watson proposed that psychology should focus only on observable behaviors.

B.F. Skinner

Skinner expanded on Watson's work in behaviorism. His primary contributions to behaviorism included studying the effect of **reinforcement** and **punishment** on particular behaviors. He noted that stimuli can be both additive or subtractive and may be used to either increase or decrease behavior frequency and strengths.

Lev Vygotsky

Vygotsky's sociocultural theory describes development as a social process in which individuals mediate knowledge through social interactions and can learn by interacting with and watching others. Vygotsky's ideas have been widely adopted in the field of education, most notably his theory of the **zone of proximal development**. This theory describes three levels of an individual's ability to do tasks, including completely incapable of performing a task, capable with assistance, and independently capable. As an individual's experience grows, he or she should progress from less capable and independent to more capable and independent.

> **Review Video: Instructional Scaffolding**
> Visit mometrix.com/academy and enter code: 989759

Bandura's Social Learning Theory

Albert Bandura's social learning theory argues against some of the behaviorist thoughts that a person has to experience stimulus and response to learn behaviors and, instead, posits that an individual can learn from other peoples' social interactions. Bandura would say that most learning takes place from observing and predicting social behavior, not through direct experience. This becomes a more efficient system for learning because people are able to learn information more synthetically.

Bowlby's Attachment Theory

Bowlby's attachment theory describes the impact that early connections have on lifelong development. Working from an evolutionary framework, Bowlby described how infants are predisposed to be attached to their caregivers because this increases chance of survival. According to Bowlby's theory, infants are predisposed to stay close to known caregivers and use them as a frame of reference to help with learning what is socially acceptable and what is safe.

Piaget's Cognitive Development Theory

Piaget's theory of cognitive development describes how as individuals develop, their cognitive processes are able to become more complex and abstract. In the early stages, an infant may be able to recognize an item, such as a glass of water, on sight only. As that individual grows, he or she is able to think, compare, and eventually develop abstract thoughts about that concept. According to Piaget, this development takes place in all individuals in predictable stages.

Maslow's Hierarchy of Needs

Maslow defined human motivation in terms of needs and wants. His **hierarchy of needs** is classically portrayed as a pyramid sitting on its base divided into horizontal layers. He theorized that, as humans fulfill the needs of one layer, their motivation turns to the layer above. The layers consist of (from bottom to top):

- **Physiological**: The need for air, fluid, food, shelter, warmth, and sleep
- **Safety**: A safe place to live, a steady job, a society with rules and laws, protection from harm, and insurance or savings for the future
- **Love/belonging**: A network consisting of a significant other, family, friends, co-workers, religion, and community
- **Esteem or self-respect**: The knowledge that you are a person who is successful and worthy of esteem, attention, status, and admiration

- **Self-actualization**: The acceptance of your life, choices, and situation in life and the empathetic acceptance of others, as well as the feeling of independence and the joy of being able to express yourself freely and competently

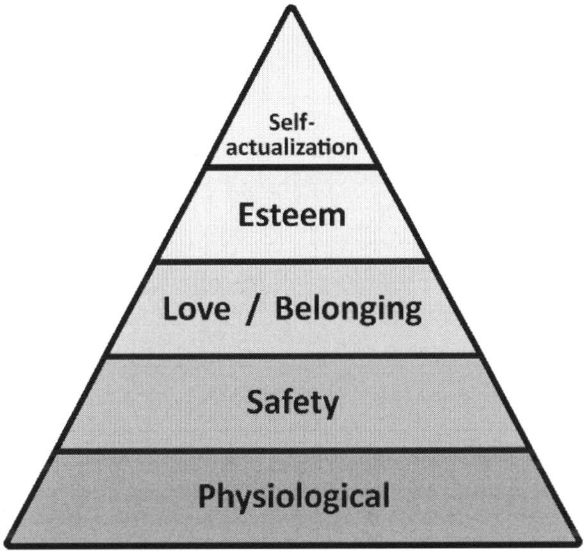

Review Video: Maslow's Hierarchy of Needs
Visit mometrix.com/academy and enter code: 461825

Cognitive Development

Piaget's Theory of Cognitive Development

Jean Piaget's theory of cognitive development consists of four stages that a child moves through throughout life. The four stages are the **sensorimotor stage** (birth-2 years), **preoperational stage** (2-7 years), **concrete operational stage** (7-11 years), and **formal operational stage** (12 years and beyond). Piaget believed that the way children think changes as they pass through these stages. In the **sensorimotor stage**, infants exist in the present moment and investigate their world for the first time through their senses, reflexes, and actions. Key skills infants acquire during this stage include object permanence and self-recognition. In the **preoperational stage**, children learn to express ideas symbolically, including through language and pretend play. Markers of this stage include engaging in animism, egocentrism, and the inability to understand conservation (the knowledge that the quantity of something does not change when its appearance does). In the **concrete operational stage**, children develop logical thought and begin understanding conservation. The **formal operational stage** brings the ability to think abstractly and hypothetically. Piaget believed that children learn through experimenting and building upon knowledge from experiences. He asserted that educators should be highly qualified and trained to create experiences that support development in each of these stages.

Review Video: Piaget's Cognitive Development Theory
Visit mometrix.com/academy and enter code: 100376

Skills Typically Acquired at Each Stage of Cognitive Development

- **Sensorimotor:** Children in the sensorimotor stage gain an increasing awareness of their bodies and the world around them and acquire a wide range of skills as they mature from infancy to toddlerhood. Early skills at this stage include sucking, tasting, smiling, basic vocalizations, and **gross motor skills** such as kicking and grasping. These skills increase in complexity over time and come to include abilities such as throwing and dropping objects, crawling, walking, and using simple words or phrases to communicate. As children near the end of this stage, they are typically able to exhibit skills such as stacking, basic problem solving, planning methods to achieve a task, and attempting to engage in daily routines, such as dressing themselves or brushing their hair.
- **Preoperational:** This stage is marked by significant leaps in **cognition** and **gross motor skills**. Children in the preoperational stage are able to use increasingly complex language to communicate, and they develop skills like jumping, running, and climbing as they gain increasing control over their bodies. Preoperational children begin learning the basic categorization of alike objects, such as animals, flowers, or foods. This stage is also characterized by the development of pretend play and includes skills such as creating imaginary friends, role playing, and using toys or objects to symbolize something else, such as using a box as a pretend house.
- **Concrete operational:** In this stage, children begin developing **logical reasoning** skills that allow them to perform increasingly complex tasks. Concrete operational children are able to distinguish subcategories, including types of animals, foods, or flowers, and can organize items in ascending or descending order based upon characteristics like height, weight, or size. Children at this stage develop the understanding that altering the appearance of an object or substance does not change the amount of it. A classic example of this is the understanding that liquid transferred from one container to another retains its volume. This concept is known as **conservation**.
- **Formal operational:** The formal operational stage is characterized by the development of **abstract** and **hypothetical** cognitive skills. Children at this stage are able to solve increasingly complex math equations, hypothesize and strategically devise a plan for engaging in science experiments, and develop creative solutions to problems. They are also able to theorize potential outcomes to hypothetical situations as well as consider the nuances of differing values, beliefs, morals, and ethics.

Substages of the Sensorimotor Stage

Piaget's sensorimotor stage is divided into six substages. In each, infants develop new skills for representing and interacting with their world. In the first substage, infants interact **reflexively** and involuntarily to stimuli in the form of muscle jerking when startled, sucking, and gripping. Subsequent stages are circular, or repetitive, in nature and are based on interactions with the self and, increasingly, the environment. **Primary circular reactions**, or intentionally repeated actions, comprise the second substage. Infants notice their actions and sounds and purposefully repeat them, but these actions do not extend past the infant's body. Interaction with the environment begins in the third substage as infants engage in **secondary circular reactions**. Here, infants learn that they can interact with and manipulate objects within their environment to create an effect, such as a sound from pressing a button. They then repeat the action and experience joy in this ability. In the fourth substage, secondary circular reactions become coordinated as infants begin planning movements and actions to create an effect. **Tertiary circular reactions** allow for exploration in the fifth substage, as infants start experimenting with cause and effect. In the sixth substage, infants begin engaging in **representational thought** and recall information from memory.

Examples of Primary, Secondary, and Tertiary Circular Reactions

The following are some common examples of primary, secondary, and tertiary circular reactions:

- **Primary:** Primary circular reactions are repeated **bodily** actions that the infant finds enjoyable. Such actions include thumb sucking, placing hands or feet in the mouth, kicking, and making basic vocalizations.
- **Secondary:** Secondary circular reactions refer to repeated enjoyable interactions between the infant and objects within their **environment** in order to elicit a specific response. Such actions include grasping objects, rattling toys, hitting buttons to hear specific sounds, banging two objects together, or reaching out to touch various items.
- **Tertiary:** Tertiary circular reactions are intentional and planned actions using objects within the environment to **achieve a particular outcome**. Examples include stacking blocks and knocking them down, taking toys out of a bin and putting them back, or engaging in a repeated behavior to gauge a caretaker's reaction each time.

Defining Characteristics of the Preoperational Stage of Development

The preoperational stage of development refers to the stage before a child can exercise operational thought and is associated with several defining characteristics including **pretend play**, **animism**, and **egocentrism**. As children learn to think and express themselves symbolically, they engage in pretend play as a means of organizing, understanding, and representing the world around them as they experience it. During this stage, children do not understand the difference between inanimate and animate objects and thus demonstrate animism, or the attribution of lifelike qualities to inanimate objects. Egocentrism refers to the child's inability to understand the distinction between him or herself and others and, consequentially, the inability to understand the thoughts, perspectives, and feelings of others. During the preoperational stage, the brain is not developed enough to understand **conservation**, which is the understanding that the quantity of something does not change just because its appearance changes. Thus, children in this stage exhibit **centration**, or the focusing on only one aspect of something at a time. Additionally, children struggle with **classification** during this stage, as they are not cognitively developed enough to understand that an object can be classified in multiple ways.

Milestones Achieved During the Concrete Operational Stage of Development

The concrete operational stage marks the beginning of a child's ability to think logically about the concrete world. In this stage, children develop many of the skills they lacked in the preoperational phase. For example, egocentrism fades as children in this stage begin to develop empathy and understand others' perspectives. Additionally, they develop an understanding of conservation, or the idea that the quantity of something does not change with its appearance. Children in this stage begin to learn to classify objects in more than one way and can categorize them based on a variety of characteristics. This allows them to practice **seriation**, or the arranging of objects based on quantitative measures.

Development of Cognitive Abilities in the Formal Operational Stage

In the formal operational stage, children can think beyond the concrete world and in terms of abstract thoughts and hypothetical situations. They develop the ability to consider various outcomes of events and can think more creatively about solutions to problems than in previous stages. This advanced cognitive ability contributes to the development of personal identity. In considering abstract and hypothetical ideas, children begin to formulate opinions and develop personal stances on intangible concepts, thus establishing individual character. The formal operational stage continues to develop through adulthood as individuals gain knowledge and experience.

Lev Vygotsky's Theory of Cognitive Development

Lev Vygotsky's theory on cognitive development is heavily rooted in a **sociocultural** perspective. He argued that the most important factors for a child's cognitive development reside in the cultural context in which the child grows up and social interactions that they have with adults, mentors, and more advanced peers. He believed that children learn best from the people around them, as their social interactions, even basic ones such as smiling, waving, or facial expressions, foster the beginning of more complex cognitive development. He is well-known for his concept of the **Zone of Proximal Development (ZPD)**, which is the gap between what a child can do independently and what the child can do with assistance from a more advanced individual or a collaborator. He believed that children could move through the ZPD and complete increasingly complicated tasks when receiving assistance from more cognitively advanced mentors. According to Vygotsky, children develop the most when passing through the ZPD. Vygotsky's contributions are heavily embedded in modern education and often take the form of teacher-led instruction and scaffolding to assist learners as they move through the ZPD.

Zone of Proximal Development

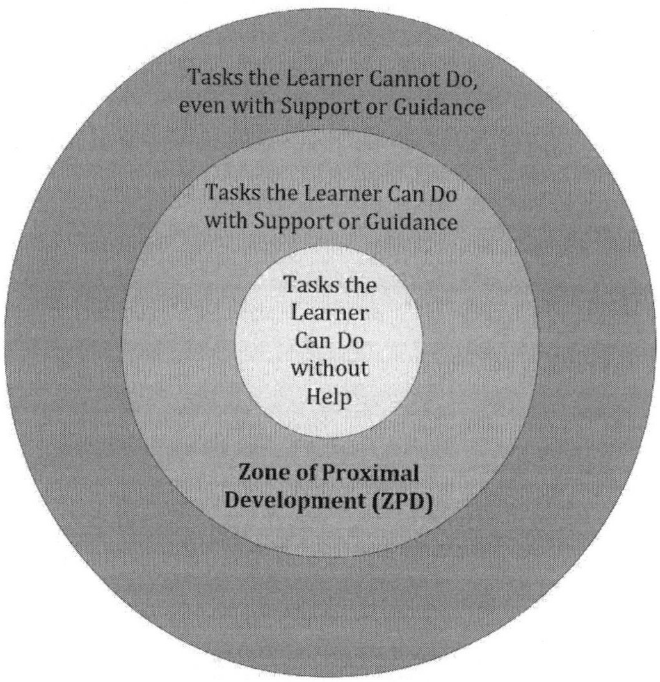

Review Video: Zone of Proximal Development (ZPD)
Visit mometrix.com/academy and enter code: 555594

Social and Emotional Development

Erik Erikson's Eight Stages of Psychosocial Development

Erik Erikson defined eight predetermined stages of psychosocial development from birth to late adulthood in which an individual encounters a crisis that must be resolved to successfully transition to the next stage. The first is **trust vs. mistrust** (0-18 months), where the infant learns that the world is safe and that caregivers can be trusted to tend to his or her basic needs. The next stage is **autonomy vs. shame** (18 months-3 years), where children learn to control their actions and establish independence. In the **initiative vs. guilt stage** (3-5 years), children acquire a sense of purpose and initiative through social interactions. Next, children enter the **industry vs. inferiority stage** (6-11 years), where they develop mastery and pride in completing a task. The next stage is **identity vs. role confusion** (12-18 years), in which children explore and develop characteristics that will comprise their identities and determine their roles in society. The sixth stage is **intimacy vs. isolation** (19-40 years), where one forms relationships by sharing the identity developed in the previous stage with others. **Generativity vs. stagnation** (40-65 years) occurs in middle adulthood and focuses on contributing to society's next generation through finding one's life purpose. The last stage is **ego integrity vs. despair** (65 to death), in which one reflects on the productivity and success of his or her life.

Expected Behaviors at Each Stage of Psychosocial Development

Stage	Examples of expected behaviors
Trust vs. mistrust	In this stage, the infant's primary goal is ensuring the fulfillment of his or her **basic needs**. Infants will cry or make other vocalizations to indicate to caregivers when they want something, such as to be fed or picked up. Separation anxiety from parents is also typical during this stage.
Autonomy vs. shame	Children in this stage begin attempting to perform daily tasks **independently**, such as making food, dressing themselves, bathing, or combing their hair. As children in this stage begin to realize they have a separate identity, they often begin attempting to assert themselves to parents and caregivers.
Initiative vs. guilt	Children at this stage often begin actively engaging and playing with other children. In play settings, these children will often assume **leadership roles** among a group of peers, create new games or activities, and devise their own rules for them. The initiative vs. guilt stage is also characterized by the development of feelings of sadness or guilt when making a mistake or hurting another's feelings.
Industry vs. inferiority	In this stage, children begin attempting to master concepts or skills with the intention of seeking **approval** and **acceptance** from others, particularly those older than themselves, in order to secure a feeling of competency. Children in this stage often become more involved in striving to succeed academically, extracurricular activities, and competitive sports.
Identity vs. role confusion	This stage is characterized by experimentation and uncertainty as young adolescents strive to establish an **independent identity**. Typical behaviors include interacting with new peer groups, trying new styles of dress, engaging in new activities, and considering new beliefs, values, and morals. As young adolescents in this stage are impressionable, they may potentially engage in risky or rebellious behavior as a result of peer pressure.
Intimacy vs. isolation	Individuals in this stage have typically established their identities and are ready to seek **long-term relationships**. This stage marks the development of a social network composed of close friends and long-term romantic partners.

Stage	Examples of expected behaviors
Generativity vs. stagnation	During this stage, individuals begin engaging in **productive** activities to benefit others and elicit personal fulfillment. Such activities include advancing in a career, parenting, or participating in community service projects.
Integrity vs. despair	This stage occurs at the end of one's life and is characterized by **reflection** upon lifetime accomplishments and positive contributions to society. Doing so allows the individual to assess whether his or her purpose was fulfilled and begin accepting death.

Incorporating Life Skills into Curriculum

In addition to academic achievement, the ultimate goal of education is to develop the whole child and provide a successful transition to independence and adulthood. Incorporating valuable life skills, such as decision-making, goal setting, organization, self-direction, and workplace communication, in early childhood through grade 12 is vital in ensuring students become productive contributors to society. Furthermore, the implementation of these life skills in early childhood is integral in allowing children to successfully progress in independence and maturity. The acquisition of such skills instills in students the self-motivation and ability to set goals, make decisions on how to effectively organize and manage time to complete them, and overcome obstacles. Additionally, teaching students to apply these skills promotes effective communication when working with others toward a goal. Through incorporating life skills into curriculum, teachers instill a growth mindset and foster self-empowered, confident lifelong learners with the necessary tools to navigate real-life situations and achieve success as they transition to adulthood. In the classroom, activities that promote leadership skills, cooperative learning, goal setting, self-monitoring, and social interaction foster an increasing sense of independence as children develop.

External Environmental Factors on Social and Emotional Development

Social and emotional development is heavily influenced by a child's home environment. Children learn social and emotional skills such as self-regulation, self-awareness, coping, and relationship building through modeling from parents and caregivers. A positive and supportive home environment is integral for proper social and emotional development. External factors, including lack of affection and attention, parental divorce, and homelessness, pose profound negative impacts on this development. In terms of social development, such external factors could lead to attachment or abandonment issues as well as distrust. Furthermore, children exposed to negative environmental factors could struggle in forging relationships, cooperating, and following societal rules. Emotionally, negative impacts on development cause aggression, poor self-regulation, insecurity, anxiety, isolation, and depression. Since developmental domains are interconnected, the impacts that external factors have on social and emotional development ultimately damage cognitive and physical development. Underdeveloped social skills impair cognitive development because the inability to properly interact with peers impedes the ability to learn from them. Additionally, inadequate emotional skills can inhibit concentration and understanding in school, thus inhibiting cognitive development. Physically, struggling to interact with others leads to impaired development of gross and fine motor skills as well as large muscle development that would be achieved through play.

Physical Development

Physical Changes Occurring in Early Childhood Through Adolescence

Early Childhood

As children pass through stages of development from early childhood through middle childhood and adolescence, they experience significant physical changes. Children in early childhood experience rapid growth in height and weight as they transition away from physical characteristics of infancy. In this stage, children begin to gain independence as they develop and improve upon gross and fine motor skills. Throughout early childhood, children develop the ability to walk and run, and as they mature through this stage, they learn to throw, catch, climb, and hop. Of the locomotive skills listed, walking comes first, running and climbing can develop simultaneously, and hopping or jumping comes last. They improve in their fine motor skills and learn to hold and manipulate small objects such as zippers and buttons and can grasp writing utensils to create shapes, letters, and drawings with increasing accuracy.

Middle Childhood

Physical growth varies for individual children in middle childhood, as some children begin experiencing prepubescent bodily changes. Children in middle childhood experience further improvements and refinements of gross and fine motor skills and coordination. Significant physical and appearance changes occur in adolescence as children enter puberty. These changes often occur quickly, resulting in a period of awkwardness and lack of coordination as adolescents adjust to this rapid development.

Impact of External Factors on Physical Development

As children pass through physical development stages from early childhood to adolescence, it is important that environmental factors are supportive of proper growth and health. Physical development can be hindered by external factors, such as poor nutrition, lack of sleep, prenatal exposure to drugs, and abuse, as these can cause significant and long-lasting negative consequences. Exposure to such factors can lead to stunted physical growth, impaired brain development and function, poor bone and muscle development, and obesity. Furthermore, the negative impacts from such external factors ultimately impedes cognitive, social, and emotional development. Impaired brain development and function negatively affect cognitive development by impacting the ability to concentrate and grasp new concepts. In terms of emotional development, physical impairments due to external factors can cause a child to become depressed, withdrawn, aggressive, prone to low self-esteem, and unable to self-regulate. Improper physical growth and health impacts social development in that physical limitations could hinder a child's ability to properly interact with and play with others. Impacted brain development and function can limit a child's ability to understand social cues and norms.

Language Development

Stages of Language Development

The first stage of language development and acquisition, the **pre-linguistic stage**, occurs during an infant's first year of life. It is characterized by the development of gestures, making eye contact, and sounds like cooing and crying. The **holophrase** or **one-word sentence stage** develops in infants between 10 and 13 months of age. In this stage, young children use one-word sentences to communicate meaning in language. The **two-word sentence stage** typically develops by the time a child is 18 months old. Each two-word sentence usually contains a noun or a verb and a modifier, such as "big balloon" or "green grass." Children in this stage use their two-word sentences to communicate wants and needs. **Multiple-word sentences** form by the time a child is two to two and a half years old. In this stage, children begin forming sentences with subjects and predicates, such as "tree is tall" or "rope is long." Grammatical errors are present, but children in this stage begin demonstrating how to use words in appropriate context. Children ages two and a half to three years typically begin using more **complex grammatical structures**. They begin to include grammatical structures that were not present before, such as conjunctions and prepositions. By the age of five or six, children reach a stage of **adult-like language development**. They begin to use words in appropriate context and can move words around in sentences while maintaining appropriate sentence structure. Language development and acquisition has a wide range of what is considered normal development. Some children do not attempt to speak for up to two years and then may experience an explosion of language development at a later time. In these cases, children often emerge from their silent stage with equivalent language development to babies who were more expressive early on. A child who does not speak after two years, however, may be exhibiting signs of a developmental delay.

Oral Language Development

Oral language development begins well before students enter educational environments. It is learned first without formal instruction, with **environmental factors** being a heavy influence. Children tend to develop their own linguistic rules as a result of genetic disposition, their environments, and how their individual thinking processes develop. Oral language refers to both speaking and listening. Components of oral language development include phonology, syntax, semantics, morphology, and pragmatics. **Phonology** refers to the production and recognition of sounds. **Morphology** refers to how words are formed from smaller pieces, called morphemes. **Semantics** refers to the meaning of words and phrases and has overlap with morphology and syntax, as morphemes and word order can both change the meaning of words. Semantic studies generally focus on learning and understanding vocabulary. **Syntax** refers to how words and morphemes are combined to make up meaningful phrases. In English, word order is the primary way that many components of grammar are communicated. Finally, **pragmatics** refers to the practical application of language based on various social situations. For instance, a college student is likely to use different vocabulary, complexity, and formality of language when speaking with a professor than when speaking with his or her peer group. Each of these five components of language are applied in oral language. Awareness and application of these components develops over time as students gain experience and education in language use. **Oral language development** can be nurtured by caregivers and teachers well before children enter educational environments. Caregivers and teachers can promote oral language development by providing environments full of language development opportunities. Additionally, teaching children how conversation works, encouraging interaction among children, and demonstrating good listening and speaking skills are good strategies for nurturing oral language development.

Review Video: Components of Oral Language Development
Visit mometrix.com/academy and enter code: 480589

Helping Students Develop Oral Language Abilities

Children pick up oral language skills in their home environments and build upon these skills as they grow. Early language development is influenced by a combination of genetic disposition, environment, and individual thinking processes. Children with **oral language acquisition difficulties** often experience difficulties in their **literacy skills**, so activities that promote good oral language skills also improve literacy skills. **Strategies** that help students develop oral language abilities include developing appropriate speaking and listening skills; providing instruction that emphasizes vocabulary development; providing students with opportunities to communicate wants, needs, ideas, and information; creating language learning environments; and promoting auditory memory. Developing appropriate speaking and listening skills includes teaching turn-taking, awareness of social norms, and basic rules for speaking and listening. Emphasizing **vocabulary development** is a strategy that familiarizes early learners with word meanings. Providing students with opportunities to **communicate** is beneficial for developing early social skills. Teachers can create **language learning environments** by promoting literacy in their classrooms with word walls, reading circles, or other strategies that introduce language skills to students. Promoting **auditory memory** means teaching students to listen to, process, and recall information.

Review Video: Types of Vocabulary Learning (Broad and Specific)
Visit mometrix.com/academy and enter code: 258753

Helping Students Monitor Errors in Oral Language

Oral language is the primary way people communicate and express their knowledge, ideas, and feelings. As oral language generally develops, their **speaking and listening skills** become more refined. This refinement of a person's language is called fluency, which can be broken down into the subdisciplines of language, reading, writing, speaking, and listening. **Speaking fluency** usually describes the components of rate, accuracy, and prosody. **Rate** describes how fast a person can speak, and **prosody** describes the inflection and expressions that a person puts into speech. **Accuracy** describes how often a person makes an error in language production. In early stages of language development, individuals generally do not have enough language knowledge to be able to monitor their own speech production for errors and require input from others to notice and correct their mistakes. As an individual becomes more proficient, he or she will be able to monitor his or her own language usage and make corrections to help improve fluency. In the classroom, the teacher needs to be an active component of language monitoring to help facilitate growth. Teachers can monitor **oral language errors** with progress-monitoring strategies. Teachers can also help students monitor their own **oral language development** as they progress through the reading curriculum. Students can monitor their oral language by listening to spoken words in their school and home environments, learning and practicing self-correction skills, and participating in reading comprehension and writing activities. Students can also monitor oral language errors by learning oral language rules for phonics, semantics, syntax, and pragmatics. These rules typically generalize to developing appropriate oral language skills.

Expressive and Receptive Language

Expressive language refers to the aspects of language that an individual produces, generally referring to writing and speaking. **Receptive language** refers to the aspects of language that an individual encounters or receives and generally refers to reading and listening. Both expressive and receptive language are needed for communication from one person to another.

	Expressive	Receptive
Written	Writing	Reading
Oral	Speaking	Listening

Expressive Language Skills

Expressive language skills include the ability to use vocabulary, sentences, gestures, and writing. People with good **expressive language skills** can label objects in their environments, put words in sentences, use appropriate grammar, demonstrate comprehension verbally by retelling stories, and more. This type of language is important because it allows people to express feelings, wants, needs, thoughts, ideas, and individual points of view. Strong expressive language skills include pragmatic knowledge, such as using gestures and facial expressions or using appropriate vocabulary for the listener or reader and soft skills, such as checks for comprehension, use of analogies, and grouping of ideas to help with clarity. Well-expressed language should be relatively easy for someone else to comprehend.

Receptive Language Skills

Receptive language refers to a person's ability to perceive and understand language. Good receptive language skills involve gathering information from the environment and processing it into meaning. People with good **receptive language skills** perceive gestures, sounds, words, and written information well. Receptive language is important for developing appropriate communication skills. Instruction that targets receptive language skills can include tasks that require sustained attention and focus, recognizing emotions and gestures, and listening and reading comprehension. Games that challenge the players to communicate carefully, such as charades or catchphrase, can be a great way to target receptive language skills. As one student tries to accurately express an idea with words or gestures, the rest of the class must exercise their receptive language skills. Lastly, focusing on **social skills and play skills instruction** encourages opportunities for children to interact with their peers or adults. This fosters receptive language skills and targets deficits in these skills.

Stages of Literacy Development

The development of literacy in young children is separated into five stages. Names and ranges of these stages sometimes vary slightly, but the stage milestones are similar. Stage 1 is the **Emergent Reader stage**. In this stage, children ages 6 months to 6 years demonstrate skills like pretend reading, recognizing letters of the alphabet, retelling stories, and printing their names. Stage 2 is the **Novice/Early Reader stage** (ages 6–7 years). Children begin to understand the relationships between letters and sounds and written and spoken words, and they read texts containing high-frequency words. Children in this stage should develop orthographic conventions and semantic knowledge. In Stage 3, the **Decoding Reader stage**, children ages 7–9 develop decoding skills in order to read simple stories. They also demonstrate increased fluency. Stage 4 (ages 8–15 years) is called the **Fluent, Comprehending/Transitional Reader stage**. In this stage, fourth to eighth graders read to learn new ideas and information. In Stage 5, the **Expert/Fluent Reader stage**, children ages 16 years and older read more complex information. They also read expository and narrative texts with multiple viewpoints.

> **Review Video: Stages of Reading Development**
> Visit mometrix.com/academy and enter code: 121184

Relationship between Language Development and Early Literacy Skills

Language development and early literacy skills are interconnected. **Language concepts** begin and develop shortly after birth with infant/parent interactions, cooing, and then babbling. These are the earliest attempts at language acquisition for infants. Young children begin interacting with written and spoken words before they enter their grade school years. Before they enter formal classrooms, children begin to make **connections** between speaking and listening and reading and writing. Children with strong speaking and listening skills demonstrate strong literacy skills in early grade school. The development of **phonological awareness** is connected to early literacy skills. Children with good phonological awareness recognize that words are made up of different speech sounds. For example, children with appropriate phonological awareness can break words (e.g., "bat" into separate speech sounds, "b-a-t"). Examples of phonological awareness include rhyming (when the ending parts of words have the same or similar sounds) and alliteration (when words all have the same beginning sound). Success with phonological awareness (oral language) activities depends on adequate development of speech and language skills.

Promoting Literacy During the Early Stages of Literacy Development

Teachers and parents can implement strategies at different stages of literacy development in order to build **good reading skills** in children with and without disabilities. During the **Emergent Reader stage**, teachers and parents can introduce children to the conventions of reading with picture books. They can model turning the pages, reading from left to right, and other reading conventions. Book reading at this stage helps children begin to identify letters, letter sounds, and simple words. Repetitive reading of familiar texts also helps children begin to make predictions about what they are reading. During the **Novice/Early Reader** and **Decoding Reader stages**, parents and teachers can help children form the building blocks of decoding and fluency skills by reading for meaning and emphasizing letter-sound relationships, visual cues, and language patterns. In these stages, increasing familiarity with sight words is essential. In the **Fluent, Comprehending/Transitional Reader stage**, children should be encouraged to read book series, as the shared characters, settings, and plots help develop their comprehension skills. At this stage, a good reading rate (fluency) is an indicator of comprehension skills. **Expert/Fluent readers** can independently read multiple texts and comprehend their meanings. Teachers and parents can begin exposing children to a variety of fiction and non-fiction texts before this stage in order to promote good fluency skills.

> **Review Video: Phonics (Encoding and Decoding)**
> Visit mometrix.com/academy and enter code: 821361
>
> **Review Video: Fluency**
> Visit mometrix.com/academy and enter code: 531179

Types of Disabilities

Medical disabilities include problems related to diseases, illnesses, trauma, and genetic conditions. **Physical disabilities** include problems related to fine and gross motor skills and can include sensory input or sensory perception disorders. Medical and physical disabilities often manifest with other disabilities, such as **learning disabilities**. Medical disabilities that affect educational performance usually fall under the "other health impairment" or "traumatic brain injury" categories of the Individuals with Disabilities Education Act (IDEA). Students with physical disabilities, such as cerebral palsy, can be eligible for special education under IDEA's "orthopedic impairment" category. However, for either medical or physical disabilities to qualify, they must **adversely affect educational performance**. For example, a student with cerebral palsy would not be eligible for special education or an **Individualized Education Program (IEP)** if the disability does not affect educational performance. The student would receive accommodations and modifications under a 504 Plan.

Review Video: Medical Conditions in Education
Visit mometrix.com/academy and enter code: 531058

Low-Incidence Disabilities and High-Incidence Disabilities

Low-incidence disabilities account for up to 20 percent of all students' disabilities. Students with low-incidence disabilities have sometimes received assistance for their disabilities starting from an early age. **Low-incidence disabilities** include intellectual disabilities, multiple disabilities, hearing impairments, orthopedic impairments, other health impairments, visual impairments, certain autism spectrum conditions, deaf-blindness, traumatic brain injury, and significant developmental delays. **High-incidence disabilities** account for up to 80 percent of all students' disabilities. While students with high-incidence disabilities present with academic, social, communication, or behavioral problems, they can often be held to the same standards as their regular education peers. Children with high-incidence disabilities may perform at the same capacities as their similar-aged peers but have deficits in reading, math, writing, handwriting, or maintaining attention. High-incidence disabilities include speech and language impairments, learning disabilities, attention-deficit/hyperactivity disorder, emotional disorders, mild intellectual disabilities, certain autism spectrum conditions, and cognitive delays.

Interventions for Students with Physical Disabilities

A physical disability refers to any disability that limits **gross mobility** and prevents **normal body movement**. For example, muscular dystrophy is a physical disability that weakens muscles over time. Students with physical disabilities require early interventions and should begin to receive them before grade school. When students with physical disabilities enter grade school, they may receive interventions and related services if they qualify for special education and receive IEPs or **504 Plans**. When physical disabilities do not affect the students' academic success, they may be put on 504 Plans to receive appropriate related services, accommodations, or modifications. When physical disabilities are present with other disabilities or the physical disabilities affect academic performance, students may be put on IEPs and receive appropriate related services, accommodations, and modifications. Teachers, intervention specialists, physiotherapists, occupational therapists, and speech language pathologists work as a team in implementing appropriate accommodations, modifications, and related services to assist students with physical disabilities.

Working with Students with Physical Disabilities

Students with physical disabilities should be included in **general education classrooms** with accommodations if their disabilities do not coexist with other disabilities, such as learning disabilities. The Individuals with Disabilities Education Act states that students must be assigned to a classroom that conforms with the student's least restrictive environment, which generally means the general education classroom, unless appropriate accommodations cannot be made. If sufficient accommodations or modifications are not able to be made within the general education classroom, a student may be placed in a more specialized environment that provides for his or her particular needs. In any of these settings, it is essential for educators to practice **instructional strategies** that facilitate the learning processes and accommodate the needs of students with physical disabilities. Classrooms should be arranged so they can be **navigated** easily by everyone. This includes giving students using wheelchairs adequate aisle space and workspace. **Partner work** is helpful for students with physical disabilities, who may struggle with handwriting or using keyboards. Partners can assist these students with skills like note-taking, which may be difficult for students with physical disabilities. Additionally, assignments can include **accommodations** or **modifications** to meet the specific needs of students with physical disabilities. For example, text-to-speech software can be provided for students who struggle with using regular keyboards.

Accommodations and Modifications

Students with **speech, language, visual,** or **hearing impairments** (including **deafness**) that adversely affect their educational performance receive **accommodations**, modifications, and related services specific to their disabilities. Students with these impairments may be educated alongside peers and provided with related services outside of the general education classroom. Accommodations, modifications, and related services are provided based on the severity of the disability.

An **orthopedic impairment (OI)** severely hinders mobility or motor activity. Accommodations, modifications, and related services in the classroom environment may be appropriate for students with OI. Students with **intellectual disabilities**, such as Down syndrome, often need supports in place for communication, self-care, and social skills. The educational implications of a **traumatic brain injury** are unique to the individual and are therefore treated on a case-by-case basis. Students with **multiple disabilities** have needs that cannot be met in any one program. Sometimes their needs are so great that they must be educated in partial inclusion or self-contained settings.

Disability Categories in IDEA

- **Specific Learning Disabilities (SLD)** is the umbrella term for children who struggle with issues in their abilities to read, write, speak, listen, reason, or do math.
- **Other Health Impairment (OHI)** is the umbrella term for a disability that limits a child's strength, energy, or alertness.
- **Autism Spectrum Disorder (ASD)** is a disability that mostly affects a child's social and communication skills, and sometimes behavior.
- **Emotional Disturbance (ED)** is a disability category for a number of mental disorders.
- **Speech or Language Impairment** covers children with language impairments.
- **Visual Impairment or Blindness** is a disability category for children with visual impairments that significantly impact their abilities to learn.
- **Deafness** is the category for students who cannot hear even with a hearing aid.
- **Hearing Impairment** describes hearing loss that is not as pervasive as deafness. This is distinguished from deafness categorically, as the types of interventions needed are very different.

- **Deaf-Blindness** covers children diagnosed with both deafness and blindness.
- Those with **Orthopedic Impairments** have impairments to their bodies that interfere with the performance of daily living skills.
- An **Intellectual Disability** is the diagnosis for children with below-average intellectual abilities or intelligence quotients (IQs).
- **Traumatic Brain Injury (TBI)** covers children who have suffered from TBIs.
- **Multiple Disabilities** as a category means a child has more than one disability defined by the Individuals with Disabilities Education Act and requires educational interventions that go beyond standard interventions for one category.

Review Video: Understanding Learning Disability Needs of Students
Visit mometrix.com/academy and enter code: 662775

SPECIFIC LEARNING DISABILITY

EARLY INDICATIONS OF A SPECIFIC LEARNING DISABILITY

Early indications of specific learning disabilities (SLDs) can include medical history, problems with speech acquisition, problems with socialization, academic delays, and behavioral delays. Delays in certain milestones may indicate learning disabilities, but these delays may also be due to other causes. Premature birth, serious childhood illnesses, frequent ear infections, and sleep disorders are **medical factors** that can influence the development of learning disabilities. Children that develop SLDs may demonstrate early delays in **speech**. Late speech development, pronunciation problems, and stuttering may indicate SLDs, but they may also be issues that are unrelated to SLDs and can be addressed by individualized speech instruction. Students with SLDs may also have problems adjusting **socially** and may demonstrate social skills that are not age appropriate. Depending on when the children enter academic settings, they may demonstrate academic delays compared to similar-aged peers. These delays are usually determined using formal and informal assessments in educational settings. **Behaviors** such as hyperactivity or difficulty following directions may also indicate a child has an SLD. However, these indicators do not definitely mean that a child has a learning disability, and some of the indicators overlap with characteristics of other disabilities.

INSTRUCTIONAL STRATEGIES FOR TEACHING STUDENTS WITH SPECIFIC LEARNING DISABILITIES

While there is no one strategy that works effectively with all students with specific learning disabilities, there are some strategies that tend to produce **positive outcomes** for these students. Direct instruction, learning strategy instruction, and a multi-sensory approach are three large-scale interventions that can be used to promote student learning. **Direct instruction** is teacher-driven instruction that targets specific skills; this is sometimes delivered in resource rooms. **Learning strategy instruction** is a method for teaching students with disabilities different tools and techniques useful for learning new content or skills. This includes techniques like chunking the content, sequencing tasks, and small group instruction. A **multi-sensory approach** ensures that students are receiving and interacting with new information and skills using more than one sense at a time. This approach is helpful for students with learning disabilities because it targets many different ways of learning.

DYSLEXIA AND DYSGRAPHIA DISORDERS

Students with dyslexia are eligible for special education under the specific learning disability category in the Individuals with Disabilities Education Act if their educational performance is significantly impacted by their disabilities. **Dyslexia** is a permanent condition that makes it difficult for people to read. This affects reading accuracy, fluency, and comprehension. Dyslexia also generalizes to difficulties in the content areas of writing, mathematics, and spelling. Children who have dyslexia often have difficulties with **phonemic awareness skills** and **decoding**. It is not a disability that affects vision or the way people see letters. Dyslexia may coexist with other conditions such as **dysgraphia**, which is a disorder that causes issues with written expression. With dysgraphia, children often struggle with holding pencils and writing letters accurately. It is difficult for students with dysgraphia to distinguish shapes, use correct letter spacing, read maps, copy text, understand spelling rules, and more.

Review Video: Disorders That Impair Reading Comprehension
Visit mometrix.com/academy and enter code: 306758

Sensory Processing Disorders

A person with a deficit in the brain's ability to interpret sensory information has a sensory processing disorder (**SPD**). In people without SPD, brain receptors can interpret sensory input, and then the person demonstrates appropriate reactions. In people with SPD, sensory input is blocked from brain receptors, resulting in abnormal reactions. Previously known as a sensory integration disorder, SPD is not a disability specifically defined or eligible under IDEA. However, many students with disabilities defined by IDEA, like autism, also experience some sort of sensory processing disorder. Students with SPD may display **oversensitive or under-sensitive responses** to their environments, stimuli, and senses. They may not understand physical boundaries, such as where their bodies are in space, and may bump into things and demonstrate clumsiness. These students may get upset easily, throw tantrums, demonstrate high anxiety, and struggle with changes.

Importance of Enforcing Word Recognition

Many students with specific learning disabilities demonstrate **deficits in their reading abilities**. This includes **word recognition abilities**. Teaching **word identification** is important for these students because developing age-appropriate word recognition skills is one of the essential building blocks for creating efficient readers. Children who do not develop adequate reading skills in elementary school are generally below-average readers as they age in school. Most districts and teachers use **basal reading programs** that teach word recognition and phonics. Teachers often supplement basal reading programs with **instructional programs** that can be used at home and at school. These are especially useful for students with disabilities or students who are at risk and struggle with word recognition abilities. Elements of basal and supplementary reading programs include instruction for helping students make connections between letters and sounds, opportunities to become comfortable with reading, alphabetic knowledge, phonemic awareness, letter-sound correlations, word identification strategies, spelling, writing, and reading fluency.

Other Health Impairments

Qualifications to Be Eligible for Special Education Under the Category of OHI

The category of other health impairment (**OHI**) under IDEA indicates that a child has **limited strength, vitality, or alertness**. This includes hyper-alertness or hypo-alertness to environmental stimuli. In order to be eligible for special education under this category according to IDEA, the disability must **adversely affect educational performance**. It must also be due to **chronic or acute health problems**, such as attention-deficit/hyperactivity disorder, diabetes, epilepsy, heart conditions, hemophilia, lead poisoning, leukemia, nephritis, rheumatic fever, sickle cell anemia, or Tourette's syndrome. Since the OHI category encompasses a number of different disabilities, teachers and parents must rely on a student's Individualized Education Program to ensure that individual academic needs are met and appropriate accommodations and modifications are provided.

Educational Implications for Students with ADHD

IDEA does **not** recognize attention-deficit/hyperactivity disorder (ADHD) in any of its 13 major disability categories. Students may be diagnosed with ADHD by a physician, but this diagnosis is not enough to qualify them for **special education services**. When ADHD is present alongside an IDEA-recognized disability, the student qualifies for special education services under that disability. A student whose ability to learn is affected by ADHD can receive services with a 504 Plan in place. **Section 504 of the Rehabilitation Act of 1973** requires that any child whose disability affects a major life activity receive appropriate **accommodations** and **modifications** in the learning environment. Parents who think a child's ADHD adversely affects educational functioning may request a formal evaluation to be performed by the school. If the child is found to qualify for special education services, they then receive services under IDEA's **other health impairment** category.

ADHD

Children with **attention-deficit/hyperactivity disorder (ADHD)** may demonstrate inattention and/or hyperactivity and impulsivity. Students with ADHD may have difficulties with attention span, following instructions, and concentrating to the point that their educational performance is affected. Since ADHD symptoms are common among children, their presence does not necessarily indicate that a child has ADHD. ADHD is not caused by certain environmental factors, such as diet or watching too much television. Symptoms may be exacerbated by these factors, but the causes can be heredity, chemical imbalances, issues with brain functions, environmental toxins, or prenatal trauma, such as the mother smoking or drinking during pregnancy.

Autism Spectrum Disorder

Autism is a **spectrum disorder**, which means the characteristics associated with the disability vary depending on the student. However, there are common repetitive and patterned behaviors associated with communication and social interactions for this population of students. Students with autism may demonstrate delayed or different speech patterns, the inability to understand body language or facial expressions, and the inability to exhibit appropriate speech patterns, body language, or facial expressions. In a classroom environment, students with autism may demonstrate **repetitive behaviors** that are distracting, such as hand flapping or making vocalizations. Some students with autism demonstrate **preoccupation** with doing activities, tasks, or routines in certain ways. This preoccupation can lead to difficulties when the students are asked to make changes to activities, tasks, or routines. Furthermore, some students with autism prefer to **participate** in a limited range of activities and may get upset when asked to participate in activities outside of their self-perceived ranges. This preference for a limited range of activities may even translate into repetitive behaviors or obsessive and fanatic focus on particular topics. Extreme interest in one topic can lead to disruptions when students with autism are asked to speak or write about different topics.

Review Video: Autism Spectrum Disorder
Visit mometrix.com/academy and enter code: 395410

Concurrent Autism Spectrum Disorder and Other Learning Disabilities

Misinformation about autism spectrum disorder (ASD) and its relation to other learning disabilities runs rampant within school communication and needs clarification to prevent harmful stereotyping of students. As a spectrum disorder, the way ASD presents varies widely and does not always affect students in the same ways. Autism spectrum disorder is frequently confused with intellectual disabilities, which is when an individual has a low IQ; however, students with ASD can have IQs ranging from significantly delayed to above average or gifted. ASD is also distinctive in that it largely involves difficulties with social understanding and communication, as well as fixations on repetitive routines and behaviors. It is important for an educational professional to understand the difference between ASD and other types of disabilities that commonly co-occur or which have overlapping symptoms. For instance, students with learning disabilities and students with ASD may both have challenges with reading nonverbal cues, staying organized, and expressing themselves, but that does not mean that they have the same underlying conditions or needs. The professional educational community must be aware and cautious when describing various disabilities to prevent the spread of misinformation and harmful stereotyping.

Early Signs of a Child Having ASD

Early signs of **autism spectrum disorder (ASD)** include impairments or delays in social interactions and communication, repetitive behaviors, limited interests, and abnormal eating habits. Students with ASD typically do not interact in conversations in the same ways as similar-aged peers without ASD. They may demonstrate inability to engage in pretend play and may pretend they don't hear when being spoken to. Hand flapping, vocal sounds, or compulsive interactions with objects are repetitive behaviors sometimes demonstrated by students with ASD. They may only demonstrate interest in talking about one topic or interacting with one object. They may also demonstrate self-injurious behavior or sleep problems, in addition to having a limited diet of preferred foods. **Early intervention** is key for these students in order to address and improve functioning. These students may also benefit from **applied behavior analysis** to target specific behaviors, and they may require speech and language therapy, occupational therapy, social skills instruction, or other services geared toward improving intellectual functioning.

Characteristics of Social Skill Delays in Students with ASD

Autism spectrum disorder (ASD) is a disability that can affect a student's social, communication, and behavioral abilities. **Social skill delays and deficits** are common for students with ASD. Social skill delays go hand in hand with **communication limitations** for students with ASD. This includes conversational focus on one or two narrow topics or ideas, which makes it difficult for students with ASD to hold two-way conversations about things that do not interest them. Some students with ASD engage in repetitive language or echolalia or rely on standard phrases to communicate with others. Their **speech and language skills** may be delayed compared to their similar-aged peers. This may also impact their abilities to engage in effective conversations. The **nonverbal skills** of students with ASD may also be misinterpreted, such as when they avoid eye contact while speaking or being spoken to.

Early Communication and Social Skill Delays in Students with ASD

Students with delays in communication development often need and receive some type of assistance or instruction with communication and social skills. Early intervention for these students is key, as communication difficulties may be a symptom of **autism spectrum disorder (ASD)**. For students with ASD, the need for communication and social skills instruction varies depending on the individual student. Key characteristics of **early communication difficulties** for a student with ASD include not responding to his or her name, not pointing at objects of interest, avoiding eye contact, not engaging in pretend play, delayed speech or language skills, or repeating words or phrases. Children with ASD may also exhibit overreaction or underreaction to environmental stimuli. Key characteristics of **early social skill difficulties** for a student with ASD may include preferring to play alone, trouble understanding personal feelings or the feelings of others, not sharing interests with others, and difficulty with personal space boundaries. Infants with ASD may not respond to their names and demonstrate reduced babbling and reduced interest in people. Toddlers with ASD may demonstrate decreased interest in social interactions, difficulty with pretend play, and a preference for playing alone.

Socratic Method for Students with ASD

With the Socratic method of teaching, students are **guided** by their teachers in their own educational discovery learning processes. This involves students intrinsically seeking knowledge or answers to problems. This method can be helpful for facilitating and enhancing the **social and emotional abilities** of students with disabilities, particularly autism spectrum disorder (ASD). The Socratic method requires **dialogue** in order to successfully facilitate the teacher/student guided learning process. This is beneficial for students with ASD, who generally struggle with appropriate communication and social skills. This method emphasizes **information seeking and communication skills** by engaging students in class discussions, assignment sharing, and group work. Communication for information-seeking purposes is often a deficit of students with ASD. Sharing of ideas is a concept that develops naturally in guided learning and often requires flexibility in the thought process, another skill that students with ASD struggle with. These skills can be taught to and reinforced in students with and without disabilities in order to develop skills essential to lifelong learning processes.

Fostering the Communication Development of Students with ASD

Students with **autism spectrum disorder (ASD)** vary in their need for communication and social skill assistance and instruction. Some students with ASD may demonstrate slight to extreme delays in language; difficulty sustaining conversations; and the inability to understand body language, tone of voice, and facial expressions. Since ASD is a **spectrum disorder**, there typically is no single instructional strategy or technique that works for all students with the disorder. Some **evidence-based strategies** are effective for teaching appropriate communication skills to students with ASD. **Applied behavior analysis (ABA)** is an evidence-based strategy that involves providing an intervention and analyzing its effectiveness for a student with ASD. **Discrete trial training (DTT)** is a teaching strategy that is more structured than ABA. It focuses on teaching and reinforcing skills in smaller increments. **Pivotal response treatment (PRT)** is an ABA-derived approach that focuses more on meaningful reinforcement when generally positive behaviors occur. Where ABA targets very specific tasks, PRT targets behaviors categorically or more generally. Furthermore, instead of using an unrelated, supplemented reward system, such as giving candy for completing a task, the rewards used should be related to the desired behavior. For instance, suppose a targeted goal is to have the individual work on politely asking for things generally. The PRT-based reward might be giving the individual the toy or desired object as a reward for asking for it.

Emotional Disturbances

A diagnosis of an emotional disturbance (**ED**) can also be referred to as a **behavioral disorder** or **mental illness**. Causes of emotional disturbances are generally unclear. However, heredity, brain disorders, and diet are some factors that influence the development of emotional disturbances. The emotional disturbance category includes psychological disorders, such as anxiety disorders, bipolar disorder, eating disorders, and obsessive-compulsive disorder. Children who have emotional disturbances that affect their educational performance are eligible for **special education** under the Individuals with Disabilities Education Act. Indicators of emotional disturbances include hyperactivity, aggression, withdrawal, immaturity, and academic difficulties. While many children demonstrate these indicators throughout their development, an emotional disturbance is associated with **prolonged demonstration** of these behaviors.

Issues Students with Emotional Disturbances Experience in the Instructional Setting

Students with the diagnosis of emotional disturbance (ED) as defined by the Individuals with Disabilities Education Act require **emotional and behavioral support** in the classroom. Students with ED may also require **specialized academic instruction** in addition to behavioral and emotional support. The amount of support given varies according to the needs of individual students. These students also need **scaffolded instruction** in social skills, self-awareness, self-esteem, and self-control. Students with ED often exhibit behaviors that impede their learning or the learning of others. **Positive behavioral interventions and supports (PBIS)** is a preventative instructional strategy that focuses on promoting positive behaviors in students. With PBIS, teachers or other professionals make changes to students' environments in order to decrease problem behaviors. PBIS involves collecting information on a problem behavior, identifying positive interventions to support the student before behaviors escalate, and implementing supports to decrease targeted negative behaviors. Supports can be implemented schoolwide or in the classroom. However, for students with ED, **classroom supports** are more effective because they can be individualized.

Speech and Language Impairments

Speech and language impairments, sometimes referred to as **communication disorders**, are disabilities recognized by the Individuals with Disabilities Education Act. Students diagnosed with communication disorders are eligible for special education if they qualify for services. Early indicators of communication disorders include but are not limited to:

- Not smiling or interacting with others
- Lack of babbling or cooing in infants
- Lack of age-appropriate comprehension skills
- Speech that is not easily understood
- Issues with age-appropriate syntax development
- Issues with age-appropriate social skills
- Deficits in reading and writing skills
- Beginning or ending words with incorrect sounds
- Hearing loss
- Stuttering

These indicators may also be linked to other disabilities, such as hearing impairments or autism spectrum disorder. Although prolonged demonstration of these indicators may suggest communication disorders, some children demonstrate delays and then self-correct over time.

Facilitating Learning for Students with Speech or Language Impairments

In order to teach students with speech or language impairments, also referred to as **communication disorders**, teachers and other professionals can use the **strategies** listed below:

- Use visuals and concrete examples to help students with communication disorders take in new information. Link the visuals with spoken words or phrases.
- Use visuals or photographs to introduce or reinforce vocabulary.
- Use repetition of spoken words to introduce or reinforce vocabulary.
- Model conversational and social skills, which helps students with communication disorders become familiar with word pronunciation.
- Speak at a slower rate when necessary, especially when presenting new information.
- Consistently check for understanding.
- Be aware that communication issues may sometimes result in other issues, such as behavioral or social skill issues.
- Pair actions and motions with words to emphasize meaning, especially for students with receptive language disorders.

RECEPTIVE LANGUAGE DISORDERS

Children with receptive language disorders often demonstrate appropriate expressive language skills and hear and read at age-appropriate levels. However, they may seem like they are not paying attention or engaging in activities, or they may appear to have difficulties following or understanding directions. They may refrain from asking questions or interrupt frequently during activities, especially during read-aloud activities. It may appear as if they are not listening, but children with receptive language disorders have difficulty perceiving **meaning** from what they hear. Children with this disorder may consistently leave tasks incomplete unless the tasks are broken down into smaller steps. This is due to issues with processing directions, especially **verbal directions**. Children with receptive language disorders may not respond appropriately or at all to questions from peers or adults. Answers to comprehension questions, especially when texts are read aloud, may be off topic or incorrect. Children with receptive language disorders have trouble gathering and connecting meaning to what they hear. A receptive language disorder is not exclusively a learning disability. However, children who have receptive disorders may have learning disabilities.

EXPRESSIVE LANGUAGE DISABILITIES

Expressive language is the ability to express wants and needs. Children with disabilities related to **expressive language disabilities** may have trouble conversing with peers and adults and have trouble with self-expression. Answers to questions may be vague or repetitive. They may not demonstrate age-appropriate social skills with peers and adults. Children with expressive language disabilities have a limited vocabulary range and rely on familiar vocabulary words in their expressive language. They can be very quiet and seclude themselves from classroom activities because of difficulties expressing their thoughts and feelings. They may not be able to accurately express what they understand because children with expressive language difficulties have trouble speaking in sentences. Expressive language disabilities indicate issues with **language processing centers** in the brain. Children with these disabilities can sometimes understand language but have trouble **expressing** it. Children with traumatic brain injuries, dyslexia, autism, or learning disabilities demonstrate issues with expressive language.

IMPLICATIONS OF LITERACY DEVELOPMENT FOR CHILDREN WITH DISABILITIES

Children may not always meet the **literacy stage milestones** at specified ages. However, this does not always indicate a disability. Children who fall significantly behind in their literacy development, continually struggle with skill acquisition, or do not consistently retain skill instruction are more likely to be identified as having **disabilities**. Furthermore, children with **speech and language disorders** are more likely to experience problems learning to read and write. These issues are typically apparent before children enter grade school but can also become evident during their early grade school years. **Early warning signs** include disinterest in shared book reading, inability to recognize or remember names of letters, difficulty understanding directions, and persistent baby talk.

EFFECTS OF DEFICITS IN LANGUAGE DEVELOPMENT ON THE LEARNING PROCESSES

Without interventions, children with deficits in language development will likely have issues with overall academic success. **Academic success** is inextricably linked with good language development. Good **language development skills** include the ability to understand spoken and written words, as well as literacy skills. When a core knowledge of language is developed in young children, it can be built upon as the children grow and develop during their grade school years. Reading and writing are language-based skills. **Phonological awareness** is an essential skill and key building block for language development. Phonological awareness is a term that refers to students' awareness of sounds, syllables, and words. Students that develop strong phonological skills typically develop good literacy skills. Students with deficits in reading, writing, or math may have difficulties with phonological awareness and miss some building blocks essential for academic success. These deficits generalize to core subject areas as students are required to demonstrate grade-level appropriate skills.

Visual Impairment or Blindness

Visual impairments range from low vision to blindness. The Individuals with Disabilities Education Act defines a **visual impairment** as an impairment in vision that is great enough to affect a child's educational performance. **Blindness** is defined as a visual acuity of 20/200 or less in the dominant eye. Some people diagnosed with blindness still have minimal sight. Early indicators of a visual impairment or blindness in children include:

- Holding things close to the eyes or face
- Experiencing fatigue after looking at things closely
- Having misaligned eyes
- Squinting
- Tilting the head or covering one eye to see things up close or far away
- Demonstrating clumsiness
- Appearing to see better during the day

Students with visual impairments benefit the most from early interventions, especially when the impairments are present with other disabilities. Appropriate interventions vary based on students' needs and whether or not they have other disabilities. Modifications, such as magnified text, Braille, auditory support, and text-tracking software, can help level the learning plane for these students.

Deafness, Hearing Impairment, and Deaf-Blindness

Deafness, hearing impairment, and deaf-blindness are each considered their own categories under the Individuals with Disabilities Education Act, as the types and levels of intervention vary widely between them. **Deafness** is defined as a complete or near-complete loss of hearing, to the degree that a hearing aid cannot help. Deaf students often need specialized interventions to help with safety and communication, such as communication aids, assistive devices, and sign language. **Hearing impairments** consist of all qualifying degrees of hearing loss that are not severe enough to qualify as deafness. Interventions may include communication aids and training, as well as hearing aids. **Deaf-blindness** is restricted to students who are both deaf and blind concurrently. Deaf-blind students usually require considerable help with communication and daily living skills.

Effect of Hearing Loss on Language Development

Hearing language is part of learning language. Children with **hearing loss** miss out on sounds associated with language, and this can affect their listening, speaking, reading, social skills, and overall school success. Hearing loss can sometimes lead to delayed speech and language, learning disabilities in school, insecurities, and issues with socialization and making friends. Children with hearing loss may:

- Have trouble learning abstract vocabulary like *since* and *before*
- Omit article words in sentences like *a* and *an*
- Fall behind in core components of learning and development without early interventions
- Have difficulty speaking in and understanding sentences
- Speak in shorter sentences
- Have difficulty including word endings like *-ing* and *-s*
- Have issues speaking clearly because they cannot accurately hear sounds

- Omit quiet sounds like *p, sh,* or *f*
- Be unable to hear what their own voices sound like

Children with hearing loss are more likely to fall behind in school due to their hearing deficits. They can easily fall behind without support from interventions, teachers, and their families. Early **hearing testing** is essential to ensure that interventions, such as sign language, can be introduced to promote school and life success for children with hearing loss.

Orthopedic Impairment

Qualifications to Receive Special Education for Orthopedic Impairment

Students who qualify to receive special education under the Individuals with Disabilities Education Act orthopedic impairment category have an orthopedic impairment that adversely affects educational performance. This includes children with congenital anomalies, impairments caused by disease, or impairments from other causes, such as cerebral palsy or amputations. An orthopedic impairment alone does not qualify a student for special education and an IEP. Once a student's educational performance is proven to be affected by the orthopedic impairment, the student becomes eligible for special education and placed on an IEP. The **IEP** determines the student's least restrictive environment, individualized goals for academic skills or adaptive behavior, and any appropriate accommodations or modifications. Students with orthopedic impairments whose educational performance is not affected may receive accommodations and modifications on **504 Plans**, if appropriate. Strategies for instruction should be determined and implemented on a case-by-case basis, as the orthopedic impairment category covers a broad range of disabilities.

Intellectual Disabilities

Determining If a Child May Have an Intellectual Disability

Intellectual disability (**ID**) is primarily diagnosed when a child displays impairments in adaptive functioning. Often, these children will score lower than 70 on an IQ test, but IQ scores are not diagnostic and are particularly inaccurate on the low end of the scale. Students diagnosed with intellectual disabilities demonstrate deficits in academic skills, abstract thinking, problem solving, language development, new skill acquisition, and retaining information. Students with ID often do not adequately meet developmental or social milestones. They demonstrate **deficits in functioning** with one or more basic living skills. Students with ID struggle conceptually and may have difficulties with time and money concepts, short-term memory, time management, pre-academic skills, planning, and strategizing. Students with ID demonstrate poor social judgment and decision-making skills because they have trouble understanding social cues and rules. They may grasp concrete social concepts before abstract ones and significantly later than their similar-aged, regular education peers. These students also tend to struggle with self-care skills, household tasks, and completing tasks that may be easy for similar-aged peers.

Determining Severity of Intellectual Disabilities

There are four levels of intellectual disabilities: mild, moderate, severe, and profound. Specific factors are used to determine whether a disability is mild, moderate, severe, or profound. Intellectual levels are measured using cognitive- and research-based assessments. An **intellectual disability (ID)** is defined as significant cognitive deficits to intellectual functioning, such as reasoning, problem solving, abstract thinking, and comprehension. A **mild intellectual disability** is the most common type of intellectual disability. People with mild to moderate ID can generally participate in independent living activities and learn practical life skills and adaptive behaviors. People diagnosed with **severe intellectual disabilities** demonstrate major developmental delays. They struggle with simple routines and self-care skills. Additionally, they often understand speech but have trouble with expressive communication. People with **profound ID** cannot live independently, and they depend heavily on care from other people and resources. They are likely to have concurrent congenital disorders that affect their intellectual functioning.

Educational Implications for Students with Intellectual Disabilities

According to IDEA, students who are eligible for special education under the category of **intellectual disability** have significantly lower intellectual abilities, along with adaptive behavior deficits. Previously, intellectual disability was referred to as "mental retardation" in IDEA. In 2010, President Obama signed **Rosa's Law**, which changed the term to "intellectual disability." The definition of the disability category remained unchanged. Educational implications of a diagnosis of an intellectual disability differ depending on students' needs as determined by their IEPs. Students with intellectual disabilities often display **limitations to mental functioning** in areas like communication, self-care, and social skills (adaptive behavior). In many cases, these skills must be addressed in the educational environments in addition to any academic skill deficits. Learning adaptive behaviors and academic skills takes longer for students with intellectual disabilities. Their special education placements depend on what environments are least restrictive. This depends on the individual student and is determined in the IEP.

Promoting a Positive Performance for Students with Intellectual Disabilities

Students with intellectual disabilities often present with skill levels that are far below those of similar-aged peers. Because of deficits in academic, behavioral, and social skills, these students require **specialized instruction**, which varies depending on the needs of each individual student. An effective strategy for promoting a positive educational performance is to collect observations and data on the academic, behavioral, and social skill levels of the individual student. Teachers usually work with professionals in related services, like speech language pathologists, to address needs and implement educational interventions that work for this population of students. These students can benefit from **communication interventions** focused on interactions they may have with adults and peers. Students may benefit from augmentative and alternative communication devices, visual activity schedules and other visual supports, and computer-based instruction when learning communication and social skills. Students with intellectual disabilities may also require **behavioral interventions** to teach appropriate behaviors or decrease negative behaviors. They may also benefit from increased **peer interactions** through structured social groups in order to promote appropriate communication skills.

Multiple Disabilities

Components of the Multiple Disability Eligibility Category According to IDEA

The multiple disabilities category according to IDEA applies to students who have two or more disabilities occurring simultaneously. The multiple disability category does not include deaf-blindness, which has its own category under IDEA. Students with **multiple disabilities** present with such **severe educational needs** that they cannot be accommodated in special education settings that address only one disability. Placement in special education programs is determined by students' **least restrictive environments** as defined in their **Individualized Education Programs**. Students with multiple disabilities often present with communication deficits, mobility challenges, and deficits in adaptive behavior and need one-on-one instruction or assistance when performing daily activities.

Intervention Strategies for the Instruction of Students with Multiple Disabilities

Working with students with multiple disabilities can be challenging. However, strategies used in other special education settings can be implemented to promote the success of students with multiple disabilities. Effective strategies include the following:

- Setting **long-term goals**, which may last for a few years depending on how long students are in the same classrooms
- Working **collaboratively** with team members, like paraprofessionals and related service professionals, to ensure that they carry out students' educational objectives consistently
- Developing and maintaining **group goals** that the adults and students in the classrooms can strive to achieve together
- Working with students and paraprofessionals and consulting paraprofessionals frequently for **feedback**
- Demonstrating **patience** when waiting for students to respond or complete tasks
- Learning about how students **communicate**, which may involve gestures, a Picture Exchange Communication System, or other methods
- Driving instruction and education goals based on how students **learn best**
- Considering how students will **respond** when designing lessons, including accounting for response time during instruction

Culture and Language Differences in Special Education

Role of Cultural Competence in Schools and Special Education

Cultural competence, the awareness and appreciation of cultural differences, helps avoid **cultural and linguistic bias**. Schools that demonstrate **cultural competence** have an appreciation of families and their unique backgrounds. Cultural competence is important because it assists with incorporating knowledge and appreciation of other cultures into daily practices and teaching. This helps increase the quality and effectiveness of services for students with unique cultural and linguistic backgrounds. It also helps produce better outcomes for these students. In special education, being culturally competent means being aware of cultural and linguistic differences, especially when considering children for the identification process. Adapting to the **diversity** and **cultural contexts** of the surrounding communities allows teachers to better understand flags for referrals. Teachers that continually assess their awareness of the cultures and diversity of the communities where they teach demonstrate cultural competence. In order for schools and teachers to be described as culturally competent, they should have a process for recognizing diversity.

Cultural and Linguistic Differences vs. Learning Difficulties

Many schools are enriched with cultural diversity. It is important for special educators to identify if a suspected learning disability may instead be a **cultural or linguistic difference**. Teachers and schools must increase awareness of cultural and linguistic differences in order to avoid overidentification of certain populations as having learning difficulties. Some ways a child's behavior may represent cultural or linguistic differences are demonstrated in the **interactions** between teachers and students. In some cultures, children are asked to make eye contact to ensure they are listening, whereas in other cultures, children are taught to look down or away when being spoken to by an adult. Certain facial expressions and behaviors may be interpreted differently by students because of their cultural backgrounds. Additionally, teaching methods that are comfortable and effective for some students may be ineffective for others due to differing cultural backgrounds. Cultural values and characteristics may vary between teachers and students and contribute to the students' school performance. It is important for teachers to be **self-aware** and constantly **assess** whether ineffective teaching methods are due to learning difficulties or cultural and linguistic diversity.

Strategies for Teaching ELLs and Students with Disabilities

English language learners (ELLs) are often at risk of being unnecessarily referred for special education services. This is frequently a result of **inadequate planning** for the needs of English language learners rather than skill deficits. To ensure that the needs of ELLs are met and discrimination is avoided, educators can implement strategies for **targeting their learning processes**. Strategies similar to those utilized in inclusive special education settings, such as using visuals to supplement instruction, are helpful. This type of nonlinguistic representation helps convey meaning to ELLs. Working in groups with peers helps students with disabilities and ELLs demonstrate communication and social skills while working toward common goals. Allowing students to write and speak in their first languages until they feel comfortable speaking in English is a scaffolding strategy that can also be implemented. Sentence frames that demonstrate familiar sentence formats help all students to practice speaking and writing in structured, formal ways.

Review Video: ESL/ESOL/Second Language Learning
Visit mometrix.com/academy and enter code: 795047

Teaching Appropriate Communication Skills to ELLs with Disabilities

Students with disabilities who are also ELLs have the additional challenge of **language barriers** affecting their access to learning. These barriers, combined with the disabilities, can make instruction for these students challenging. For ELL students with disabilities, it is important for teachers to rely on **appropriate instructional strategies** in order to determine what is affecting the students' access to information. Strategies for teaching ELLs are similar to those for teaching nonverbal students. Pairing **visuals** with words helps students make concrete connections between the written words and the pictures. Consistently seeing the words paired with the visuals helps the students interpret word meanings. Using sign language or other gestures is another way teachers can facilitate understanding of word meanings. When used consistently, students make connections between the visual word meanings and the written words. Teachers can also provide opportunities for ELLs to access language by having all students in the classroom communicate in a **consistent manner**. The goal of this instructional strategy is for peers to model appropriate verbal communication as it applies to different classroom situations.

Social and Functional Living Skills

Targeting and Implementing Social Skills Instruction

Developing good social skills is essential for lifelong success, and people with disabilities often struggle with these skills. Addressing social skill behavior is most effective when specific **social skill needs** are identified, and **social skills instruction** is implemented as a collaborative effort between parents and teachers.

Evaluating **developmental milestones** is helpful in targeting social skills that need to be addressed and taught. If a child with a disability is not demonstrating a milestone, such as back-and-forth communication, the skill can be evaluated to determine if it should be taught. However, meeting milestones is not a reliable way to measure a student's social skill ability, as some children naturally progress more slowly. **Social skill deficits** may be acquisition deficits, performance deficits, or fluency deficits. A student with an **acquisition deficit** demonstrates an absence of a skill or behavior. A student with a **performance deficit** does not implement a social skill consistently. A student with a **fluency deficit** needs assistance with demonstrating a social skill effectively or fluently. Once a student's social skill need is identified, teachers, parents, and other professionals can collaborate to address it by establishing a routine or a behavior contract or implementing applied behavior analysis.

Using Instructional Methods to Address Independent Living Skills

When applicable, goals for independent living skills are included in the **transition section** of students' Individualized Education Programs (IEPs). However, **independent living skills education** should begin well before students reach high school, regardless of whether these skills are addressed in their IEP goals. **Functional skills instruction** is necessary to teach students skills needed to gain independence. Instructional methods used to address independent living skills for students with disabilities include making life skills instruction part of the daily curriculum. An appropriate **task analysis** can be used to determine what skills need to be taught. **Functional academic skills**, especially in the areas of math and language arts, should also be included in the curriculum. Telling time, balancing a checkbook, and recognizing signs and symbols are just some examples of basic skills that students can generalize outside of the classroom environment. The goal of **community-based instruction** is to help students develop skills needed to succeed in the community, such as skills needed when riding a bus or shopping. This type of instruction may be harder to implement than basic social skills training, which should be part of the daily curriculum.

Purposes and Benefits of Social Skills Groups

Social skills groups are useful for helping students with social skill deficits learn and practice appropriate skills with their peers. Social skills groups are primarily composed of similarly aged peers with and without disabilities. An adult leads these groups and teaches students skills needed for making friends, succeeding in school and life, and sometimes obtaining and maintaining a job. Other professionals, such as school psychologists or speech language pathologists, may also lead social skills groups. Social skills groups work by facilitating **conversation** and focusing on **skill deficits**. These groups can help students learn to read facial cues, appropriately greet others, begin conversations, respond appropriately, maintain conversations, engage in turn-taking, and request help when needed.

Evidence-Based Methods for Promoting Self-Determination

Students with disabilities often need to be taught **self-determination** and **self-advocacy** skills. These skills may not come easily to students with specific disorders, like Autism Spectrum Disorder. Self-determination involves a comprehensive understanding of one's own **strengths and**

limitations. Self-determined people are **goal-oriented** and intrinsically motivated to **improve themselves**. Teachers can facilitate the development of these skills in a number of ways, starting in early elementary school. In early elementary school, teachers can promote self-determination by teaching choice-making skills and providing clear consequences for choices. Teachers can also promote problem-solving and self-management skills, like having students evaluate their own work. At the middle school and junior high school level, students can be taught to evaluate and analyze their choices. They can also learn academic and personal goal-setting skills and decision-making skills. At the high school level, teachers can promote decision-making skills, involvement in educational planning (e.g., students attending their Individualized Education Program meetings), and strategies like self-instruction, self-monitoring, and self-evaluation. Throughout the education process, teachers should establish and maintain high standards for learning, focus on students' strengths, and create positive learning environments that promote choice and problem-solving skills.

Teaching Self-Awareness Skills

Students engage in private self-awareness and public self-awareness. Some students with disabilities have the additional challenge of needing instruction in **self-awareness skills**. Special educators and other professionals can facilitate the instruction of self-awareness skills by teaching students to be **aware** of their thoughts, feelings, and actions; to recognize that other people have needs and feelings; and to recognize how their behaviors **affect other people**. Students can be taught self-awareness by identifying their own strengths and weaknesses and learning to self-monitor errors in assignments. They can also be taught to identify what materials or steps are needed to complete tasks and to advocate for accommodations or strategies that work for them. Special educators or other professionals should frequently talk with students about their performance and encourage them to discuss their mistakes without criticism.

Importance of Learning Self-Advocacy Skills

Self-advocacy is an important skill to learn for people entering adulthood. For students with disabilities, **self-advocacy skills** are especially important for success in **postsecondary environments**. Teaching and learning self-advocacy skills should begin when students enter grade school and be reinforced in the upper grade levels. Students with disabilities who have the potential to enter postsecondary education or employment fields need to learn self-advocacy skills in order to **communicate** how their disabilities may affect their education or job performance and their need for supports and possible accommodations. Students with disabilities who graduate or age out of their Individualized Education Programs do not receive the **educational supports** they received at the grade school level. It is essential for students to advocate for themselves in the absence of teachers or caregivers advocating for them, especially when students independently enter postsecondary employment, training, or educational environments. Many colleges, universities, communities, and workplaces offer services to students with disabilities, but it is up to the students to advocate for themselves and seek them out.

Teaching Functional Living Skills

Also known as life skills, functional living skills are skills that students need to live independently. Ideally, students leave high school having gained functional skills. For students with special needs, **functional living skills instruction** may be needed to gain independent living skills. Students with developmental or cognitive disabilities sometimes need to acquire basic living skills, such as self-feeding or toileting. **Applied behavior analysis** is a process by which these skills can be identified, modeled, and taught. Students must also learn functional math and language arts skills, such as managing money and reading bus schedules. Students may also participate in **community-based instruction** to learn skills while completing independent living tasks in the community. These skills include grocery shopping, reading restaurant menus, and riding public transportation. **Social skills instruction** is also important for these students, as learning appropriate social interactions is necessary to function with community members.

Adaptive Behavior Skills Instruction

Adaptive behavior skills refer to age-appropriate behaviors that people need in order to live independently and function in daily life. **Adaptive behavior skills** include self-care, following rules, managing money, making friends, and more. For students with disabilities, especially severely limiting disabilities, adaptive behavior skills may need to be included in daily instruction. Adaptive behavior skills can be separated into conceptual skills, social skills, and practical life skills. **Conceptual skills** include academic concepts, such as reading, math, money, time, and communication skills. **Social skills** instruction focuses on teaching students to get along with others, communicate appropriately, and maintain appropriate behavior inside and outside the school environment. **Practical life skills** are skills needed to perform the daily living tasks, such as bathing, eating, sitting and standing, and using the bathroom. Adaptive behavior assessments are useful in assessing what adaptive behavior skills need to be addressed for each student. These assessments are usually conducted using observations and questionnaires completed by parents, teachers, or students.

Social Skill Deficits

Social skills generally develop alongside language development and emotional development, as they are a major component of communication and awareness. Social skills need to be taught to some students with disabilities, such as students with autism. **Social skills instruction** involves the teaching of basic communication skills, empathy and rapport skills, interpersonal skills, problem-solving skills, and accountability. These are skills that do not come naturally to students with social skill deficits.

- **Basic communication skills** include listening, following directions, and taking turns in conversations.
- **Emotional communication skills** include demonstrating empathy and building rapport with others.
- **Interpersonal skills** include sharing, joining activities, and participating in turn-taking.
- **Problem-solving skills** include asking for help, apologizing to others, making decisions, and accepting consequences.
- **Accountability** includes following through on promises and accepting criticism appropriately.

Instructional Methods for Teaching Students with Social Skill Deficits

Students with social skill deficits may or may not require explicit social skills instruction. These deficits can be addressed in inclusive settings. **Social skills instruction** can be delivered to entire classes or individual students, depending on the needs of the students. Also, **one-on-one** or **small group social skills instruction** can be delivered by professionals like speech-language pathologists. In both settings, it is important to model appropriate manners, hold students responsible for their actions, and have clear and concise rules and consequences. This creates educational environments that are both predictable and safe. Social situations that produce undesired outcomes can be remediated by **role-playing** the situations and teaching students positive responses. **Social stories** are another way to foster social skills growth. Often, these social stories demonstrate appropriate responses to specific social situations. The goal is for the students to generalize learned concepts to their school and home environments.

Assessment Methodology

Assessment Methods

Effective teaching requires multiple methods of assessment to evaluate student comprehension and instructional effectiveness. Assessments are typically categorized as diagnostic, formative, summative, and benchmark and are applicable at varying stages of instruction. **Diagnostic** assessments are administered before instruction and indicate students' prior knowledge and areas of misunderstanding to determine the path of instruction. **Formative** assessments occur continuously to measure student engagement, comprehension, and instructional effectiveness. These assessments indicate instructional strategies that require adjustment to meet students' needs in facilitating successful learning and include strategies like checking for understanding, observations, total participation activities, and exit tickets. **Summative** assessments are given at the end of a lesson or unit to evaluate student progress in reaching learning targets and identify areas of misconception for reteaching. Such assessments can be given in the form of exams and quizzes or be project-based activities in which students demonstrate their learning through hands-on, personalized methods. Additionally, portfolios serve as valuable summative assessments in allowing students to demonstrate their progress over time and provide insight regarding individual achievement. **Benchmark** assessments occur less frequently and encompass large portions of curriculum. These assessments are intended to evaluate the progress of groups of students in achieving state and district academic standards.

Assessment Types

- **Diagnostic:** These assessments can either be formal or informal and are intended to provide teachers with information regarding students' level of understanding prior to beginning a unit of instruction. Examples include pretests, KWL charts, anticipation guides, and brainstorming activities. Digital resources, such as online polls, surveys, and quizzes are also valuable resources for gathering diagnostic feedback.
- **Formative:** These assessments occur throughout instruction to provide the teacher with feedback regarding student understanding. Examples include warm-up and closure activities, checking frequently for understanding, student reflection activities, and providing students with color-coded cards to indicate their level of understanding. Short quizzes and total participation activities, such as four corners, are also valuable formative assessments. Numerous digital resources, including polls, surveys, and review games, are also beneficial in providing teachers with formative feedback to indicate instructional effectiveness.
- **Summative:** Summative assessments are intended to indicate students' levels of mastery and progress toward reaching academic learning standards. These assessments may take the form of written or digital exams and include multiple choice, short answer, or long answer questions. Examples also include projects, final essays, presentations, or portfolios to demonstrate student progress over time.
- **Benchmark:** Benchmark assessments measure students' progress in achieving academic standards. These assessments are typically standardized to ensure uniformity, objectivity, and accuracy. Benchmark assessments are typically given as a written multiple choice or short answer exam, or as a digital exam in which students answer questions on the computer.

Review Video: Formative and Summative Assessments
Visit mometrix.com/academy and enter code: 804991

Determining Appropriate Assessment Strategies

As varying assessment methods provide different information regarding student performance and achievement, the teacher must consider the most applicable and effective assessment strategy in each stage of instruction. This includes determining the **desired outcomes** of assessment as well as the information the teacher intends to ascertain and how they will apply the results to further instruction. **Age-** and **grade-level-**appropriateness must be considered when selecting which assessment strategies will enable students to successfully demonstrate their learning. Additionally, the teacher must be cognizant of students' individual differences and learning needs to determine which assessment model is most **accommodating** and reflective of their progress. It is also important that teachers consider the practicality of assessment strategies and methods they will use to implement the assessment for maximized feedback regarding individual and whole-class progress in achieving learning goals.

Assessments That Reflect Real-World Applications

Assessments that reflect **real-world applications** enhance relevancy and students' ability to establish personal connections to learning that deepen understanding. Implementing such assessments provides authenticity and enhances engagement by defining a clear and practical purpose for learning. These assessments often allow for hands-on opportunities for demonstrating learning and can be adjusted to accommodate students' varying learning styles and needs while measuring individual progress; however, assessments that focus on real-world applications can be subjective, thus making it difficult to extract concrete data and quantify student progress to guide future instructional decisions. In addition, teachers may have difficulty analyzing assessment results on a large scale and comparing student performance with other schools and districts, as individual assessments may vary.

Diagnostic Tests

Diagnostic tests are integral to planning and delivering effective instruction. These tests are typically administered prior to beginning a unit or lesson and provide valuable feedback for guiding and planning instruction. Diagnostic tests provide **preliminary information** regarding students' levels of understanding and prior knowledge. This serves as a baseline for instructional planning that connects and builds upon students' background knowledge and experiences to enhance success in learning. Diagnostic tests allow the teacher to identify and clarify areas of student misconception prior to engaging in instruction to ensure continued comprehension and avoid the need for remediation. They indicate areas of student strength and need as well as individual instructional aids that may need to be incorporated into lessons to support student achievement. In addition, these tests enable the teacher to determine which instructional strategies, activities, groupings, and materials will be most valuable in maximizing engagement and learning. Diagnostic tests can be **formal** or **informal** and include pre-tests, pre-reading activities, surveys, vocabulary inventories, and graphic organizers (such as KWL charts). These tests are used to assess student understanding prior to engaging in learning. Diagnostic tests are generally not graded, as there is little expectation that all students in a class possess the same baseline of proficiency at the start of a unit.

Formative Assessments

Formative assessments are any assessments that take place in the **middle of a unit of instruction**. The goals of formative assessments are to help teachers understand where a student is in his or her progress toward **mastering** the current unit's content and to provide the students with **ongoing feedback** throughout the unit. The advantage of relying heavily on formative assessments in instruction is that it allows the teacher to continuously **check for comprehension** and adjust instruction as needed to ensure that the whole class is adequately prepared to proceed at the end of the unit. To understand formative assessments well, teachers need to understand that any interaction that can provide information about the student's comprehension is a type of formative assessment which can be used to inform future instruction.

Formative assessments are often a mixture of formal and informal assessments. **Formal formative assessments** often include classwork, homework, and quizzes. Examples of **informal formative assessments** include simple comprehension checks during instruction, class-wide discussions of the current topic, and exit slips, which are written questions posed by teachers at the end of class, which helps the teacher quickly review which students are struggling with the concepts.

Summative Assessments

Summative assessment refers to an evaluation at the end of a discrete unit of instruction, such as the end of a course, unit, or semester. Classic examples of summative assessments include end-of-course assessments, final exams, or even qualifying standardized tests such as the SAT or ACT. Most summative assessments are created to measure student mastery of particular **academic standards**. Whereas formative assessment generally informs current instruction, summative assessments are used to objectively demonstrate that each individual has achieved adequate mastery of the standards in question. If a student has not met the benchmark, he or she may need extra instruction or may need to repeat the course.

These assessments usually take the form of **tests** or formal portfolios with rubrics and clearly defined goals. Summative assessments are usually high-stakes, heavily-weighted, and they should always be formally graded. These types of assessments often feature a narrower range of question types, such as multiple choice, short answer, and essay questions to help with systematic grading.

Project-based assessments are beneficial in evaluating achievement, as they incorporate several elements of instruction and highlight real-world applications of learning. This allows students to demonstrate understanding through a hands-on, individualized approach that reinforces connections to learning and increases retainment. **Portfolios** of student work over time serve as a valuable method for assessing individual progress toward reaching learning targets. Summative assessments provide insight regarding overall instructional effectiveness and are necessary for guiding future instruction in subsequent years but are not usually used to modify current instruction.

Review Video: Assessment Reliability and Validity
Visit mometrix.com/academy and enter code: 424680

Benchmark Assessments

Benchmark assessments are intended to quantify, evaluate, and compare individual and groups of students' achievement of school-wide, district, and state **academic standards.** They are typically administered in specific intervals throughout the school year and encompass entire or large units of curriculum to determine student mastery and readiness for academic advancement. Benchmark assessments provide data that enable the teacher to determine students' progress toward reaching academic goals to guide current and continued instruction. This data can be utilized by the school and individual teachers to create learning goals and objectives aligned with academic standards. It can also be used to plan instructional strategies, activities, and assessments to support students in achieving these academic standards. In addition, benchmark assessments provide feedback regarding understanding and the potential need for remediation to allow the teacher to instill necessary supports in future instruction that prepare students for success in achieving learning targets.

Alignment of Assessments with Instructional Goals and Objectives

To effectively monitor student progress, assessments must align with **instructional goals** and **objectives**. This allows the teacher to determine whether students are advancing at an appropriate pace to achieve state and district academic standards. When assessments are aligned with specific learning targets, the teacher ensures that students are learning relevant material to establish a foundation of knowledge necessary for growth and academic achievement. To achieve this, teachers must determine which instructional goals and objectives their students must achieve and derive instruction, content, and activities from these specifications. Instruction must reflect and reinforce learning targets, and the teacher must select the most effective strategies for addressing students' needs as they work to achieve them. Assessments must be reflective of content instruction to ensure they are aligned with learning goals and objectives, as well as to enable the teacher to evaluate student progress in mastering them. The teacher must clearly communicate learning goals and objectives throughout all stages of instruction to provide students with clarity on expectations. This establishes a clear purpose and focus for learning that enhances relevancy and strengthens connections to support student achievement.

Clearly Communicating Assessment Criteria and Standards

Students must be clear on the purpose of learning throughout all stages of instruction to enhance understanding and facilitate success. When assessment **criteria** and **standards** are clearly communicated, the purpose of learning is established, and students are able to effectively connect instructional activities to learning goals and criteria for assessment. Communicating assessment criteria and standards provides students with clarity on tasks and learning goals they are expected to accomplish as they prepare themselves for assessment. This allows for more **focused instruction** and engagement in learning, as it enhances relevancy and student motivation. Utilizing appropriate forms of **rubrics** is an effective strategy in specifying assessment criteria and standards, as it informs students about learning goals they are working toward, the quality of work they are expected to achieve, and skills they must master to succeed on the assessment. Rubrics indicate to students exactly how they will be evaluated, thus supporting their understanding and focus as they engage in learning to promote academic success.

Rubrics for Communicating Standards

The following are varying styles of rubrics that can be used to communicate criteria and standards:

- **Analytic:** Analytic rubrics break down criteria for an assignment into several categories and provide an explanation of the varying levels of performance in each one. This style of rubric is beneficial for detailing the characteristics of quality work as well as providing students with feedback regarding specific components of their performance. Analytic rubrics are most effective when used for summative assessments, such as long-term projects or essays.
- **Holistic:** Holistic rubrics evaluate the quality of the student's assignment as a whole rather than scoring individual components. Students' scores are determined based upon their performance across multiple performance indicators. This style of rubric is beneficial for providing a comprehensive evaluation but limits the amount of feedback that students receive regarding their performance in specific areas.

- **Single-point:** Single-point rubrics outline criteria for assignments into several categories. Rather than providing a numeric score to each category, however, the teacher provides written feedback regarding the students' strengths and ways in which they can improve their performance. This style of rubric is beneficial in providing student-centered feedback that focuses on their overall progress.
- **Checklist:** Checklists typically outline a set of criteria that is scored using a binary approach based upon completion of each component. This style increases the efficiency of grading assignments and is often easy for students to comprehend but does not provide detailed feedback. This method of grading should generally be reserved for shorter assignments.

Communicating High Academic Expectations in Assessments

The attitudes and behaviors exhibited by the teacher are highly influential on students' attitudes toward learning. Teachers demonstrate belief in students' abilities to be successful in learning when they communicate **high academic expectations**. This promotes students' **self-concept** and establishes a **growth mindset** to create confident, empowered learners that are motivated to achieve. High expectations for assessments and reaching academic standards communicates to students the quality of work that is expected of them and encourages them to overcome obstacles as they engage in learning. When communicating expectations for student achievement, it is important that the teacher is aware of students' individual learning needs to provide the necessary support that establishes equitable opportunities for success in meeting assessment criteria and standards. Setting high expectations through assessment criteria and standards while supporting students in their learning enhances overall achievement and establishes a foundation for continuous academic success.

Effective Communication and Impact on Student Learning

Communicating high academic expectations enhances students' self-concept and increases personal motivation for success in learning. To maximize student achievement, it is important that the teacher set high academic expectations that are **clearly** communicated through **age-appropriate** terms and consistently reinforced. Expectations must be reflected through learning goals and objectives and must be **visible** at all times to ensure student awareness. Teachers must be **specific** in communicating what they want students to accomplish and clearly detail necessary steps for achievement while assuming the role of facilitator to guide learning and provide support. Providing constructive **feedback** throughout instruction is integral in reminding students of academic expectations and ensuring they are making adequate progress toward reaching learning goals. When high academic expectations are communicated and reinforced, students are empowered with a sense of confidence and self-responsibility for their own learning that promotes their desire to learn. This ultimately enhances achievement and equips them with the tools necessary for future academic success.

Analyzing and Interpreting Assessment Data

Teachers can utilize multiple techniques to effectively analyze and interpret assessment data. This typically involves creating charts and graphs outlining different data subsets. They can list each learning standard that was assessed, determine how many students overall demonstrated proficiency on the standard, and identify individual students who did not demonstrate proficiency on each standard. This information can be used to differentiate instruction. Additionally, they can track individual student performance and progress on each standard over time.

Teachers can take note of overall patterns and trends in assessment data. For example, they can determine if any subgroups of students did not meet expectations. They can consider whether the data confirms or challenges any existing beliefs, implications this may have on instructional planning and what, if any, conclusions can be drawn from this data.

Analyzing and interpreting assessment data may raise new questions for educators, so they can also determine if additional data collection is needed.

Using Assessment Data to Differentiate Instruction for Individual Learners

By analyzing and interpreting assessment data, teachers can determine if there are any specific learning standards that need to be retaught to their entire classes. This may be necessary if the data shows that all students struggled in these specific areas. Teachers may consider reteaching these standards using different methods if the initial methods were unsuccessful.

Teachers can also form groups of students who did not demonstrate proficiency on the same learning standards. Targeted instruction can be planned for these groups to help them make progress in these areas. Interventions can also be planned for individual students who did not show proficiency in certain areas. If interventions have already been in place and have not led to increased learning outcomes, the interventions may be redesigned. If interventions have been in place and assessment data now shows proficiency, the interventions may be discontinued.

If assessment data shows that certain students have met or exceeded expectations in certain areas, enrichment activities can be planned to challenge these students and meet their learning needs.

Aligning Assessments with Instructional Goals and Objectives

Assessments that are congruent to instructional goals and objectives provide a **clear purpose** for learning that enhances student understanding and motivation. When learning targets are reflected in assessments, instructional activities and materials become more **relevant**, as they are derived from these specifications. Such clarity in purpose allows for more focus and productivity as students engage in instruction and fosters connections that strengthen overall understanding for maximized success in learning. Aligning assessments with instructional goals and objectives ensures that students are learning material that is relevant to the curriculum and academic standards to ensure **preparedness** as they advance in their academic careers. In addition, it enables the teacher to evaluate and monitor student progress to determine whether they are progressing at an ideal pace for achieving academic standards. With this information, the teacher can effectively modify instruction as necessary to support students' needs in reaching desired learning outcomes.

Norm-Referenced Tests

On **norm-referenced tests**, students' performances are compared to the performances of sample groups of similar students. Norm-referenced tests identify students who score above and below the average. To ensure reliability, the tests must be given in a standardized manner to all students.

Norm-referenced tests usually cover a broad range of skills, such as the entire grade-level curriculum for a subject. They typically contain a few questions per skill. Whereas scores in component areas of the tests may be calculated, usually overall test scores are reported. Scores are often reported using percentile ranks, which indicate what percentage of test takers scored lower than the student being assessed. For example, a student's score in the 75th percentile means the student scored better than 75% of other test takers. Other times, scores may be reported using grade-level equivalency.

One advantage of norm-referenced tests is their objectivity. They also allow educators to compare large groups of students at once. This may be helpful for making decisions regarding class placements and groupings. A disadvantage of norm-referenced tests is that they only indicate how well students perform in comparison to one another. They do not indicate whether or not students have mastered certain skills.

Criterion-Referenced Tests

Criterion-referenced tests measure how well students perform on certain skills or standards. The goal of these tests is to indicate whether or not students have mastered certain skills and which skills require additional instruction. Scores are typically reported using the percentage of questions answered correctly or students' performance levels. Performance levels are outlined using terms such as *below expectations*, *met expectations*, and *exceeded expectations*.

One advantage of criterion-referenced tests is that they provide teachers with useful information to guide instruction. They can identify which specific skills students have mastered and which skills need additional practice. Teachers can use this information to plan whole-class, small-group, and individualized instruction. Analyzing results of criterion-referenced tests over time can also help teachers track student progress on certain skills. A disadvantage of criterion-referenced tests is that they do not allow educators to compare students' performances to samples of their peers.

Ways That Standardized Test Results Are Reported

- **Raw scores** are sometimes reported and indicate how many questions students answered correctly on a test. By themselves, they do not provide much useful information. They do not indicate how students performed in comparison to other students or to grade-level expectations.
- **Grade-level equivalents** are also sometimes reported. A grade-level equivalent score of 3.4 indicates that a student performed as well as an average third grader in the fourth month of school. It can indicate whether a student is performing above or below grade-level expectations, but it does not indicate that the student should be moved to a different grade level.
- **Standard scores** are used to compare students' performances on tests to standardized samples of their peers. Standard deviation refers to the amount that a set of scores differs from the mean score on a test.
- **Percentile ranks** are used on criterion-referenced tests to indicate what percentage of test takers scored lower than the student whose score is being reported.
- **Cutoff scores** refer to predetermined scores students must obtain in order to be considered proficient in certain areas. Scores below the cutoff level indicate improvement is needed and may result in interventions or instructional changes.

Formal and Informal Assessments

Assessments are any method a teacher uses to gather information about student comprehension of curriculum, including improvised questions for the class and highly-structured tests. **Formal assessments** are assessments that have **clearly defined standards and methodology** and which are applied consistently to all students. Formal tests should be objective and scrutinized for validity and reliability since they tend to carry higher weight for the student. Summative assessments, such as end-of-unit tests, lend themselves to being formal tests because it is necessary that a teacher test the comprehension of all students in a consistent and thorough way.

Although formal assessments can provide useful data about student performance and progress, they can be costly and time-consuming to implement. Administering formal assessments often interrupts classroom instruction and may cause testing anxiety.

Informal assessments are assessments that do not adhere to formal objectives, and they do not have to be administered consistently to all students. As a result, they do not have to be scored or recorded as a grade and generally act as a **subjective measure** of class comprehension. Informal assessments can be as simple as asking the students to raise their hands if they are ready to proceed to the next step or asking a particular question of an individual student.

Informal assessments do not provide objective data for analysis, but they can be implemented quickly and inexpensively. Informal assessments can also be incorporated into regular classroom instruction and activities, making them more authentic and less stressful for students.

Using Various Assessments

The goal of **assessment** in education is to gather data that, when evaluated, can be used to further student learning and achievement. **Standardized tests** are helpful for placement purposes and to reflect student progress toward goals set by a school district or state. If a textbook is chosen to align with district learning standards, the textbook assessments can provide teachers with convenient, small-scale, regular checks of student knowledge against the target standard.

In order be effective, teachers must know where their students are in the learning process. Teachers use a multitude of **formal and informal assessment methods** to do this. Posing differentiated discussion questions is an example of an informal assessment method that allows teachers to gauge individual student progress rather than their standing in relation to a universal benchmark.

Effective teachers employ a variety of assessments, as different formats assess different skills, promote different learning experiences, and appeal to different learners. A portfolio is an example of an assessment that gauges student progress in multiple skills and through multiple media. Teachers can use authentic or performance-based assessments to stimulate student interest and provide visible connections between language-learning and the real world.

Assessment Reliability

Assessment reliability refers to how well an assessment is constructed and is made up of a variety of measures. An assessment is generally considered **reliable** if it yields similar results across multiple administrations of the assessment. A test should perform similarly with different test administrators, graders, test-takers, and over multiple iterations. Factors that affect reliability include the day-to-day wellbeing of the student (students can sometimes underperform), the physical environment of the test, the way it is administered, and the subjectivity of the scorer (with written-response assessments).

Perhaps the most important threat to assessment reliability is the nature of the **exam questions** themselves. An assessment question is designed to test knowledge of a certain construct. A question is reliable in this sense if students who understand the content answer the question correctly. Statisticians look for patterns in student marks, both within the single test and over multiple tests, as a way of measuring reliability. Teachers should watch out for circumstances in which a student or students answer correctly a series of questions about a given concept (demonstrating their understanding) but then answer a related question incorrectly. The latter question may be an unreliable indicator of concept knowledge.

Measures of Assessment Reliability

- **Test-retest reliability** refers to an assessment's consistency of results with the same test-taker over multiple retests. If one student shows inconsistent results over time, the test is not considered to have test-retest reliability.

- **Intertester reliability** refers to an assessment's consistency of results between multiple test-takers at the same level. Students at similar levels of proficiency should show similar results.
- **Inter-rater reliability** refers to an assessment's consistency of results between different administrators of the test. This plays an especially critical role in tests with interactive or subjective responses, such as Likert-scales, cloze tests, and short answer tests. Different raters of the same test need to have a consistent means of evaluating the test-takers' performance. Clear rubrics can help keep two or more raters consistent in scoring.
- **Intra-rater reliability** refers to an assessment's consistency of results with one rater over time. One test rater should be able to score different students objectively to rate subjective test formats fairly.
- **Parallel-forms reliability** refers to an assessment's consistency between multiple different forms. For instance, end-of-course assessments may have many distinctive test forms, with different questions or question orders. If the different forms of a test do not provide the same results, the test is said to be lacking in parallel-forms reliability.
- **Internal consistency reliability** refers to the consistency of results of similar questions on a particular assessment. If there are two or more questions targeted at the same standard and at the same level, they should show the same results across each question.

Assessment Validity

Assessment validity is a measure of the relevancy that an assessment has to the skill or ability being evaluated and the degree to which students' performance is representative of their mastery of the topic of assessment. In other words, a teacher should ask how well an assessment's results correlate to what it is looking to assess. Assessments should be evaluated for validity on both the **individual question** level and as a **test overall**. This can be especially helpful in refining tests for future classes. The overall validity of an assessment is determined by several types of validity measures.

An assessment is considered **valid** if it measures what it is intended to measure. One common error that can reduce the validity of a test (or a question on a test) occurs if the instructions are written at a reading level the students can't understand. In this case, it is not valid to take the student's failed answer as a true indication of his or her knowledge of the subject. Factors internal to the student might also affect exam validity: anxiety and a lack of self-esteem often lower assessments results, reducing their validity as a measure of student knowledge.

An assessment has content validity if it includes all the **relevant aspects** of the subject being tested—if it is comprehensive, in other words. An assessment has **predictive validity** if a score on the test is an accurate predictor of future success in the same domain. For example, SAT exams purport to have validity in predicting student success in a college. An assessment has construct validity if it accurately measures student knowledge of the subject being tested.

Measures of Assessment Validity

- **Face validity** refers to the initial impression of whether an assessment seems to be fit for the task. As this method is subjective to interpretation and unquantifiable, it should not be used singularly as a measurement of validity.

- **Construct validity** asks if an assessment actually assesses what it is intended to assess. Some topics are more straightforward, such as assessing if a student can perform two-digit multiplication. This can be directly tested, which gives the assessment a strong content validity. Other measures, such as a person's overall happiness, must be measured indirectly. If an assessment asserted that a person is generally happy if he or she smiles frequently, it would be fair to question the construct validity of that assessment because smiling is unlikely to be a consistent measure of all peoples' general happiness.
- **Content validity** indicates whether the assessment is comprehensive of all aspects of the content being assessed. If a test leaves out an important topic, then the teacher will not have a full picture as a result of the assessment.
- **Criterion validity** refers to whether the results of an assessment can be used to **predict** a related value, known as **criterion.** An example of this is the hypothesis that IQ tests would predict a person's success later in life, but many critics believe that IQ tests are not valid predictors of success because intelligence is not the only predictor of success in life. IQ tests have shown validity toward predicting academic success, however. The measure of an assessment's criterion validity depends on how closely related the criterion is.
- **Discriminant validity** refers to how well an assessment tests only that which it is intended to test and successfully discriminates one piece of information from another. For instance, a student who is exceptional in mathematics should not be able to put that information into use on a science test and gain an unfair advantage. If the student is able to score well due to his or her mathematics knowledge, the science test did not adequately discriminate science knowledge from mathematics knowledge.
- **Convergent validity** is related to discriminant validity, but takes into account that two measures may be distinct but correlated. For instance, a personality test should distinguish self-esteem from extraversion so that they can be measured independently, but if an assessment has convergent validity, it should show a correlation between related measures.

Practicality

An assessment is **practical** if it uses an appropriate amount of human and budgetary resources. A practical exam doesn't take very long to design or score, nor does it take students very long to complete in relation to other learning objectives and priorities. Teachers often need to balance a desire to construct comprehensive or content-valid tests with a need for practicality: lengthy exams consume large amounts of instruction time and may return unreliable results if students become tired and lose focus.

Assessment Bias

An assessment is considered biased if it disadvantages a certain group of students, such as students of a certain gender, race, cultural background, or socioeconomic class. A **content bias** exists when the subject matter of a question or assessment is familiar to one group and not another. For example, a reading comprehension passage that discusses an event in American history would be biased against students new to the country. An **attitudinal bias** exists when a teacher has a pre-conceived idea about the likely success of an assessment of a particular individual or group. A **method bias** arises when the format of an assessment is unfamiliar to a given group of students. **Language bias** occurs when an assessment utilizes idioms, collocations, or cultural references unfamiliar to a group of students. Finally, **translation bias** may arise when educators attempt to translate content-area assessments into a student's native language—rough or hurried translations often result in a loss of nuance important for accurate assessment.

Authentic Assessments

An authentic assessment is an assessment designed to closely resemble something that a student does, or will do, in the real world. For example, students will never encounter a multiple-choice test requiring them to choose the right tense of a verb, but they will encounter contexts in which they have to write a narration of an event that has antecedents and consequents spread out in time—like narrating their version of what caused a traffic accident. The latter is an example of a potential **authentic assessment**.

Well-designed authentic assessments require a student to exercise **advanced cognitive skills** (e.g., solving problems, integrating information, performing deductions), integrate **background knowledge**, and confront **ambiguity**. Research has demonstrated that mere language proficiency is not predictive of future language success—learning how to utilize knowledge in a complex context is an essential additional skill.

The terms "authentic" and "performance-based" are often used interchangeably when describing assessments; however, a performance-based assessment doesn't necessarily have to be grounded in a possible authentic experience.

Performance-Based Assessments

A performance-based assessment is one in which students demonstrate their learning by performing a **task** rather than by answering questions in a traditional test format. Proponents of **performance-based assessments** argue that they lead students to use **high-level cognitive skills** since they focus on how to put their knowledge to use and plan a sequence of stages in an activity or presentation. They also allow students more opportunities to individualize their presentations or responses based on preferred learning styles. Research suggests that students welcome the chance to put their knowledge to use in real-world scenarios.

Advocates of performance-based assessments suggest that they avoid many of the problems of language or cultural bias present in traditional assessments, allowing more accurate assessment of how well students learned the underlying concepts. In discussions regarding English as a second language, they argue that performance assessments come closer to replicating what should be the true goal of language learning—the effective use of language in real contexts—than do more traditional exams. Critics point out that performance assessments are difficult and time-consuming for teachers to construct and for students to perform. Finally, performative assessments are difficult to grade in the absence of a well-constructed and detailed rubric.

Technology-Based Assessments

Technology-based assessments provide teachers with multiple resources for evaluating student progress to guide instruction. They are applicable in most formal and informal instructional settings and can be utilized as formative and summative assessments. Technology-based assessments simplify and enhance the efficiency of determining comprehension and instructional effectiveness, as they quickly present the teacher with information regarding student progress. This data enables the teacher to make necessary adjustments to facilitate student learning and growth. Implementing this assessment format simplifies the process of aligning them to school and district academic standards. This establishes objectivity and uniformity for comparing results and progress among students. It also helps ensure that all students are held to the same academic expectations. While technology-based assessments are beneficial, there are some shortcomings to consider. This format may not be entirely effective for all learning styles in demonstrating understanding, as individualization in technology-based assessment can be limited. These assessments may not illustrate individual students' growth over time but rather their mastery of an academic standard, thus hindering the ability to evaluate overall achievement. As technology-based evaluation limits hands-on opportunities, the real-world application and relevancy of the assessment may be unapparent to students.

Advantages and Disadvantages of Technology-Based Assessments

Technology-based assessments can have many advantages. They can be given to large numbers of students at once, limited only by the amounts of technological equipment schools possess. Many types of technology-based assessments are instantly scored, and feedback is provided quickly. Students are sometimes able to view their results and feedback at the conclusion of their testing sessions. Data can be quickly compiled and reported in easy-to-understand formats. Technology-based assessments can also often track student progress over time.

Technology-based assessments can have some disadvantages as well. Glitches and system errors can interfere with the assessment process or score reporting. Students must also have the necessary prerequisite technological skills to take the assessments, or the results may not measure the content they are designed to measure. For example, if students take timed, computer-based writing tests, they should have proficient typing skills. Otherwise, they may perform poorly on the tests despite strong writing abilities. Other prerequisite skills include knowing how to use a keyboard and mouse and understanding how to locate necessary information on the screen.

Portfolio Assessments

A **portfolio** is a collection of student work in multiple forms and media gathered over time. Teachers may assess the portfolio both for evidence of progress over time or in its end state as a demonstration of the achievement of certain proficiency levels.

One advantage of **portfolio assessments** is their breadth. Unlike traditional assessments, which focus on one or two language skills, portfolios may contain work in multiple forms, such as writing samples, pictures, and graphs designed for content courses, video and audio clips, student reflections, teacher observations, and student exams. A second advantage is that they allow a student to develop work in authentic contexts, including in other classrooms and at home.

In order for portfolios to function as an objective assessment tool, teachers should negotiate with students in advance of what genres of work will be included and outline a grading rubric that makes clear what will be assessed, such as linguistic proficiency, use of English in academic contexts, and demonstrated use of target cognitive skills.

Curriculum-Based Assessments

Curriculum-based assessments, also known as **curriculum-based measurements (CBM)**, are short, frequent assessments designed to measure student progress toward meeting curriculum **benchmarks**.

Teachers implement CBMs by designing **probes**, or short assessments that target specific skills. For example, a teacher might design a spelling probe, administered weekly, that requires students to spell 10 unfamiliar but level-appropriate words. The data from these assessments can be tracked over time to measure student progress toward defined grade-level goals.

CBM has several clear advantages. If structured well, the probes have high reliability and validity. Furthermore, they provide clear and objective evidence of student progress—a welcome outcome for students and parents who often grapple with less-clear and subjective evidence. Used correctly, CBMs also motivate students and provide them with evidence of their own progress; however, while CBMs are helpful in identifying areas of student weaknesses, they do not identify the causes of those weaknesses or provide teachers with strategies for improving instruction.

TEXTBOOK ASSESSMENTS

Textbook assessments are the assessments provided at the end of a chapter or unit in an approved textbook. **Textbook assessments** present several advantages for a teacher: they are already made; they are likely to be accurate representations of the chapter or unit materials; and, if the textbook has been prescribed or recommended by the state, it is likely to correspond closely to Common Core or other tested standards.

Textbook assessments can be limiting for students who lag in the comprehension of academic English or whose preferred learning style is not verbal. While textbooks may come with DVDs or recommended audio links, ESOL teachers will likely need to supplement these assessment materials with some of their own findings. Finally, textbook assessments are unlikely to represent the range of assessment types used in the modern classroom, such as a portfolio or performance-based assessments.

PEER ASSESSMENT

A peer assessment is when students grade one another's work based on a teacher-provided framework. **Peer assessments** are promoted as a means of saving teacher time and building student metacognitive skills. They are typically used as **formative** rather than summative assessments, given concerns about the reliability of student scoring and the tensions that can result if student scores contribute to overall grades. Peer assessments are used most often to grade essay-type written work or presentations. Proponents point out that peer assessments require students to apply metacognition, build cooperative work and interpersonal skills, and broaden the sense that the student is accountable to peers and not just the teacher. Even advocates of the practice agree that students need detailed rubrics in order to succeed. Critics often argue that low-performing students have little to offer high-performing students in terms of valuable feedback—and this disparity may be more pronounced in ESOL classrooms or special education environments than in mainstream ones. One way to overcome this weakness is for the teacher to lead the evaluation exercise, guiding the students through a point-by-point framework of evaluation.

Developmental Screening

TYPES OF DEVELOPMENTAL ASSESSMENTS

Developmental assessments measure the development of infants, toddlers, and preschoolers. These **norm-referenced tests** measure fine and gross motor skills; communication and language; and social, cognitive, and self-help milestones that young children should achieve at certain ages. When a child is suspected of having a **developmental delay**, a developmental assessment is useful in identifying the child's strengths and weaknesses. These assessments map out the **progress** of a child compared to the progress of similar-aged children. Developmental assessments are also useful in identifying if the delay is significant or can be overcome with time. These assessments can be used to determine what **educational placement** is most appropriate for a child with a developmental delay. Developmental assessments are administered via observations and questionnaires. Parents, legal guardians, caregivers, and instructors who are most familiar with the child provide the most insight on developmental strengths and weaknesses.

Review Video: Identifying Appropriate Evaluation Strategies
Visit mometrix.com/academy and enter code: 100353

Screening Tests for Identifying Students Who Need Special Education

When determining if a child needs special education, **screening tests** are the first step. The Individuals with Disabilities Education Act offers guidance for schools to implement screening tests. Districts and schools often have school-wide processes in place for screening students for **special education**. Screening tests can also be used to identify students who are falling behind in class. The advantage of screening tests is that they are easily administered. They require few materials and little time and planning in order to administer. Additionally, they can be used to quickly assess students' strengths and weaknesses, they do not have to be administered one-on-one, and they can be used for everyone in the class. Screening tests can be as simple as paper-and-pencil quizzes assessing what students know. They are used for measuring visual acuity, auditory skills, physical health, development, basic academic skills, behavioral problems, risk of behavioral problems, language skills, and verbal and nonverbal intelligence.

Individual Intelligence Tests vs. Individual Academic Achievement Tests

Intelligence tests measure a student's capacity for abstract thinking, mental reasoning, judgment, and decision-making. These **norm-referenced tests** help determine a student's **overall intelligence**, which correlates with **potential academic performance**. Intelligence tests can be used to determine if a student's deficits are due to intellectual disabilities or related to specific learning disabilities or emotional disorders. They can also measure verbal skills, motor performance, and visual reasoning. Intelligence tests are also known as **intelligence quotient tests (IQ tests)**. IQ tests should be administered by trained professionals to ensure the tests are administered accurately. Unlike intelligence tests, individual academic achievement tests measure a student's strengths and weaknesses in individual skills. They are also norm referenced and used to determine if a student needs **special education services**. Results from individual academic tests help determine areas of concern or possible deficits for an individual student. Unlike intelligence tests, individual academic tests can be administered by teachers.

Adaptive Behavior Scale Assessments

Adaptive behavior scales are useful for diagnosing a student with an **intellectual disability** that affects the development or progression of adaptive behavior. They are used in preschools and for determining eligibility for **special education** in grade schools. They are also used in planning the **curriculum** for students with intellectual disabilities. Adaptive behavior scales are standardized but not always norm referenced because of difficulties comparing expectations for some adaptive and maladaptive skills exhibited by similar-aged peers. In terms of curriculum planning, these assessments can determine the type and quantity of assistance a student may need. Adaptive behavior scale assessments identify a student's level of **independence**. Adaptive behavior scales can be used to determine **skill abilities** associated with daily living, community functioning, social skills, communication, motor functions, and basic academic skills. Teachers and other professionals can administer adaptive behavior scales to students with intellectual disabilities to determine starting points for improving their adaptive behavior deficits.

Curriculum-Based Measurement of Student Academic Progress

Curriculum-based measurement (**CBM**) is a way for teachers to track how students are **progressing** in mathematics, language arts, social studies, science, and other skills. It is also useful for communicating progress to parents or legal guardians. CBM results can determine whether or not current **instructional strategies** are effective for particular students. In the same respect, CBM can determine if students are meeting the **standards** laid out in their Individualized Education Program goals. If CBM results show that instructional strategies are not effective or goals are not being met, teachers should change instructional strategies. CBM can be revisited to determine whether or not the newly implemented strategies are effective. Progress can sometimes be charted to present a visual for how a student is progressing in a particular content area or with a specific skill.

Woodcock-Johnson Tests

High-Incidence Disabilities

Woodcock-Johnson tests can be used as diagnostic tools for identifying children with **high-incidence disabilities**. The Woodcock-Johnson Tests of Achievement, the Woodcock-Johnson Tests of Cognitive Abilities, and the Woodcock-Johnson Tests of Oral Language are comprehensively useful for assessing children's:

- Intellectual abilities
- Cognitive abilities
- Aptitude
- Oral language
- Academic achievements

These norm-referenced tests are valuable in understanding children's strengths and weaknesses and how they compare to cohorts of normally progressing, similar-aged peers. For example, **Woodcock-Johnson tests (WJ tests)** are useful in identifying children with language disorders because children with language disorders typically score lower on the listening comprehension and fluid reasoning test sections. The WJ tests are useful diagnostic tools for identifying children with attention-deficit/hyperactivity disorder (ADHD) as well. While children with ADHD may perform similarly to children with learning disabilities, their key deficits are in the cognitive efficiency, processing speed, academic fluency, short-term memory, and long-term retrieval test sections.

Prenatal, Perinatal, and Neonatal Disabilities

Prenatal, perinatal, and neonatal risk factors can be genetic or environmental. These factors put infants at risk for developing **intellectual disabilities** that affect their day-to-day lives. An intellectual disability is a disability that significantly limits a child's overall cognitive abilities. **Prenatal** risk factors include genetic syndromes (e.g., Down syndrome), brain malformation, maternal diseases, and environmental influences. Drugs, alcohol, or poison exposure can all affect an unborn child. **Perinatal** (during delivery) risk factors include labor and delivery trauma or anoxia at birth. **Neonatal** (post-birth) risk factors include hypoxic ischemic brain injury, traumatic brain injury, infections, seizure disorders, and toxic metabolic syndromes. Early screening and applicable assessments are tools used to identify young children with intellectual disabilities and can assist with providing special education services under the Individuals with Disabilities Education Act. These tools can also help assess the severity of deficits and the need for special services, such as occupational therapy.

Learning Disabilities in Reading and Mathematics

The Woodcock-Johnson tests (WJ tests) include tests of achievement, cognitive abilities, and oral language. Together, these assessments are useful in the diagnostic process of identifying a student with a **disability**. Additionally, they are helpful for identifying specific **deficits** in a student's reading or math skills. WJ tests are norm-referenced and compare the results of a child's performance to that of a cohort of children of similar age and average intellectual abilities. These assessments provide information about **reading disorders**, such as dyslexia, because they measure phonological awareness, rapid automatized naming, processing speed, and working memory. WJ tests report on a child's cognitive functioning in these test areas. These assessments also provide useful information for students with learning deficits in **mathematics**. Performance on the math calculation skills and math reasoning test sections provides information on specific deficits in general comprehension, fluid reasoning, and processing speed. Deficits in these areas are correlated with learning disabilities in mathematics.

The Wechsler Intelligence Scales

The Wechsler Intelligence Scales are assessments that measure the cognitive abilities of children and adults. The **Wechsler Intelligence Scale for Children (WISC)**, now in its fifth edition (WISC-V), is used for children ages 6–16 and measures the child's intellectual ability through 10 primary subtests and 6 secondary subtests. The result is an overall composite score, the Full-Scale Intelligence Quotient (FSIQ), as well as index scores in subcategories such as verbal comprehension, fluid reasoning, and quantitative reasoning. WISC-V results are useful tools for evaluating a student with a disability. Test results can be used to measure and report on a student's general intelligence and provide insight into the student's cognitive abilities in order to determine an appropriate educational pathway. Results can be reported in a student's Evaluation Team Report (ETR) and Individualized Education Program (IEP) in order to justify special education services or have a starting point for IEP goals. WISC-V results are especially important in an ETR, and they are generally completed at least once every three years, because they contribute to describing the **overall performance profile** of a student with a disability.

Kaufman Assessment Battery for Children

The Kaufman Assessment Battery for Children (KABC), updated to a second edition in 2008 with a normative update in 2014 (**KABC-II NU**) is a unique standardized test because it is used to evaluate preschoolers, minority groups, and children with learning disabilities. The KABC-II NU can be used to assess children ages 3–18 and is meant to be used with children who are nonverbal, bilingual, or English-speaking. However, it is especially useful in assessing the abilities of students who are **nonverbal**. The KABC-II NU can be used to help determine students' educational placements and assist with their educational planning. This assessment consists of subtests that may be combined and interpreted according to one of two different models depending on the child's language background. The subtests lead to both individual scaled scores and a global score. The scales are:

- Simultaneous
- Sequential
- Planning
- Learning
- Knowledge

The KABC-II NU is also unique because it includes a **nonverbal scale** that can be administered to children with hearing or speech impairments and children who do not speak English.

Vineland Adaptive Behavior Scales

The Vineland Adaptive Behavior Scales, Third Edition (**Vineland-3**), assesses the personal and social skills of children and adults. **Adaptive behavior** refers to the skills needed for day-to-day activities and independent living. Children with disabilities sometimes have deficits in adaptive behavior, and the Vineland-3 is useful for planning their **educational pathways**. It is an especially useful tool for developing **transition plans and goals** for students of appropriate ages on Individualized Education Programs. The Vineland-3 is a process that involves people who know the students best, like parents and teachers. The teacher version and parent version of this assessment can be delivered via interview or survey. The parent version focuses on a student's adaptive behavior at home, while the teacher version focuses on adaptive behavior in the school setting. Vineland-3 assesses four **domains**: communication, activities of daily living, social relationships, and motor skills. A student's parents or caregivers fill out a form pertaining to home life, and a teacher fills out a form pertaining to school settings. The comprehensive score from both the teacher and parent version are used to report abilities in the four domains.

Types of Cognitive Assessments

Cognitive tests assess the **cognitive functioning abilities** of children and adults. They are useful tools for diagnosing or identifying children with disabilities who are eligible for **special education services** under the Individuals with Disabilities Education Act. Examples of cognitive tests used in diagnosing or identifying children with disabilities include aptitude tests and intelligence quotient (IQ) tests. There are also cognitive assessments that measure verbal reasoning, numerical reasoning, abstract reasoning, spatial ability, verbal ability, and more. Children's cognitive abilities are related to how quickly they **process** information. Assessment results can be good measurements of how quickly children may learn new information or tasks. Cognitive assessments provide specific information about children's cognitive functioning by providing measurements of their intelligence, attention, concentration, processing speed, language and communication, visual-spatial abilities, and short- and long-term memory capabilities. Results can also be used on a child's Evaluation Team Report or to develop goals for an Individualized Education Program.

Advantages and Disadvantages of Curriculum-Based Assessments

Curriculum-based assessments (**CBAs**) determine if students are making adequate progress through the curriculum. They can be administered by a teacher, special educator, or school psychologist. CBAs have advantages over norm-referenced assessments, like developmental assessments, because they are not used to compare performance between students. Other types of assessments measure a student's cumulative abilities across multiple skills instead of assessing individual skills. CBAs measure student progress in more **individualized** ways. They are especially useful for measuring IEP goal progress. Since CBAs are **teacher-created assessments**, they provide opportunities to assess students informally and formally on IEP goals. For example, a teacher may verbally quiz a student on ten addition problems to determine if the student is making progress on math IEP goals. CBAs are also used in the "response to intervention" process to identify students with special needs by measuring the effectiveness of interventions provided to them.

Assessment for Students with Disabilities

Alternate Assessments

Students with and without disabilities are typically expected to take the same standardized tests, sometimes with accommodations and modifications. Some students with disabilities take **alternate assessments**, which are forms of the standardized tests that other students take. Students that participate in alternate assessments are unable to participate in state standardized tests even with accommodations. Less than one percent of students in public school districts participate in alternate assessments. They are mostly intended for students with **intellectual disabilities** or **severe cognitive delays**. Alternate assessments are based on **alternate achievement standards**, which are modified versions of state achievement standards. Alternate assessments are a way for students' progress to be assessed with standards that are more appropriate for their skills. For example, a state standard for math may not be appropriate for a student with an intellectual disability. Instead, the student may have the alternate standard of demonstrating the ability to count money to make a purchase. Teachers, parents, and students work collaboratively to demonstrate that the achievement standards are met.

Role of Formal Assessments in the Education of a Student with Disabilities

Formal assessments measure how well a student has mastered learning material and are useful in detecting if a student is **falling behind** in general or at the end of a unit. Formal test results can be used to compare the performance of a student with disabilities against other students of similar demographics. **Developmental assessments** are norm-referenced tests that are designed to assess the development of young children. Developmental assessments are used to identify the strengths and weaknesses of a child suspected of having a disability. **Intelligence tests** are another type of norm-referenced test that can determine a student's potential to learn academic skills. Intelligence tests, sometimes called IQ tests, also indicate a student's specific level of intelligence. This is helpful in knowing if a student's learning problems are associated with sub-average intellectual abilities or other factors, such as an emotional disturbance. A student with an emotional disturbance or specific learning disability would have an average or above-average intelligence score, whereas a student with intellectual disabilities would have a sub-average score. **Curriculum-based assessments** are also helpful in determining where, specifically, a student needs the most help within a content area.

Interest Inventories

Interest inventories are tools for measuring people's interests or preferences in activities. They are useful for gathering information about a student's likes and dislikes. In special education, interest inventories are sometimes used to help develop the **transition portion** of an Individualized Education Program (IEP). A student's interests as determined by an interest inventory can be used to drive the entire IEP. For an older student with a driving interest in mind, interest inventories can also be reflected in the annual IEP goals. Interest inventories can come in the form of observations, ability tests, or self-reported inventories. They can also work as age-appropriate **transition assessments** used in the transition statement section of the IEP. An advantage of interest inventories is that they help students get to know their own strengths and interests. They are also useful in guiding students with disabilities into thinking about postsecondary careers, education, or independent living.

Role of Informal Assessments in the Education of a Student with Disabilities

Informal assessments are a little more flexible for teachers, particularly in the ways they can be administered in the classroom. In special education, informal assessments play an important role in **adjusting instruction** to meet the specific needs of a student. Using informal assessment outcomes to drive instruction helps ensure that academic or behavioral student needs are met. Informal assessments are also helpful in adjusting instruction to meet **specific goals or objectives** on a student's IEP. Checklists, running records, observations, and work samples are all informal assessments from which data for IEP goals can be collected. **Checklists** can include behaviors or academic skills the student is meant to achieve. **Running records** help provide insight into student behavior over time by focusing on a sequence of events. **Work samples** are helpful in providing a concrete snapshot of a student's academic capabilities.

Individualized Education Programs

Developing and Writing Measurable IEP Goals

According to the Individuals with Disabilities Education Act, students eligible for special education receive Individualized Education Program (IEP) goals, which must contain specific **components**. Components of a **measurable IEP goal** include condition, performance, criteria, assessment, and standard. Measurable goals also include how skill mastery will be **assessed**, such as through observations or work samples. In the provided example below, the criterion is clearly measurable, as Jacob will either succeed or fail at multiple trials, and the ratio of successes to numbers of attempts should be recorded and dated throughout the IEP year to show his progress. Goals should also be **standards-based** whenever possible and may be required.

For example, an IEP goal may state, "By the end of this IEP, Jacob will use appropriate skills to communicate his needs in four out of five trials."

- **Condition** refers to when, where, and how the disability will be addressed. "By the end of this IEP" is the condition of the goal.
- **Performance** is what the student is expected to accomplish during the condition of the goal. In this case, that is "Jacob will use appropriate skills to communicate his needs."
- The last part of the goal stating "in four out of five trials" is the **criterion** that outlines how well the goal will be performed.

Review Video: IEPs
Visit mometrix.com/academy and enter code: 153484

Role of Local Education Agency Representatives in IEP Meetings

A local education agency (**LEA**) representative is a member of the IEP team who is trained in special education curriculum, general education curriculum, and community resources. In many cases, a school building leader or principal may fulfill the role of LEA representative. An LEA rep must be a licensed professional who knows the student and is familiar with the IEP process. The role of LEA representatives in IEP meetings is to make sure the information presented is compliant with the Individuals with Disabilities Education Act (IDEA) standards. LEA representatives are also responsible for ensuring that the school district is **compliant** with procedural components of IDEA and that eligible students are receiving free and appropriate public educations. This role is necessary on the IEP team because whereas the whole IEP team should have the students' best interests in mind, they may not understand the doctrines of IDEA and be able to consider compliance. As a result, the LEA representative must act as the primary advocate for effective implementation of the IEP.

Involvement of Students with IEPs in the Transition Process in High School

Most states require **transition statements** to be made when students reach age 14 during the IEP year. Federal law requires students 16 years of age or older to have transition statements; postsecondary goals for independent living, employment, and education; and summaries of performance that include the results of the most recent transition assessments. Per federal law, students of transition age must be invited to their **IEP meetings**. It is important for students on IEPs to **participate** in the transition process because it helps them figure out what they want to do after they graduate from high school. Participation in the process gets them thinking about living independently, postsecondary education options, and employment options. Students usually have opportunities to participate in formal and informal assessments like interest inventories that help them define their interests. Transition goals for independent living, employment, and education should be based on the results of these assessments and any other interests the students have expressed. The students participate in the **implementation** of the transition goals by completing activities associated with their indicated interests.

Student Support Teams

A **student support team (SST)** is a team made up of parents and educational professionals who work to support students in the general education classroom who are struggling with academics, discipline, health problems, or any other anticipated or actual problem that does not qualify the student for special education or supports from an Individualized Education Program. In this support team model, a group of educators works to identify and provide early intervention services for any student exhibiting academic or behavioral problems. The purpose of this kind of SST is to offer different supports, such as monitoring student progress, developing intervention plans, and referring students for intervention services. While the primary goal of this kind of SST is to provide support for students **struggling with school**, it can also shift focus to supporting students at risk of **dropping out of school**. Another primary objective of an SST is to identify students who are likely to have disabilities or who may need 504 Plans to succeed in school and to recommend them for referrals so they are not left without necessary supports.

Amendments to an Individualized Education Program

A student's IEP is in effect for one year. Academic goals, objectives, benchmarks, transition goals, and any accommodations and modifications are to be in place for the student for the duration of the IEP. An **amendment** to the IEP can be made when a change is needed before the year is over. An amendment is an agreement between the student, parents or legal guardians, and the IEP team. IEP meetings for amendments can be requested at any time. IEP amendments can be requested if a student is not making adequate progress toward the goals, if the goals become inappropriate in some way for the student, or when the student has met all IEP goals and requires new ones. If new information about the student becomes available, the IEP can be amended. Students, parents, and other team members may also request amendment meetings if they think that other accommodations and modifications are needed or should be removed.

How the Needs of Students with IEPs Are Met in the School Environment

IEPs communicate what **services** are to be provided for children with disabilities in the school setting, the children's **present levels of performance**, and how their disabilities affect **academic performance**. IEPs also specify **annual goals** appropriate to the students' specific needs and any accommodations or modifications that need to be provided. Schools and teachers have the responsibility to implement these IEP components when working with students with disabilities. Additionally, schools and teachers working with students with disabilities must ensure that students' individualized annual goals are met within a year of the students' IEP effective dates. It is up to the IEP teams to determine what classroom settings would most benefit the students while also appropriately meeting their IEP goals with the fewest barriers. Special educators must determine how data is collected and then obtain and record data on how the students are meeting their IEP goals. Special educators are responsible for providing intervention services based on the data results. They must also ensure that any accommodations or modifications listed on the IEPs are implemented in both general education and self-contained classrooms.

Accommodation vs. Modification in IEPs

Formal accommodations, adaptations, and modifications for a student with a disability are listed on the Individualized Education Program. **Accommodations** change *how* a student learns the material, while an **adaptation** or **modification** changes *what* a student is taught or expected to learn.

- **Accommodations** are changes to the instruction or assessment that do *not* alter the curricular requirements. For instance, a student with accommodations may be allowed to answer a test orally instead of writing the answers or might be given pre-structured notes to help organize thoughts during instruction. These types of changes do not fundamentally change the information taught or the requirements for passing.
- **Adaptations** or **modifications** are changes to the instruction or assessment that fundamentally change the curricular requirements, but which enable a student with a disability to participate. Examples of adaptations include substitution of activities for related materials, exemption from answering particular types of questions on assessments, and removing or reducing time limits when taking tests.

For state standardized tests, accommodations like extra time and frequent breaks can be provided. Students that need modifications to state tests may complete alternate assessments that may not cover the same material as the standard exams.

Review Video: Adapting and Modifying Lessons or Activities
Visit mometrix.com/academy and enter code: 834946

Determining the Placement of a Student with a Disability

With every student, the ideal goal is placement in the **general education classroom** as much as possible while still meeting the student's educational needs and ensuring a successful educational experience. The Individuals with Disabilities Education Act does not require that students be placed in the regular education classroom, but it does require that students be placed in their **least restrictive environment** as defined by the student's IEP team. Ultimately, the IEP team determines what **environment** best suits the student based on the student's specific needs. The IEP team is responsible for determining what educational environment would provide the student with the maximum appropriate educational benefit. While justification for removing a student from the regular education classroom is common and appropriate, as occurs when a student is placed in a resource room, the IEP team must explain the reasoning in the student's IEP. **Justification** must specifically state why the student cannot be educated with accommodations and services in the regular education classroom during any part of the school day. Justification for removal cannot be the perceived instructional limitations of the regular education teacher or concerns over extra instructional time needed to educate a student with a disability.

Creating a SMART Annual Goal in an IEP

A good IEP goal describes how far the student is expected to **progress** toward the goal by the next IEP. Since IEPs should be revised once a year, a good annual IEP goal should describe what the student is capable of doing in a one-year time frame. Creating **SMART** IEP goals can help the student determine realistic expectations of what can be achieved in a year. SMART IEP goals are specific, measurable, attainable, relevant, and time-bound. Goals are **specific** when they list the targeted result in the skill or subject area. Goals should also be specific to the student's needs. Goals that are **measurable** state the way a student's progress will be measured. Measurable goals list how accurately a student should meet the goal. **Attainable** goals are realistic for the student to achieve in one year. **Relevant** goals outline what a student needs to do to accomplish the goal. For example, a SMART goal may state, "During the school week, Robert will use his device to communicate greetings 80 percent of the time in four out of five trials." **Time-bound** goals include a time frame for the student to achieve the goal. They also list when and how often progress will be measured.

Review Video: SMART Goals
Visit mometrix.com/academy and enter code: 100378

Role of an Initial Evaluation Assessment in Qualifying for Special Education

When a student is determined to need special education, it means the student has a disability or disabilities adversely affecting educational performance. It may also mean the student's needs cannot be addressed in the general education classroom with or without accommodations and that **specially designed instruction** is required. An **initial evaluation** of the student is required for special education eligibility. The evaluation is comprehensive and includes existing data collected on the student and additional assessments needed to determine eligibility. Individual school districts decide what assessments should be completed for the student's initial evaluation. Each district is responsible for and should provide assessments that measure functional, developmental, and academic information. The student's parents or legal guardians are responsible for providing outside information relevant to the student's education, such as medical needs assessed outside of the school district by qualified providers.

Purpose of an IEP

The purpose of an IEP is to guide the learning of a student with a **disability** in the educational environment. An IEP is a written statement for a student eligible for **special education**. An initial IEP is **implemented** once the child has been evaluated and determined to be in need of special education. After the initial IEP, **IEP meetings** are conducted annually (or more often) in order to update the plan to meet the needs of the student. IEPs are created, reviewed, and revised according to individual state and federal laws. These plans include the amount of time the student will spend in the special education classroom based on the level of need. They also include any related services the student might need (such as speech-language therapy) as well as academic and behavioral goals for the year. As the student learns and changes, performance levels and goals change as well. A student's present levels of performance are included and updated yearly, as are the academic and behavioral goals.

Members of an Individualized Education Program Team

IEPs are updated **annually** following the initial IEP. IEP team members meet at least once a year to discuss a student's progress and make changes to the IEP. The required members of a student's IEP team include the student's parents or legal guardians, one of the student's general education teachers, the special education teacher, a school representative, an individual who can interpret the instructional implications of evaluation results, and if appropriate, the student. Anyone else who has knowledge or expertise about the student may also attend. **Parents and legal guardians** contribute unique expertise about the student, typically having the benefit of knowing the child well. **General education teachers** can speak to how the student is performing in the general education classroom. The **special education teacher** can report on progress made toward academic and behavioral goals and present levels of performance. A **school representative** must be qualified to provide or supervise specially designed instruction, be knowledgeable of the general education curriculum, and be knowledgeable about school resources. The **individual who can interpret evaluation results** can be an existing team member or someone else who is qualified to report on evaluation results. **Advocates**, such as counselors or therapists who see the student outside the school day, can also attend the meeting to speak on the student's behalf.

LEGAL RIGHTS OF PARENTS OR LEGAL GUARDIANS

IEP meetings occur annually for each student. However, it is a **parent or legal guardian's right** to request a meeting at any point during the school year. The student's school is responsible for identifying and evaluating the child; developing, reviewing, or revising the IEP; and determining what placement setting best suits the needs of the student. It is within the parent or legal guardian's rights to have **input** in all processes related to the student. Under the Individuals with Disabilities Education Act, parents have the right to participate in IEP meetings, have an independent evaluation in addition to the one the school provides, give or deny consent for the IEP, contest a school's decision, and obtain private education paid for by the public school. In specific circumstances, if the student is determined to need services that the public school cannot provide, the public school district may need to pay for the student's tuition at a private school where the student's needs can be met.

COLLABORATIVE CONSULTATION BETWEEN EDUCATIONAL PROFESSIONALS

Collaborative consultation refers to the special educator or other professional providing advice to the general education teacher about a student on an IEP. Special educators and other IEP team members, such as school psychologists and related service professionals, serve as the **experts** and have knowledge about how individual students learn and behave. This is especially important when students with IEPs are included in the general education classroom. Special educators and general education teachers must work collaboratively to ensure that students are reaching their potential in the general education setting. Examples of **collaborative consultation** include the special educator serving as a consultant to the general education teacher by providing advice on a student's IEP, accommodations, modifications, and IEP goal tracking. Another way the special educator or other professional can assist the general educator is by providing skill and strategy instruction to students on IEPs outside the general education classroom. The idea behind this method is for students to generalize these skills and strategies to the general education classroom.

> **Review Video: Collaborating with Other Professionals**
> Visit mometrix.com/academy and enter code: 100351

PUBLIC SCHOOL RESPONSIBILITIES TO PARENTS OF STUDENTS ON IEPS

The school must invite the parents or legal guardians to any **IEP meetings** and provide advance notice of the meetings. Each meeting notice is required to include the purpose of the meeting, its time and location, and who will attend. The location of the meeting is likely the student's school, but legally it must be held at a mutually agreed-upon place and time. If the parent or legal guardian cannot attend the IEP meeting, the school must ensure participation in another way, such as video or telephone conference. The meeting can be conducted without the parent or legal guardian if the school district cannot get the parent or legal guardian to attend. A parent or legal guardian can request a meeting, and the school can refuse or deny the request. If denied, the school must provide a **prior written notice** explaining their refusal. A prior written notice is a document outlining important school district decisions about a student on an IEP.

Chapter Quiz

Ready to see how well you retained what you just read? Scan the QR code to go directly to the chapter quiz interface for this study guide. If you're using a computer, simply visit the online resources page at **mometrix.com/resources719/texesspedsupp** and click the Chapter Quizzes link.

Promoting Student Learning and Development

Transform passive reading into active learning! After immersing yourself in this chapter, put your comprehension to the test by taking a quiz. The insights you gained will stay with you longer this way. Scan the QR code to go directly to the chapter quiz interface for this study guide. If you're using a computer, simply visit the online resources page at **mometrix.com/resources719/texesspedsupp** and click the Chapter Quizzes link.

Special Education Settings

Least Restrictive Environment

The Individuals with Disabilities Education Act (IDEA) requires a free and appropriate public education to be provided in a student's **least restrictive environment (LRE)**. This means that a student with a disability who qualifies for special education should be educated in a free, appropriate, and public setting and be placed in an instructional setting that meets the LRE principle. IDEA states that LRE means students with disabilities should participate in the general education classroom "to the maximum extent appropriate." **Mainstreaming** and **inclusion** are ways for students with disabilities to participate in general education classrooms while receiving appropriate accommodations, modifications, interventions, and related services. The amount of time students spend in an LRE suitable for their individual needs is stated in their Individualized Education Program (IEP). The accommodations, modifications, interventions, and related services the student should receive are also outlined in the IEP. Students who need special education services for more than 50% of the day may be placed in other instructional settings that meet their LRE needs, such as resource rooms or self-contained classrooms.

Review Video: Least Restrictive Environment
Visit mometrix.com/academy and enter code: 100354

Continuum of Special Education Services

IDEA mandates that school systems educate students with disabilities with students who do not have disabilities to the maximum extent that is appropriate. IDEA also mandates that schools not take students out of regular education classes unless the classes are not benefiting the students. Supplementary aids and support services must be in place before students can be considered for removal. Schools must offer a **continuum of special education services** that range from restrictive to least restrictive. In a typical continuum of services, regular education classrooms offer the **least restrictive access** to students with disabilities. Next on the continuum are resource rooms, followed by special classes that target specific deficits. Special schools, homebound services, hospitals, and institutions are the most restrictive education environments. The number of students at each stage of the continuum decreases as restriction increases. Fewer students benefit more from being educated in hospitals or institutions than in resource rooms.

Inclusion Classroom Setting

The principle of least restrictive environment (LRE) is a right guaranteed under IDEA to protect a student from unnecessary restriction or seclusion from the general population. IDEA does not expressly define an LRE for each specific disability, so it is the responsibility of the IEP team of professionals, including the student's parent or legal guardian, to determine the best **LRE setting** possible for an individual student. **Mainstreaming** or **inclusion** is the practice of keeping students with disabilities in the general education setting for the entire school day. The students may receive supports and services like aides, assistive technology, accommodations, and modifications that are appropriate for their individual needs. These supports and services are intended to help students with disabilities gain access to the general education curriculum with the fewest possible barriers. The principle of LRE also sits on a spectrum and allows for variable inclusion or separation throughout parts of the day depending on a student's particular needs. As this is a student right, any more restrictive setting must be **justified by necessity** in students' IEPs and cannot be determined by convenience or financial considerations of the school or staff.

Collaborative Teaching in an Inclusion Classroom

If determined by an IEP, a student with a disability may participate in an **inclusive setting**. In some classrooms, students participate in **co-taught settings**. In this **collaborative teaching environment**, the general educator and special educator work together to meet the goals of the students with disabilities in the regular education classroom. Students in this setting are all taught to the same educational standards. However, accommodations and modifications may be implemented for students with disabilities. In a successful collaborative teaching model, the special educator and general educator may cooperatively implement the accommodations and modifications for these students. A two-teacher setting also gives students more opportunities to receive individualized instruction, work in small groups, or receive one-on-one attention. Collaborative teaching in the co-taught setting can facilitate differentiated instruction, help teachers follow the universal design for learning framework, and provide individualized learning opportunities.

Implementing Modifications and Accommodations in an Inclusion Classroom

General educators can work with special educators to create an effective **co-teaching model**. In an effective co-teaching model, both general educators and special educators are guided by the **universal design for learning framework**. This helps ensure that the needs of the diverse group of learners are being met. Students' IEPs expressly document any required modifications, such as reduced work. In a co-teaching model, student modifications are communicated to the **general educator**. The **special educator** can work with the general educator to provide the modifications in an inclusive classroom setting. Students' IEPs also expressly document any required **accommodations**. These accommodations may or may not be used in an inclusive setting, depending on the relevancy of the accommodation. For example, the accommodation of using a calculator would be utilized in a math class but not a social studies class. In addition to expressly written accommodations, special educators and general educators can work together in an inclusive setting to provide appropriate accommodations during the learning process. These accommodations may be part of informal assessments used to adjust instruction.

Role of Paraeducators

Paraeducators, sometimes referred to as aides or paraprofessionals, are part of students' education teams. **Paraeducators** work under the supervision of special educators or principals and are key contributors to the learning process for certain students. Their primary role, especially if their positions are funded by the Individuals with Disabilities Education Act, is to provide **educational support** for students. The use of paraeducators is noted in students' IEPs. Paraeducators can facilitate the learning process for students by removing learning barriers, keeping track of goal progress, and organizing goal-tracking activities. Paraeducators cannot introduce new concepts or take over the role of teachers. Paraeducators cannot make changes to what students are learning unless specific modifications are listed in students' IEPs. They cannot provide accommodations unless the accommodations are appropriate for what is written in students' IEPs. Paraeducators may also be instructed by supervising teachers or principals to facilitate and monitor accommodations or modifications for students and reinforce learned concepts.

Self-Contained Classroom Setting

According to the Individuals with Disabilities Education Act, LRE standards require students to spend as much time as possible with their nondisabled peers in the **general education setting**. This means students should receive general education "to the maximum extent appropriate," and special classes, special schools, or removal from the general education classroom should only be considered when students' needs are greater than what can be provided by supplementary aids and services. A **self-contained classroom setting** can be a separate class within a school or a separate school for students with disabilities whose needs are greater than what can be offered in the general education classroom even with educational supports. These settings may provide specialized instruction and support for students with similar needs. Placement in self-contained classrooms must be justified in students' IEPs.

Partial Mainstream/Inclusion Classroom Setting

It is generally up to the IEP team of professionals and the parent or legal guardian to determine the LRE that best suits the needs of a student. In a partial mainstream/inclusion classroom setting, a student spends part of the day in the general education classroom and part of the day in a separate, special education classroom. This type of LRE is appropriate when a student's needs are greater than what can be provided in the general education classroom even with educational supports or services in place. For example, a student with severe deficits in mathematical skills may receive math instruction in a separate classroom or receive one-on-one or small group instruction. Placement in partial mainstream/inclusion classrooms must be justified in students' IEPs.

Specialized Education Settings

School districts sometimes offer specialized education settings for students with disabilities, such as **special preschools**. Preschools for children with disabilities typically focus on children aged 3–5 years. They are important resources for teaching early learning, communication, and social skills that are essential for children with disabilities. In **life skills settings**, students with disabilities can receive specialized instruction in academic, social, behavioral, and daily-living skills. **Social behavior skills settings** are sometimes called "applied behavior skills settings" or "behavior skills settings." In this setting, the primary focus is on social and decision-making skills. **Transition settings** are available for students making the transition from high school to life after high school. Students with IEPs can stay in high school until the age of 21 or 22, depending on the calendar month they turn 22. Transition settings assist students with work experiences, postsecondary education experiences, and independent living skills.

Instructional Planning

Designing Lesson Plans and Units to Align with Instructional Goals

The effective sequencing of units and lesson plans is key to developing coherent, comprehensible instruction that aligns with instructional goals and fosters success in learning. Teachers must first determine the instructional goals that students will be expected to achieve based on state academic standards as a framework and students' individual needs, knowledge, and abilities. Teachers must then logically arrange specific units of instruction aimed toward achieving the determined instructional goals. Each unit should build upon knowledge from the prior unit. Within each unit, teachers must determine what students must achieve as they work toward instructional goals and determine objectives that facilitate success based on individual need and ability. Once objectives are defined, teachers must design lesson plans in a logical sequence that will facilitate students in reaching these objectives and increasingly build upon knowledge as students work toward achieving the learning goal. When planning lessons, teachers must decide which activities, procedures, and materials are necessary for successfully completing lesson objectives while ensuring that individual learning needs are met. The teacher must also decide what will be assessed at the end of each lesson and unit to determine student success in achieving instructional goals.

Review Video: Creating Effective Lesson Plans
Visit mometrix.com/academy and enter code: 100377

Creating Developmentally Appropriate Learning Experiences and Assessments

Multiple factors must be considered when designing developmentally appropriate learning experiences and assessments that effectively facilitate student growth and achievement. Teachers must consider the general cognitive, physical, social, and emotional developmental levels of students as well as individual differences in background, skill, knowledge, and learning needs. With this understanding, teachers must then evaluate whether learning experiences are simultaneously appropriate to students' developmental levels and individual needs. This includes ensuring that learning activities and teaching strategies are varied in approach, are tailored to students' interests, and that they incorporate student choice in learning. Learning experiences must build upon students' background knowledge and experiences and provide challenging yet attainable learning opportunities based on individual skills and abilities. Additionally, teachers must consider whether learning experiences promote student participation and engagement as well as cooperative learning to ensure development across domains. Just as with learning experiences, the developmental appropriateness of assessments must also be evaluated. The teacher must consider whether assessments allow for choice in how students demonstrate their learning so as to address individual learning needs. Furthermore, it is important that teachers consider the purpose of each assessment regarding the feedback they are seeking and how it can help determine further instruction.

Role of Learning Theory in Instructional Process and Student Learning

Multiple learning theories exist to explain how people acquire knowledge, abilities, and skills. Each theory proposes its own approach for best practices in teaching and learning, and their effectiveness varies depending on the context of learning and individual student needs. These theories serve as frameworks for the instructional process and facilitating student learning. Teachers must understand the principles of various learning philosophies as well as their students' unique learning needs to effectively design and implement instruction from the perspective of the most applicable theory. Upon identifying desired learning outcomes, teachers can draw on applicable learning theories to make informed decisions about designing instruction, activities, and assessments that are most effective based on their students' learning styles, skills, and abilities.

The following are examples of some common learning theories that can be used as a framework in the instructional process:

- **Constructivism (Jean Piaget):** This theory proposes that students learn by interacting with the learning environment and connecting new information to their background knowledge to build understanding. This active process allows students to personalize their learning and construct their own perceptions of the world through the lens of their previous experiences.
- **Humanism (Abraham Maslow, Carl Rogers):** This theory proposes that learning should take a person-centered approach, with a focus on the individual's innate capacity for personal growth and self-actualization. It operates axiomatically from the principle that all humans have a natural desire to learn; therefore, a failure to learn is due to the learning situation or environment rather than a person's inability to learn. Teachers should act as facilitators and strive to create a safe, accepting learning environment, celebrate students' differences, and praise academic and personal achievement.
- **Connectivism (George Siemens, Stephen Downes):** This theory proposes that learning occurs by making a series of connections across pieces of information, ideas, concepts, and perspectives. Connectivism is rooted in the notion that learning occurs externally, and technology facilitates connections by giving learners access to several outlets for acquiring and processing new information.
- **Experiential Learning (David Kolb):** This theory proposes that students learn and retain information best through physical exploration and interaction with the learning environment. In the classroom, teachers can facilitate this student-led approach by providing students with varying relevant experiences and opportunities for hands-on learning, such as projects or learning centers.
- **Multiple Intelligences (Howard Gardner):** Gardner's theory proposes there are several versions of intelligence, and as such, the process of learning differs among individuals. Some learners may have a stronger intelligence in one domain but have difficulty in another and, therefore, learn best when instruction is presented through the lens of their dominant intelligence. Intelligences are categorized as logical-mathematical, verbal-linguistic, visual-spatial, bodily-kinesthetic, interpersonal, intrapersonal, musical, and naturalistic.

Connecting New Information and Ideas to Prior Knowledge

When students connect new information to prior knowledge, learning becomes relevant and engaging. Effective instruction encourages students to connect learning to background knowledge and experiences, which increases retainment, deepens understanding, and enhances the effectiveness of the overall learning experience. Fostering personal connections to learning is achieved through incorporating an array of strategies and technologies into instruction. Activities including KWL charts, anticipatory guides, graphic organizers, and brainstorming encourage students to consider what they know before learning new concepts, thus allowing them to build upon their prior knowledge and ability to make connections that strengthen learning. Cooperative learning strategies promote sharing and building prior knowledge with other students, thus increasing students' connections to new information. Numerous technologies exist to enhance the learning experience by fostering connections between prior knowledge and new information. Teachers can incorporate a wide range of apps and games across subject areas that build upon prior knowledge by providing activities with increasing levels of difficulty. Online polls, surveys, and word association websites allow students to demonstrate prior understanding of a topic to begin making connections. Self-reflection and closure opportunities at the end of instruction further strengthen learning by encouraging students to connect new material to prior knowledge and experiences.

Making Learning Meaningful and Relevant

Effective instruction occurs when learning is meaningful and relevant. When the purpose of learning is clear, students are engaged, motivated, and retain new information. Instruction must be student-centered, foster personal connections, and be applicable to real-life situations to create meaningful and relevant instruction. Teachers achieve this through an array of methods and technologies that are tailored to students' learning needs. Through forging positive relationships with students, teachers learn their unique interests, preferences, and experiences. Activities such as interest inventories, surveys, and community building develop a positive rapport between teachers and students. This allows teachers to make learning meaningful by creating learner-centered instruction that facilitates personal connections and builds upon prior knowledge. Field trips and community outreach programs are effective in enhancing relevancy through demonstrating the real-world applications of instruction. Additionally, technologies including virtual field trips and tours, videos, and documentaries assist in increasing students' understanding the purpose of learning by illustrating the real-world applications of instruction. Self-assessments make learning meaningful and relevant through encouraging student ownership and responsibility over learning as students seek areas for improvement. Moreover, closure activities serve to demonstrate overall purpose for learning through encouraging students to connect learning to the lesson's objective and their prior knowledge.

Intradisciplinary and Interdisciplinary Instruction

Intradisciplinary and interdisciplinary instruction are both valuable strategies for teaching and learning. In **intradisciplinary** instruction, several elements of a single broad subject area are incorporated into the lesson. For example, in a science lesson, the teacher could incorporate elements of chemistry, biology, and physics into instruction. This method of instruction is beneficial in deepening students' understanding of the nuances of a particular subject area through demonstrating the various components that comprise the overarching discipline. **Interdisciplinary** instruction refers to the simultaneous integration of ideas, knowledge, and skills from several subject areas when approaching an idea, problem, or theme and applying principles of one subject area to another. For example, in an interdisciplinary unit on food, the teacher could incorporate elements of math by teaching students to measure ingredients, language arts by teaching them to read or write a recipe, science through examining chemical reactions of the cooking process, and social studies through having students explore the impact of food agriculture on economy and society. Interdisciplinary instruction is beneficial in deepening students' understanding across subject areas and developing real-world critical thinking skills by encouraging them to make connections between disciplines and teaching them to consider an idea or problem from multiple perspectives.

Examples of Intradisciplinary Instruction

- **Language arts:** A single language arts lesson can incorporate components of reading, writing, grammar, and listening skills. For example, a lesson on a particular poem can include a close reading of the poet's use of grammar, symbolism, imagery, and other literary techniques as well as an audio recording of the poet reading aloud. At the end of the unit, students can be assigned to use what they learned to compose their own original poems.

- **Social studies:** Social studies units can incorporate elements of history, anthropology, archaeology, sociology, psychology, or any other field that involves the study of humans, civilizations, cultures, and historical events. For example, a unit on the Aztec people may include an examination of their religious beliefs, customs, architecture, and agricultural practices.
- **Science:** Intradisciplinary units in science can include several branches within the field, such as chemistry, biology, physics, earth science, botany, or geology. For example, a unit on volcanoes may incorporate lessons on plate tectonics, the Earth's layers, chemicals released during a volcanic eruption, islands formed from cooled volcanic rock, as well as plants that grow best near volcanoes.
- **Mathematics:** An intradisciplinary math lesson may simultaneously include several branches within the field, such as arithmetic, algebra, or geometry. For example, in a geometry lesson on the Pythagorean theorem, students must utilize algebraic equations and arithmetic to determine the length of the sides of a right triangle.

Examples of Interdisciplinary Instruction

- **Language arts:** A unit based in language arts may also incorporate several other disciplines, such as social studies, art, or music. For example, a unit on William Shakespeare's *Romeo and Juliet* may include a reading of the play, an analysis of the use of literary techniques within it, and study of William Shakespeare's life and the society in which he lived, thereby incorporating social studies into the language arts lesson. Students can also act out the play to incorporate the arts and participate in a rhythmic study on iambic pentameter to incorporate music.
- **Social studies:** Units based in social studies can include lessons focused on multiple disciplines, including language arts, music, science, and math. For example, an interdisciplinary unit on Ancient Egypt may include a historical study of the culture, religion, architecture, and practices of the Ancient Egyptians while integrating other subject areas, such as a study of hieroglyphics to incorporate language arts and creating Egyptian masks to incorporate art. Students can also study the scientific advancements of the Ancient Egyptians and incorporate math to study how the ancient pyramids were constructed.
- **Science:** Scientific units can also incorporate elements of art, math, social studies, and language arts in order to become interdisciplinary. For example, a unit on Punnett squares focuses on biology and genetics but can also include several other subject areas. Math can be incorporated by integrating lessons on probability or students can be assigned to research their genetics, create a family tree, and write a report on their findings to incorporate language arts and social studies. Art can also be incorporated by having students create portraits of the potential outcomes from Punnett squares.
- **Mathematics:** Interdisciplinary units in mathematics can also include lessons focused on art, social studies, science, and music. For example, a geometry unit on measuring triangles may also incorporate songs to memorize equations, lessons on the pyramids of Ancient Egypt to incorporate social studies, as well as an art project in which students use only triangles to create an original piece.

Incorporating Cooperative Learning and Consideration from Multiple Viewpoints

In any classroom, teachers will encounter a wide range of diversities among students' backgrounds, cultures, interests, skills, and abilities. Thus, providing students with several opportunities for cooperative learning gives them access to others' perspectives and is highly valuable in teaching students to consider ideas from multiple viewpoints. As each student has different experiences and background knowledge, collaborative learning allows them to share their views on ideas with others. Additionally, in working together, students have the opportunity to work with others from different backgrounds that they may have otherwise never encountered and gain exposure to approaching ideas from multiple viewpoints. Cooperative learning opportunities allow students to understand and appreciate others' perspectives and teach them that there are multiple approaches to problem solving and ideas.

Learning Experiences That Develop Real-World Life Skills

The ultimate goal of education is to develop the whole child into a productive, contributing member of society; therefore, it is imperative to provide learning experiences that will develop life skills that are applicable and beneficial in the real world. In an increasingly fast-paced global society, students must be prepared to enter the professional and societal world as confident, independent, responsible, and adaptive individuals. They must have the leadership skills necessary to compete in the professional arena. Students must be able to work cooperatively with others, respect and value multiple perspectives, and be effective problem solvers and critical thinkers in order to be successful outside of the classroom. Teachers must also aim to help students develop the skills necessary to become lifelong learners to ensure continuous growth and development as they enter society; therefore, learning experiences that promote the development of real-world life skills in addition to academic skills are necessary in adequately preparing students for success.

Cross-Curricular Instruction for Exploring Content from Varied Perspectives

Cross-curricular instruction allows teachers to demonstrate that elements from one subject area can be applied to ideas or problems in another. Thus, this instructional strategy is highly valuable in developing students' abilities to explore content from varied perspectives. As this method incorporates several disciplines in approaching a topic, it deepens students' understanding that there are several perspectives that one can take when solving a problem and that elements of one subject area are relevant in another. In addition, cross-curricular instruction prepares students for the real world through developing critical thinking skills and allowing them to make connections between disciplines, thus allowing them to understand how to successfully approach ideas from varied perspectives.

Benefits of Multicultural Learning Experiences

Multicultural learning experiences demonstrate to students the array of diversities that exist both inside and outside of the classroom. Just as each culture has its own values, norms, and traditions, each has its own perspectives and approaches to ideas and problem solving. Incorporating multicultural experiences in the classroom exposes students to cultures and groups that they may have otherwise never encountered and teaches them to respect and value perspectives outside of their own. As students learn other cultures' beliefs, customs, and attitudes, they develop the understanding that each culture solves problems and considers ideas from multiple viewpoints and that each approach is valuable. As students learn other perspectives, they can apply this knowledge and build problem solving and critical thinking skills that will be beneficial in developing successful lifelong learning habits.

Incorporating Multiple Disciplines into a Thematic Unit

In **cross-curricular** (or **interdisciplinary**) instruction, multiple disciplines are incorporated into a thematic unit in order to deepen students' understanding through fostering connections and demonstrating multiple perspectives and methods of problem solving. Effective interdisciplinary instruction requires careful planning to ensure that all activities are relevant to the overall lesson theme and effectively support students in achieving desired learning outcomes. Teachers must first select a thematic unit based on state academic standards and then determine desired learning outcomes. Then, teachers must design lessons and activities for students to reach learning goals and objectives. When integrating multiple disciplines into a thematic unit, teachers must seek out materials, resources, and activities from various subject areas that are applicable to the main topic and reinforce lesson objectives. Teachers can then integrate these elements into lesson planning to create multifaceted instruction. Additionally, teachers can create activities that approach the overarching lesson theme from the perspective of different subject areas. The activities and materials should be coordinated and relate to one another in order to deepen students' understanding of the overall concept.

Effectively Allocating Time When Creating Lessons and Units

Effective time management is vital for successful teaching and learning. To ensure that all academic standards are covered within a school year, teachers must consider how to best allocate specific amounts of time for units and lessons that allow for review, enrichment, and reteaching. A unit plan for the school year is an effective strategy in allowing the teacher to visualize and plan the amount of content that must be covered. A unit plan can also be utilized on a smaller scale, as a framework for designing and allotting time for instructional goals, objectives, and lessons within each unit. By setting learning goals and daily objectives within individual units, teachers can determine the amount of time available for completing each unit. This ensures more effective lesson planning by allowing teachers to develop daily schedules with dedicated time for teaching and learning. When planning lessons, teachers must consider how much instructional time is necessary to cover each topic and the time students will need to complete lesson activities. Additionally, teachers must ensure that they allow time at the end of each lesson for reteaching if students have misconceptions, as extra time can be utilized for enrichment if reteaching is unnecessary.

Opportunities for Reflection

Opportunities for reflection within lesson plans enhance learning experiences through strengthening student understanding and influencing further instruction. When students are given the opportunity to reflect, they are able to connect their learning back to the original objective and better understand the overall purpose for learning, thus fostering engagement. Reflection deepens students' understanding by allowing them to connect new concepts to their own personal experiences, which ultimately helps in comprehension and retainment by making learning relevant. Reflecting on performance empowers students to become self-motivated lifelong learners by allowing them to analyze what they understood and did well. Reflection also encourages students to identify areas for improvement. Teachers can utilize students' reflections to influence and drive further instruction. Students' reflections allow teachers to identify areas in which students excelled and areas in which they need improvement. They can also aid teachers in tailoring future lesson plans to adapt to students' needs and interests.

Opportunities for Self-Assessment

Including self-assessments within lessons is a valuable formative assessment strategy that enriches student learning and provides insight to the teacher. Providing students with the opportunity to monitor their progress and assess their learning supports them in developing a wide range of skills that are beneficial both inside and outside of the classroom. Self-assessments create a sense of ownership and responsibility over learning, which foster self-motivation and engagement. They also serve to create a sense of independence and objectivity within students to effectively review their own work and identify areas of improvement, which is a vital skill needed to become a lifelong learner. When students evaluate their own performance, teachers are able to effectively assess student understanding, thus allowing them to identify areas of weakness or misconception for reteaching.

Opportunities for Closure Activities

Closure activities at the end of each lesson or topic are short activities that allow teachers to formatively assess student understanding of content covered within a lesson and identify areas of misconception for reteaching. Additionally, closure activities are valuable in measuring whether the intended lesson objective was achieved before moving to the next topic. For students, closures at the end of a lesson provide structure and organization to learning as well as emphasize the purpose for instruction by allowing them to connect what they learned back to the original objective. Moreover, in having students restate what they have learned in a closure activity, learning is strengthened by giving students the opportunity to internalize new information. In demonstrating their understanding, they can better make personal connections between their own learning, background knowledge, and experiences.

Instructional Techniques

Implementing Multiple Instructional Techniques to Maximize Student Learning

Incorporating multiple instructional techniques into the classroom maximizes student learning by enhancing intellectual involvement and overall engagement. When instructional material is presented through a variety of means, it facilitates an **active learning** environment in which students' interest is captured and they are motivated to participate in learning. Varying teaching strategies stimulates engagement and fosters achievement by encouraging students to actively participate in their own learning and implement critical thinking skills to consider information more deeply. Students' understanding is strengthened when content is presented in different ways through various instructional techniques by providing them with multiple frames of reference for making connections and internalizing new concepts. In addition, utilizing multiple instructional techniques allows the teacher to effectively **differentiate instruction** to access multiple learning styles and address individual student needs to ensure understanding and enhance the overall learning process.

Instructional Strategies to Differentiate Instruction

Implementing a variety of strategies for differentiation helps to ensure that instruction appeals to students' varying learning styles and needs. By incorporating **multiple modalities** into direct instruction, such as visual representations, written directions, video or audio clips, songs, graphs, or mnemonic devices, teachers can differentiate the presentation of new concepts and information. Using strategies to differentiate instructional activities is also beneficial in diversifying the learning experience. By providing opportunities for **independent, collaborative**, and **hands-on** learning, teachers can ensure that learning is accessible and engaging to all students. In addition, learning activities should allow for a degree of flexibility in order to appeal to students' varying needs and preferences. Activities such as task cards, educational technology resources, and learning stations provide this **flexibility** and allow for a student-directed experience in which students can choose to learn in the way that best suits their needs. Similarly, assigning open-ended projects as summative assessments allows for a degree of **student-choice**, thus differentiating the method in which students demonstrate their understanding.

Varying the Teacher and Student Roles in the Instructional Process

Varying the roles of the teacher and students as an instructional technique is beneficial in creating an engaging, dynamic classroom environment that maximizes learning. When different roles are implemented, instruction is diversified, thus stimulating student interest and engagement. In addition, certain teacher and student roles are most applicable and effective in specific learning situations. When teachers acknowledge this and understand when to adopt and assign particular roles, they can effectively deliver instruction in a way that deepens student understanding and fosters success in learning. In presenting new content, directions, or modeling new skills, for example, the roles of **lecturer** and student **observer** are effective. In hands-on learning situations, students can take on the role of **active participant** while the teacher acts as a **facilitator** to create a student-centered and engaging learning environment in which students are given ownership over their own learning. Such variation enhances intellectual involvement by promoting critical thinking and problem-solving skills through self-directed learning. Skillfully assigning different roles throughout the learning process also allows the teacher to effectively address students' individual learning needs and preferences to promote engagement and enhance the learning experience.

Fostering Intellectual Involvement and Engagement

Effective instruction includes a variety of strategies for fostering intellectual involvement and engagement to promote academic success. Presenting instruction using various approaches provides multiple avenues for learning new content, thus ensuring and strengthening student understanding to facilitate achievement. In addition, diversifying instructional strategies creates variety in the classroom that effectively stimulates students' interest and motivation to engage in learning. Strategies such as **cooperative learning**, **discussion**, and **self-directed opportunities** encourage active student participation that enhances intellectual involvement by allowing students to build on background knowledge, deepen understanding by exploring others' perspectives, and take ownership over their own learning. This ultimately increases student engagement and motivation for success in learning. Similarly, incorporating **inquiry**, **problem-solving**, and **project-based** strategies promotes curiosity in learning, creativity, and the development of critical thinking skills that stimulate intellectual participation and engagement to create a productive learning environment. Implementing **digital resources** and media throughout instruction is integral in enhancing academic success by making learning relevant, interesting, and differentiated to accommodate various learning needs. At the end of a lesson or activity, allowing students the opportunity to reflect is a valuable strategy in increasing intellectual involvement, retainment, and academic success by facilitating personal connections with learning to build understanding.

Actively Engaging Students by Incorporating Discussion into Instruction

Classroom discussion is a valuable instructional technique in engaging students throughout the learning process. When teachers skillfully pose higher-level questions in discussions, they establish an active learning environment in which students are encouraged and motivated to participate, thus enhancing overall engagement. Effective discussions prompt students to become **intellectually invested** in instruction by promoting the use of **critical** and **higher-order thinking** skills to consider information more deeply and devise creative solutions to problems. In addition, discussions stimulate engagement by providing students the opportunity to express their own thoughts and reasoning regarding a given topic to establish a sense of ownership over their learning. Furthermore, discussions foster a collaborative learning environment that actively engages students by prompting them to understand others' perspectives, consider alternative approaches, and build on one another's experiences to make deeper connections to learning.

Promoting Student Inquiry

The promotion of inquiry is a valuable instructional technique in enhancing student engagement and intellectual involvement. In an **inquiry-based** learning environment, students are encouraged to explore instructional material and devise their own conclusions or solutions to problems. This increases the effectiveness of the learning process by providing students with a sense of agency over their own learning. In addition, implementing this strategy fosters curiosity, self-motivation, and active participation, as it allows for hands-on, **student-led** learning that increases overall engagement. Incorporating inquiry into the classroom stimulates critical and higher-order thinking skills as students construct their own understanding by interacting with learning materials, analyzing their findings, and synthesizing their learning to create new conclusions, results, and responses. To effectively incorporate inquiry into the learning process, the teacher must provide several opportunities for self-directed learning, project-based learning, and student choice to stimulate curiosity. Questions must be open-ended, and students must be encouraged to hypothesize, predict, and experiment in their learning. The teacher must be flexible in instruction to allow space and opportunity for exploration and allow time for reflection and extended learning opportunities to facilitate further inquiry.

Incorporating Problem-Solving into Instruction

Providing opportunities for creative problem solving within instruction effectively creates an engaging and successful learning experience. Students become more **intellectually involved** when encouraged to actively participate in learning and utilize **critical thinking skills** to test hypotheses, analyze results, and devise creative solutions to problems. This hands-on, **student-directed** approach promotes success in learning by allowing students to interact with learning materials as they seek answers to complex ideas and problems in an engaging environment. Problem-solving enables students to make deeper connections to their learning to enhance understanding, as this strategy prompts them to employ and develop background knowledge. In addition, problem-solving activities allow for collaborative learning in which students can actively engage with peers to build on one another's knowledge and experience, thus enhancing successful learning.

Intellectual Involvement, Active Student Engagement, and Success in Learning

A productive learning environment is composed intellectually involved students that are actively engaged in successful learning. A strong correlation exists between **intellectual involvement**, **active student engagement**, and **success in learning**, and each component is necessary for effective instruction. Effective instruction consists of challenging students based on their abilities and teaching them to think deeply about new ideas and concepts. This ultimately encourages students' intellectual involvement, as it prompts them to utilize their critical thinking skills to build on their background knowledge, consider alternative perspectives, and synthesize their learning to devise creative solutions. When students are intellectually involved in instruction, they become more personally invested and engaged, as learning becomes relevant, interesting, and challenging. Engaged students are active participants in their learning, thus enhancing their overall productivity and academic success.

Effectively Structuring Lessons

When developing instruction, it is imperative that the teacher is knowledgeable on how to effectively structure lessons to maximize student engagement and success. Each lesson must include a clear **objective** and explicitly state the process for achieving it. To initiate engagement, effective lessons begin with an **opening**, or "warm-up," activity to introduce a new topic, diagnose student understanding, and activate prior knowledge. Instruction of new material must be delivered through a variety of teaching strategies that are consciously tailored to students' individual learning needs to enhance participation and ensure comprehension. Direct instruction should be followed by **active learning** activities with clear directions and procedures to allow students to practice new concepts and skills. Throughout a successful lesson, the teacher checks frequently for understanding and comprehension by conducting a variety of **formative assessments** and adjusts instruction as necessary. Including **closure** activities is essential to successful learning, as it gives students the opportunity to reflect, process information, make connections, and demonstrate comprehension. In structuring lessons effectively according to students' learning needs, the teacher establishes a focused and engaging learning environment that promotes academic success.

Example of a Daily Lesson Plan Structure

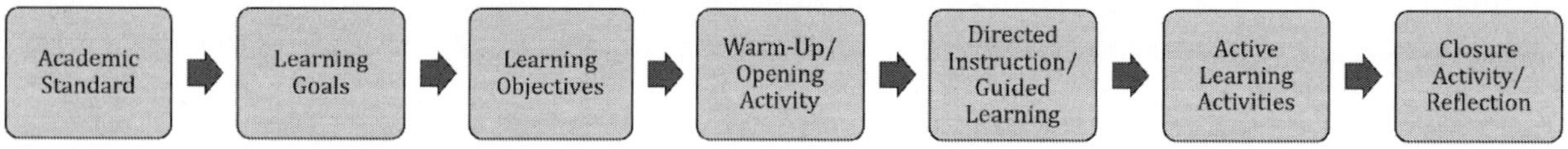

Flexible Instructional Groupings

Flexible instructional groupings provide the teacher and students with a versatile, engaging environment for successful learning. Skillfully grouping students allows for productive, cooperative learning opportunities in which individual strengths are enhanced and necessary support is provided, thus enhancing motivation and engagement. When working in groups, students' understanding of instruction is strengthened, as they are able to learn and build upon one another's background knowledge, perspectives, and abilities. Instructional groups can include students of the **same** or **varied abilities** depending on the learning objective and task to increase productivity and provide scaffolding as necessary for support. This strategy is effective in enabling the teacher to **differentiate** instruction and adjust groups as needed to accommodate varying learning styles, abilities, and interests to maximize engagement and success in learning.

Effective Pacing of Lessons and Importance of Flexibility to Students' Needs

Effective pacing is imperative to focused and engaging instruction. Teachers must be conscientious of the pace of their instruction and ensure that it is reflective of their students' learning needs and sustains their attention. Instruction that is delivered too quickly results in confusion and discouragement, whereas if instruction is too slow, students will lose interest and become disengaged. A well-paced lesson states clear learning goals and objectives while clearly outlining the means to achieve them to elicit student motivation. The teacher must consider the most **efficient** and **engaging** instructional strategies for presenting new material to establish a steady pace and maintain it by incorporating smooth **transitions** from one activity to the next. It is important that teachers are conscious of the rate of instruction throughout all stages of learning while maintaining **flexibility** in pacing in order to be responsive to their students. As individual students have different learning needs and processing times, they may require a faster or slower rate of instruction to understand new concepts and remain engaged in learning. Frequent checks for understanding and reflection activities are essential strategies in determining if the pace of instruction must be adjusted to accommodate students' needs.

Connecting Content to Students' Prior Knowledge and Experiences

Implementing effective instructional strategies for connecting content to students' prior knowledge and experiences enhances the relevancy of learning and fosters deeper connections that strengthen understanding. To achieve this, teachers must educate themselves on students' backgrounds, experiences, communities, and interests to determine what is important and interesting to them. With this knowledge in mind, teachers can successfully locate and implement **authentic materials** into instruction to enhance relevancy. Additionally, encouraging students to bring materials to class that reflect their backgrounds and including these materials in instruction makes learning relevant by allowing students to make **personal connections** to content. Instructional strategies such as brainstorming, KWL charts, prereading, and anticipation guides allow the teacher to determine what students know prior to learning a new concept, thus enabling them to connect content to students' background knowledge in a relevant way. Incorporating digital resources further enhances relevancy in learning. Teachers can locate videos or audio clips that relate to instruction and reflect students' background experiences and interests. Using digital resources to introduce a new concept is a valuable strategy in developing students' **schema** on a topic to build prior knowledge and make learning meaningful by fostering connections.

Making Learning Relevant and Meaningful

For learning to be relevant and meaningful, it is essential that teachers present content in a way that connects with students' **prior knowledge** and experiences. When students are able to apply new ideas and information to what they already know through effective instructional techniques, it facilitates strong **personal connections** that make learning relevant and meaningful. In addition, personal connections and **relevancy** are strengthened when teachers consciously incorporate materials to reflect students' individual backgrounds and experiences in instruction. Linking content to students' background experiences enables them to relate instruction to real-world situations, thus establishing a sense of purpose for learning by making it applicable to their lives. Intentionally connecting content with students' prior knowledge and experiences enhances the effectiveness of the instructional process and fosters positive attitudes toward learning.

Enhancing Student Engagement and Success in Learning

Engaging instruction employs a variety of instructional strategies and materials to create a relevant, meaningful, and successful learning experience. Effective content establishes a clear and applicable purpose for instruction that increases student participation in the learning process. Presenting relevant and meaningful content enhances understanding and engagement by enabling students to create real-world, **personal connections** to learning based upon their own backgrounds and experiences. In addition, when instruction is tailored to reflect students' unique interests and preferences, content becomes more appealing and students' willingness to learn is enhanced. When students can perceive content through their own frames of reference with instructional materials that reflect their unique differences, they are able to effectively internalize and relate information to their lives, thus increasing engagement. Engaged learning ultimately facilitates academic success in that when students are motivated to learn, they demonstrate positive attitudes toward learning and are more likely to actively participate.

Adapting Instruction to Individual Needs

Evaluating Activities and Materials to Meet Learning Needs

The careful selection of instructional activities and materials is integral to accommodating students' varying characteristics and needs. When evaluating the appropriateness of activities and materials, several considerations must be made. Teachers must consider whether activities and materials align with state and district **academic standards**. Teachers must also evaluate the quality and effectiveness of the activities and materials in supporting students' unique differences as they achieve learning goals and objectives. All materials and activities must be **developmentally appropriate** across domains yet adaptable to individual students' learning needs. In addition, they must be challenging yet feasible for student achievement relative to students' grade levels and abilities to promote engagement and the development of critical and **higher-order thinking** skills. Teachers must evaluate activities and materials for versatility to allow for student choice and differentiation in order to address varying characteristics and needs. Teachers must also ensure that activities and materials are accurate, **culturally sensitive**, and reflective of students' diversities to foster an inclusive learning environment that promotes engagement.

Instructional Resources and Technologies

The implementation of varied instructional resources and technologies is highly valuable in supporting student engagement and achievement. Effective use of resources and technologies requires teachers to evaluate their appropriateness in addressing students' individual characteristics and learning needs for academic success. Teachers must be attuned to students' unique differences in order to seek high quality technologies and resources that address their students' needs and support the achievement of learning goals and objectives. Technologies and resources must be **accurate**, **comprehensible**, easily **accessible** to students, and **relevant** to the curriculum and the development of particular skills. Teachers must also consider the grade-level and **developmental appropriateness** of technologies and resources as well as their adaptability to allow for differentiation. Effective technologies and resources are interactive, engaging, and multifaceted to allow for varying levels of complexity based on students' abilities. This allows teachers to provide appropriate challenges while diversifying instruction to appeal to varied characteristics and learning needs, thus fostering an engaging environment that supports success in learning for all students.

Adapting Activities and Materials to Meet Individual Characteristics and Needs

In effective instruction, activities and materials are adapted to accommodate students' individual characteristics and needs. Teachers must be attuned to students' unique differences and understand how to adjust activities and materials accordingly to facilitate academic success and growth. To achieve this, teachers must incorporate a **variety** of activities and materials that appeal to all styles of learners. Activities and materials should provide **student choice** for engagement in learning and demonstration of understanding. By differentiating instruction, teachers can effectively scaffold activities and materials to provide supports as necessary as well as include extensions or alternate activities for enrichment. **Chunking** instruction, allowing extra time as necessary, and accompanying activities and materials with aids such as graphic organizers, visual representations, and anticipation guides further differentiates learning to accommodate students' learning characteristics and needs. Conducting **formative assessments** provides teachers with valuable feedback regarding student understanding and engagement, thus allowing them to modify and adjust the complexity of activities and materials as necessary to adapt to varied characteristics and learning differences.

Instructional Resources and Technologies

When teachers understand students' individual characteristics and needs, they can adapt instructional resources and technologies accordingly to maximize learning. To do so effectively, the teacher must incorporate a diverse array of **multifaceted** resources and technologies that support and enhance learning through a variety of methods. This ensures that varying learning needs are met, as students of all learning styles are provided with several avenues for building and strengthening understanding. Additionally, the teacher can adapt resources and technologies to accommodate individual students by **varying the complexity** to provide challenges, support, and opportunities for enrichment based on ability level. Supplementing technologies and resources with **scaffolds**, such as extra time, visual representations, or opportunities for collaborative learning, further enables the teacher to adapt to individual learning needs. When effectively implemented and adapted to students' characteristics and needs, instructional technologies and resources serve as valuable tools for differentiating curriculum to enhance the learning experience.

Modifications, Accommodations, and Adaptations

ACCOMMODATIONS AND MODIFICATIONS

Accommodations and modifications are different types of educational supports put in place to help a student participate effectively in school. An **accommodation** changes *how* a student is taught or assessed by providing more time or other supports that remove barriers to the material. Students who receive accommodations are taught and assessed to the same standards as students without accommodations. A **modification** changes *what* is taught or assessed by changing or omitting parts of the materials. Students with modifications may receive fewer problems to solve or lower-rigor versions of the materials compared to other students.

MODIFICATIONS

Modifications are changes to *what* students are taught or expected to learn. Students with disabilities can receive modifications as determined by their specific needs and as written out in their Individualized Education Programs.

- **Curriculum modifications** allow students to learn material that is different from what their general education peers learn. For example, students with classroom modifications may receive assignments with fewer math problems or with reading samples appropriate for their reading levels. Students with curriculum modifications may receive different grading tiers than their peers. The ways teachers grade their assignments may be different from how the teachers grade their peers' assignments. Students may also be excused from particular projects or given project guidelines that are different and better suited to their individual needs.
- **Assignment modifications** include completing fewer or different homework problems than peers, writing shorter papers, answering fewer questions on classwork and tests, and creating alternate projects or assignments.

ENVIRONMENTAL MODIFICATIONS

Students with disabilities may need environmental modifications in order to be successful in their classrooms, homes, and communities. **Environmental modifications** are adaptations that allow people with disabilities to maneuver through their environments with as little resistance as possible. They allow for more **independent living experiences**, especially for those with limited mobility. Environmental modifications ensure the health, safety, and welfare of the people who need them. Examples of environmental modifications in the home, community, or school include ramps, hydraulic lifts, widened doorways and hallways, automatic doors, handrails, and grab bars. Roll-in showers, water faucet controls, worktable or work surface adaptations, and cabinet and shelving adaptations are also environmental modifications that can be provided if necessary. Other adaptations include heating and cooling adaptations and electrical adaptations to accommodate devices or equipment. Environmental modifications in the home are typically provided by qualified agencies or providers. The Americans with Disabilities Act ensures that environmental modifications are provided in the **community** to help avoid discrimination against people with disabilities.

ACCOMMODATIONS

Accommodations are flexible classroom tools because they can be used to provide **interventions** without time or location boundaries. They remove **barriers** to learning for students with disabilities, and they change how students learn. Accommodations do not change what students are learning or expected to know. Classroom accommodations may be outlined in students' Individualized Education Programs (IEPs) and 504 Plans or simply provided as needed by special educators or general educators. Accommodations are put into place to ensure that students with disabilities are accessing the learning process with the fewest barriers, putting them on the same levels as their peers without disabilities. **Presentation accommodations** include allowing students to listen to oral instructions, providing written lists of instructions, and allowing students to use readers to assist with comprehension. **Response accommodations** include allowing students to provide oral responses, capture responses via audio recording, and use spelling dictionaries or spell-checkers when writing. **Accommodations to setting** include special seating (wherever the students learn best), use of sensory tools, and special lighting.

Types of Accommodations

Timing, schedule, and organizational accommodations change the ways students with disabilities have access to classrooms with the fewest barriers to learning. Students who need these accommodations receive them as written statements in their IEPs, 504 Plans, or as teachers see fit during classroom time.

- **Timing accommodations** allow students more time to complete tasks or tests and/or process instructions. They also allow students to access frequent breaks during assignments or tests.
- **Schedule accommodations** include taking tests in chunks over periods of time or several days, taking test sections in different orders, and/or taking tests during specific times of day.
- **Organizational skill accommodations** include assistance with time management, marking texts with highlighters, maintaining daily assignment or work schedules, and/or receiving study skills instruction.

When accommodations are written in a student's IEP, the student has access to them for state standardized tests. When and how accommodations are put into place is left to the discretion of the teacher unless specifically written in the student's IEP or 504 Plan.

Obtaining Accommodations

When parents or legal guardians of children with disabilities believe that **accommodations** may help their children, they can arrange to speak with teachers about informal supports. **Informal supports** are strategies teachers can put into place to assist students with their learning processes. These changes do not require paperwork and can be implemented during classroom instruction. Teachers can experiment with informal supports to determine what will be most helpful for removing the barriers to learning students might be experiencing. If it is determined that students need bigger changes to how they learn, **formal evaluations** can take place. Students who do not already have IEPs or 504 Plans may be evaluated to collect data on their needs. For students with IEPs or 504 Plans, accommodations can be included the next time these plans are updated. The IEPs or 504 Plans can also be **amended** if the need for the accommodations is immediate, such as when they need to be put in place before standardized testing time. **Data** supporting the need for the accommodations must be provided and listed in the comprehensive initial evaluations and all versions of IEPs and 504 Plans.

Parents and Legal Guardians Ensuring Accommodations Are Being Provided

Accommodations are changes to the ways children with disabilities learn, not changes to what the children are learning. While parents and legal guardians may only receive **formal updates** on how accommodations are being provided or helping the students during specified reporting times (unless students' IEPs or 504 Plans specifically state otherwise), they can ask for **reports** on goal progress or accommodations for their students at any time. Parents and legal guardians can ensure that accommodations are successfully implemented by using the progress reports and asking the right questions. Parents and legal guardians can ensure that accommodations are being provided in a number of ways. They can **advocate** for their students by making sure the accommodations are being implemented on a regular basis. Parents and legal guardians also have the right to ask if their students are using the accommodations on a **regular basis**. If they are being used on a regular basis, parents and legal guardians can explore additional options that might help their students. Parents and legal guardians can work with special education teachers and the IEP teams to ensure that their students' accommodations are being received and are effective.

INFORMAL SUPPORTS VS. FORMAL ACCOMMODATIONS

Informal supports are generally easier to implement in the classroom setting. They do not necessarily have to be implemented only for students with Individualized Education Programs or students with disabilities. Students who have not been evaluated for special education services can receive **informal supports** to ensure classroom success. Teachers may use informal supports to help students who are struggling with the ways they are learning. They may demonstrate that the students are able to learn with the accommodations in place. Informal supports are often the first step to indicating that students are in need of **special education services**.

Formal accommodations are put in place when students become eligible for IEPs or 504 Plans. Formal supports are written into the IEPs or 504 Plans and then required by law to be provided. Examples of informal supports include frequent breaks, special seating, quiet areas for test taking or studying, teacher cues, and help with basic organizational skills. These informal supports may eventually turn into formal supports if students become eligible for special education services.

REASONABLE ACCOMMODATIONS ACCORDING TO ADA

According to the Americans with Disabilities Act (ADA), a **reasonable accommodation** is a change to workplace conditions, equipment, or environment that allows an individual to effectively perform a job. Title I under the ADA requires businesses with more than 15 employees to abide by certain regulations, ensuring that their needs are reasonably met. Any change to the work environment or the way a job is performed that gives a person with a disability access to **equal employment** is considered a reasonable accommodation. Reasonable accommodations fall into **three categories**: changes to a job application process, changes to the work environment or to the way a job is usually done, and changes that enable employee access to equal benefits and privileges that employees without disabilities receive. These effectively level the playing field for people with disabilities to receive the same benefits as their peers. It also allows for the fewest barriers to success in the workplace. Many communities have resources available to help people with disabilities find jobs. They also have resources that help employers make their workplaces accessible for people with disabilities.

TYPES OF ASSISTIVE TECHNOLOGY

Assistive technology (AT) tools can be physical objects and devices or online resources that assist students with disabilities in their learning. The purpose of AT tools is to provide students with disabilities **equal access to the curriculum** by accommodating their individual needs to promote positive outcomes. **Personal listening devices (PLDs)**, sometimes called FM systems, are devices that clarify teachers' words. With a PLD, a teacher speaks into a small microphone and the words transmit clearly into a student's headphone or earpiece. **Sound field systems** amplify teachers' voices to eliminate sound issues in classroom environments. **Noise-cancelling headphones** are useful for students who need to work independently and limit distractions or behavioral triggers. **Audio recorders** allow students to record lectures or lessons and refer to the recordings later at their own pace. Some note-taking applications will transcribe audio into written words. Captioning is available to pair visual words with spoken words. **Text-to-speech (TTS) software** lets students see and hear words at the same time. TTS and audiobook technology can help students with fluency, decoding, and comprehension skills.

Voice Recognition Software

Voice recognition software and communication software can assist students who struggle with speaking or communicating. **Voice recognition software** allows people to speak commands into microphones to interact with the computer instead of using a keyboard. This feature helps create a **least restrictive environment** for a student with a disability because it removes the sometimes challenging aspect of using a keyboard while working on a computer. Voice recognition software allows users to carry out actions such as opening documents, saving documents, and moving the cursor. It also allows users to "write" sentences and paragraphs by speaking into the microphones in word processing programs. In order for voice recognition software to be effective, the user must learn to dictate words distinctly into a microphone. This ensures that the correct word is heard and dictated by the voice-to-text software. Some programs collect information and familiarize themselves with people's particular voice qualities. Over time, the systems adapt to people's voices and become more efficient.

Effectively Instructing Students Using Assistive Technology

Assistive technology (**AT**) refers to tools that are effective for teaching students with learning disabilities, as they address a number of potential special needs. The purpose of AT is to level the playing field for students with **learning disabilities**, particularly when they are participating in general education classrooms. AT can address learning difficulties in math, listening, organization, memory, reading, and writing. **AT for listening** can assist students who have difficulties processing language. For example, a personal listening device can help a student hear a teacher's voice more clearly. **AT for organization and memory** can help students with self-management tasks, such as keeping assignment calendars or retrieving information using handheld devices. **AT for reading** often includes text-to-speech devices that assist with students' reading fluency, decoding, comprehension, and other skill deficits. **AT for writing** assists students who struggle with handwriting or writing development. Some AT writing devices help with actual handwriting, while others assist with spelling, punctuation, grammar, word usage, or text organization.

Augmentative and Alternative Communication Systems

Students with communication disorders may require the use of augmentative or alternative communication systems. Communication systems are used to help the students effectively demonstrate **expressive and receptive language** and engage in **social skills**. Teaching appropriate communication skills is a collaborative effort between the students' caretakers, teachers, and other professionals. Typically, **speech services** are written into students' IEPs, and the services are delivered by **speech language pathologists (SLPs)**. Depending on the requirements in the IEPs, the SLPs may work one-on-one with students or work with the teachers to incorporate speech and language skills throughout students' school days. In order for communication systems to work for nonverbal students, measures must be taken to ensure that the particular systems are appropriate for what the students need. It is important for the caretakers, teachers, other professionals, and even classmates to model using the devices so the students can learn how to "talk" appropriately. Students must also have constant access to the systems and receive consistent opportunities to communicate using the systems at home and at school.

Use of Visual Representation Systems with Students with Autism

Assistive technology (AT) helps increase learning opportunities for students with autism by eliminating barriers to learning. AT can help improve students' expressive communication skills, attention skills, motivation skills, academic skills, and more. **Visual representation systems** in the form of objects, photographs, drawings, or written words provide concrete representations of words for students with autism. Visual representations, such as simple pictures paired with words, can be used to create visual schedules for students with autism. Photographs can be used to help students learn vocabulary words and the names of people and places. Written words should be paired with the visual representations in order to create links between the concrete objects and the actual words. The goal is for students to eventually recognize the words without the pictures. Visual representation systems can also help facilitate easier transitions between activities or places, which can be difficult for students with autism.

Communication Systems

Students who are nonverbal may have access to **communication systems** implemented by trained professionals. Teachers, caretakers, and other professionals work with the students to use the communication systems effectively. The goal of a communication system is to teach a nonverbal student how to "talk" and engage in **age-appropriate social skills**. In order for nonverbal students to learn appropriate social interactions, they must spend time learning communication skills, just as they learn academic content. Communication skills can be taught in isolation or as part of students' daily activities. Giving nonverbal students opportunities to foster communication skills in **familiar environments** makes it easier for them to learn appropriate social interactions. Teachers, caregivers, and other professionals must demonstrate how to use communication systems to engage in conversations, make requests, and answer questions. Most importantly, nonverbal students must be instructed to **access** their "words" (communication systems) at all times throughout the school and home environments.

Accessibility Components of a Picture Exchange Communication System

A Picture Exchange Communication System (**PECS**) is a communication system for people with little or no **communicative abilities**. This system is a way for the students to access their environments using **picture symbols** to communicate meaning, wants, and needs. For example, a child may point to a picture symbol to request a book. A PECS provides a way for students with communication disorders to develop their **verbal communication** without actually speaking. It reduces frustration and problem behaviors by providing students with an avenue to express what they want to say. It is commonly used for students with autism spectrum disorder in the form of augmentative communication devices. It can also be used for students with other impairments whose communicative abilities are affected. A PECS focuses on **functional communication skills** and can be practiced in home, school, and community environments.

Supporting Nonverbal Students

Nonverbal students have extra challenges in addition to learning content. These students may need extra instruction in academic areas as well as specialized instruction in the area of communication skills. Students with **nonverbal disabilities** may also need social skills instruction, struggle with abstract concepts, and dislike changes to their routines. Teachers can **facilitate learning** for nonverbal students by making changes to their classroom environments, by teaching strategies for comprehending concepts, and by providing materials to accommodate their needs. Teachers can also provide accommodations or modifications to classwork and tests to make the content accessible to nonverbal students. Using visuals to represent actions, words, or concepts is a helpful instructional strategy for teaching nonverbal students, especially when teaching new material. Additionally, teachers can assist nonverbal students by taking measures to prevent undesirable behaviors from occurring.

Strategies and Accommodations for Students with Working Memory Deficits

Working memory is critical for remembering letters and numbers, listening to short instructions, reading and understanding content, completing homework independently, and understanding social cues. When **working memory skills** are absent or slow to develop, learning may be difficult. This may get worse for children over time. As they fail to develop or retain working memory capabilities, their overall **cognitive abilities** begin to suffer. Working memory deficits vary among people with disabilities, but accommodations can make up for missing or underdeveloped skills. Educators can implement **strategies** like reducing the children's workload; being aware of when children might be reaching memory overload; and providing visual cues, positive feedback, testing alternatives, and extra time. **Accommodations** in an Individualized Education Program for a student with working memory deficits might include frequent breaks, small group instruction, and extended time for tests and assignments.

Life Stage Transitions

Supporting Students Through Transitions

Transitioning to life after high school can be a difficult process, particularly for students with disabilities. It is important for teachers to facilitate and support these **transitions** before students exit their special education programs. **Structured learning environments** that include independent workstations and learning centers provide opportunities for independent learning to occur. **Independent workstations** give students chances to practice previously introduced concepts or perform previously introduced tasks. **Learning centers** provide small group settings where new skills can be taught. Students can also rotate through different learning centers that offer art lessons, focus on academic skills, or provide breaks or leisure activities. **Classroom layout** also plays an important role. Teachers should plan their classroom layouts based on individual student needs in order to create comfortable, predictable environments for students with disabilities. **Visual schedules** help students transition between centers by providing them with concrete schedule references.

Benefits of Vocational Education

Students with disabilities often participate in vocational education in order to gain **independent living skills**. Often, schools and communities offer services that provide vocational training for people with disabilities. These programs offer students **job-specific skills training** and opportunities to earn certifications, diplomas, or certificates. They often involve **hands-on learning experiences** focused on building skills specific to certain occupations. These programs are beneficial to students with disabilities who may struggle with grasping abstract concepts learned in typical classroom environments. Hands-on training in vocational programs can be a meaningful way for students with disabilities to learn academic concepts and gain living skills needed to function in postgraduate life. Vocational education opportunities offer alternatives for students with disabilities who might otherwise drop out of high school. These programs also serve as a viable option for younger students to work towards, as most vocational education programs are offered to students in upper grade levels.

Vocational Skills Needed to Be Successful in Work Environments

Informal vocational training often begins before students even get to high school. Teachers include informal vocational training skills in their classrooms by teaching academic and communication skills. **Academic skills** can both spark and strengthen students' career interests and provide learning platforms to build upon. **Communication skills**, like giving and following instructions and processing information, generalize to work environments. **Social and**

interpersonal skills, like problem-solving abilities and participating in phone conversations, are important for performance in workplaces. Students need to learn important **vocational and occupational skills** required by most jobs, such as interacting appropriately with coworkers and keeping track of worked hours. Students also need formal or informal training in completing resumes, cover letters, and tax forms. Training may also include interview practice and job search guidance.

Resources to Promote Successful Transitions to Life after High School

In some states, **statements of transition** should be included in Individualized Education Programs (IEPs) at age 14 for students with disabilities. In most states, the Individuals with Disabilities Education Act mandates that transition plans be put in place for students with IEPs at age 16 and every year thereafter. Some schools and communities have programs and resources available to facilitate students' successful transitions to life after high school. Throughout the transition process, it is important that students and their caregivers participate in any decision-making processes. **Vocational education courses**, sometimes called career and technical education courses, offer academic course alternatives. The courses usually specialize in specific trades or occupations. They can serve to spark or maintain students' interests in vocational fields. Some schools offer **postsecondary enrollment options**, where students can participate in college courses, earning both high school and college credits. **Career assessments**, including interest inventories and formal and informal vocational assessments, serve to gauge students' career interests. These can be worked into students' transitional goals in their IEPs and should be conducted frequently, as students' interests change.

Components of a Transition Plan

Transition plans are flexible but formal plans that help a student identify his or her goals for after school and act as a roadmap to help the support team advocate for the student's future. They generally include postsecondary goals and expected transition services. The four goal areas are vocational training, postsecondary education, employment, and independent living. **Transition goals** must be results oriented and measurable. Goals can be general, but the transition activities need to be quantified to reflect what the student can complete in the IEP year. It is common for interests to change from year to year; therefore, goals and plans may change as well. **Transition services** are determined once the goals are established. Transition services include types of instruction the student will receive in school, related services, community experiences, career or college counseling, and help with adaptive behavior skills. Goals and transition services must be reviewed and updated each year. Academic goals in the IEP can also support transition goals. For example, math goals can focus on money management skills as part of a transition plan.

Factors That Influence Successful Transitions to Postsecondary Life

Parents or legal guardians, teachers, school professionals, community members, and students themselves can all contribute to successful transitions to postsecondary life. Key **factors** that help students successfully transition include the following:

- Participation in standards-based education
- Work preparation and career-based learning experiences
- Leadership skills
- Access to and experience with community services, such as mental health and transportation services
- Family involvement and support

Standards-based education ensures that students receive consistent and clear expectations with a curriculum that is aligned to the universal design for learning standards. Exposure to work preparation and career-based learning experiences ensures that students receive opportunities to discover potential career interests or hobbies. Connections and experiences with community activities provide students with essential postsecondary independent living skills. Family involvement and support ensure that students have advocates for their needs and interests. Families can also help students connect with school and community-based supports that facilitate their career interests.

Instructional Design for Students with Disabilities

Developmentally Appropriate Curriculum

Choosing a developmentally appropriate curriculum is challenging for educators. Special educators have the additional challenge of finding a curriculum that meets the needs of the **individual students with disabilities**. The end result is not usually a one-size-fits-all curriculum because that goes against the intentions of Individualized Education Programs (IEPs) designed to meet the needs of students with special needs. Instead, special educators often pick and choose curriculum components that best meet the needs of differing abilities in the classroom. When selecting an appropriate curriculum, special educators should consider the following:

- Standards and goals that are appropriate to the needs of the students
- Best practices that have been found effective for students
- Curricula that are engaging and challenging
- Instruction and activities that are multimodal
- IEP goals
- Real-world experiences
- Different ways of learning that help teachers understand students' learning processes
- Collaboration with co-teachers to deliver appropriate instruction

In some special education settings, the curriculum is already chosen. In these settings, teachers can collaborate with co-teachers to find ways to provide instruction that meets standards and the individual needs of the students.

Components of Differentiated Instruction

Differentiated instruction is different from individualized instruction. It targets the strengths of students and can work well in both special education and general education settings. **Differentiated instruction** is also useful for targeting the needs of students with **learning and attention deficits**. With differentiated instruction, teachers adjust their instructional processes to meet the needs of the individual students. Teaching strategies and classroom management skills are based largely on each particular class of students instead of on methods that may have been successful in the past. Teachers can differentiate content, classroom activities, student projects, and learning environments. For example, students may be encouraged to choose topics of personal interest to focus on for projects. Students are held to the same standards but have many choices in terms of project topics. **Differentiated content** provides access to a variety of resources to encourage student choice over what and how they learn. **Differentiated learning environments** are flexible to meet the ever-changing needs of the students.

Review Video: Differentiated Instruction
Visit mometrix.com/academy and enter code: 100342

Effectiveness of Differentiated Instruction

Differentiated instruction is effective in general education settings, team-teaching settings, and special education settings because it targets the **strengths** of students. Differentiated instruction is used to target the different ways that students learn instead of taking a one-size-fits-all approach. Differentiated instruction is used in lieu of individualized instruction because it uses a variety of instructional approaches and allows students to use a variety of materials to help them access the curriculum. **Effective differentiated instruction** includes small group work, reciprocal learning, and continual assessment.

Small group work allows for the individual learning styles and needs of students to be addressed. In small groups, students receive instruction by rotating through groups. Group work should be used sparingly or be well-regulated to ensure that all of the students in the group are learning for themselves and contributing to group work sufficiently. Groups may be shuffled or have assigned roles within the group to ensure a good division of labor. In **reciprocal learning**, students play the role of the teacher, instructing the class by sharing what they know and asking content questions of their peers. Teachers who practice **continual assessment** can determine if their differentiated instructional methods are effective or if they need to be changed. Assessments can determine what needs to be changed in order for students to participate in effective classroom environments.

Different Educational Levels and Learning Styles

Learning styles of students differ, regardless of whether or not the students have disabilities. When addressing groups of students in inclusion settings, it is important for teachers to organize and implement teaching strategies that address learning at **different educational levels**. Students generally fall into one or more learning modes. Some are visual learners, some are auditory learners, some are kinesthetic or tactile learners, and some learn best using a combination of these approaches. Teachers can address students' educational levels by creating lessons that allow learning to take place visually, auditorily, and kinesthetically. **Visual learners** prefer information that has been visually organized, such as in graphic organizers or diagrams. **Auditory learners** prefer information presented in spoken words. Lessons that target auditory learners provide opportunities for students to engage in conversations and question material. **Kinesthetic learners** prefer a hands-on approach to learning. These learners prefer to try out new tasks and learn as they go. Lessons that include opportunities for these three types of learning to occur can successfully target different educational levels.

Multiple Modality Instruction and Activities

The purpose of multiple modality instruction is to engage students by offering different ways to learn the same material. **Multiple modality teaching** also addresses students' unique learning styles. Learning modalities are generally separated into four categories: **visual** (seeing), **auditory** (hearing), **kinesthetic** (moving), and **tactile** (touch) modalities. This way of teaching targets students who may have deficits in one or more modalities. It is also helpful for students who struggle in one or more of the learning categories. If a student struggles with understanding content that is presented visually, a lesson that includes auditory, kinesthetic, and tactile components may engage learning. Additionally, presenting lesson material and activities in a multimodal approach helps improve student memory and retention by solidifying concepts through multiple means of engagement. This approach is also useful for students with **attention disorders** who may struggle in environments where one mode of teaching is used. The multiple modality approach ensures that activities, such as kinesthetic or tactile activities, keep more than one sense involved with the learning process.

Review Video: Teaching Through Multiple Modalities
Visit mometrix.com/academy and enter code: 100371

Using Visual Supports to Facilitate Instruction and Self-Monitoring Strategies

Many students learn best when provided with instruction and activities that appeal to multiple senses. A **multimodal approach** is especially important for students with developmental disabilities, who may need supports that match their individual ways of learning. **Visual supports** are concrete representations of information used to convey meaning. Teachers can use visual supports to help students with developmental disabilities understand what is being taught and communicated to them. Visual supports can help students with understanding classroom rules, making decisions, communicating with others, staying organized, and reducing frustrations. **Visual schedules** show students visual representations of their daily schedules. This assists with transitions between activities, which can sometimes be difficult for students with disabilities. Visuals can be used to help students share information about themselves or their school days with their peers and parents. Visual supports can also be used with checklists to help facilitate independence. For example, behavior checklists can be used to help students monitor their own behaviors.

Universal Design for Learning

Universal design for learning (UDL) is a flexible approach to learning that keeps students' individual needs in mind. Teachers that utilize **UDL** offer different ways for students to access material and engage in content. This approach is helpful for many students but particularly those with learning and attention issues. The **principles of UDL** all center on varying instruction and assessment to appeal to the needs of students who think in various ways.

	Principles of the Universal Design for Learning
Multiple means of *representation*	*Instructional content* should be demonstrated in various ways so that students may learn in a mode that is effective for them.
Multiple means of *expression*	*Assessment* should be administered in a variety of ways to adequately allow students to demonstrate their knowledge. This includes quizzes, homework, presentations, classwork, etc.
Multiple means of *engagement*	Instruction should include a variety of *motivational factors* that help to interest and challenge students in exciting ways.

Review Video: Universal Design for Learning
Visit mometrix.com/academy and enter code: 523916

Evaluating, Modifying, and Adapting the Classroom Setting Using the UDL

The **universal design for learning (UDL)** is a framework that encourages teachers to design their instruction and assessment in ways that allow **multiple means** for the student to learn and express their knowledge. The UDL model is most successful when the teacher prepares a classroom setting that encourages the success of students with and without disabilities. Knowledge of the **characteristics** of students with different disabilities, as well as the unique **learning needs** of these students, enables the teacher to address these needs in the classroom setting. Setting clear short- and long-term goals for students is one way to meet the UDL standards. A traditional classroom may offer one assignment for all students to complete, but a UDL-compliant classroom may offer **different assignments** or **different ways** for students to complete assignments. UDL-compliant classrooms often offer **flexible workspaces** for students to complete their classwork and may offer quiet spaces for individual work or group tables for group work. UDL-compliant teachers recognize that students access information differently and provide different ways for students to gain **access** to the information, such as through audio text or physical models to work with. The universal design for learning assumes students learn in a variety of ways, even if those ways have not been clearly identified; it follows that all instruction and assessment can be improved by making it more varied and accessible.

Modifying Classroom Curriculum and Materials for UDL

In order for a **universal design for learning (UDL) model classroom** to be successful, the teacher must evaluate, modify, and adapt the **curriculum** and **materials** to best suit the needs of the individual students. UDL contrasts with a one-size-fits-all concept of curriculum planning, where lesson plans are developed and implemented strictly based on how teachers expect students to learn. Instead, a successful UDL model addresses the many **specific needs** of the students. These needs vary depending on the unique abilities each classroom of students presents. UDL-compliant teachers can evaluate the success of lessons by checking for comprehension throughout lessons instead of only upon lesson completion. Evaluation methods used informally can provide a lot of information about whether students are grasping the concepts. Teachers use the results of the evaluations to modify and adapt classroom instruction to meet the needs of the students. Other means for diversifying the materials include using multiple assignment completion options and varied means of accessing the materials, such as both written, digital, and audio forms of a text. These means of instruction can take place simultaneously. For instance, a UDL-compliant teacher may choose to pair audio output and text for all students during a reading assignment in order to target students with listening or comprehension difficulties.

Principles of the Universal Design for Learning Model

The universal design for learning (UDL) model contains three principles that aim to level the playing field for all learners. **Principle I** of the UDL model primarily focuses on what **representation or version** of information is being taught. This principle aims to target an audience of diverse learners. By providing multiple ways for students to approach content, teachers can ensure that the unique needs of all learners in their classrooms are met. **Principle II** examines how people learn. This principle focuses on the concept that students learn best when provided with **multiple ways** to demonstrate what they have learned. In classrooms compliant with Principle II, students are given more than one option for expressing themselves. **Principle III** focuses on providing multiple ways for students to engage in the learning process. Teachers compliant with Principle III provide options for keeping content **interesting and relevant** to all types of learners. Effective UDL-model classrooms provide multiple ways to present content, engage in learning, and express what was learned.

Specially Designed Instruction

Specially designed instruction (**SDI**) in special education refers to specialized teaching given to students in a co-taught inclusion classroom. While a teacher teaches the class, the special education teacher provides specialized instruction in parallel to a student to help clarify the information. This is distinctive from adaptation and modification, as the content and its medium do not change for SDI. While the general education class engages in instruction, a special education teacher provides SDI to meet the specific needs of learners who may not be successful learning in the same ways as their similar-aged peers. The main purpose of SDI is to provide a student with access to the general education setting without substantially changing the content as it is aligned with state standards.

Diagnostic Prescriptive Method

The diagnostic prescriptive approach to teaching is based on the fact that all students are unique learners. The **diagnostic prescriptive approach** examines factors that impede student learning and how to remedy specific issues. A successful approach begins with a **diagnosis** of what students are bringing to the classroom. This can be completed through careful observations and assessments. Once the skill deficits are clear, **prescriptive teaching** can be put into effect. In this process, teachers examine what will help students the most. It may be switching materials, changing to group settings, or recognizing the need for specialized interventions due to disabilities. In order to address multiple needs in the classroom, lesson plans should be **multimodal**. Developing strategies in advance to address students' needs is also a highlight of this method. Another important part of this method is evaluating results to determine what was effective or ineffective for entire classes and individual students.

Guided Learning

Guided learning is practice or instruction completed by the teacher and students together. The goal of **guided learning** is to help students engage in the learning process in order to learn more about how they think and acquire new information. **Guided practice** occurs when the teacher and students complete practice activities together. The advantage of guided practice is that students can learn ways to approach concepts they have just learned. It allows students to understand and ask questions about lesson-related activities before working independently. Guided practice is useful in classrooms for students with and without disabilities because it helps teachers gauge how students learn and what instructional methods work best for them. Additionally, guided practice allows teachers to understand how students are learning the material. It also allows teachers to revisit concepts that are unclear or fine tune any missed lesson objectives.

How Cooperative Learning Works

Cooperative learning is an interpersonal group learning process where students learn concepts by working together in **small groups**. Cooperative learning involves collaboration among small groups to achieve common goals. With **formal cooperative learning**, an instructor oversees the learning of lesson material or completion of assignments for students in these small groups. With **informal cooperative learning**, the instructor supervises group activities by keeping students cognitively active but does not guide instruction or assignments. For example, a teacher might use a class period to show a movie but provide a list of questions for students to complete during the movie. In the special education classroom, cooperative learning is helpful when students need specific skills targeted or remediated. It is also helpful for separating students who are learning different content at different levels. For example, a cooperative learning activity may involve multiple groups of students with differing levels of mathematic abilities. Group work also promotes development of interpersonal skills as students interact with one another.

Intrinsic Motivation

Intrinsic motivation is a person's inner drive to engage in an activity or behavior. Students with special needs often struggle with intrinsic motivation as a skill. This requires special educators and other professionals to promote and teach intrinsic motivation to students. Teachers can **promote intrinsic motivation** by giving students opportunities to demonstrate **achievement**. This can be done by challenging students with intellectual risks and helping them focus on difficult classwork or tasks. Teachers can build upon students' strengths by providing daily opportunities in the classroom for students to demonstrate their **strengths** instead of focusing on their weaknesses. Offering choices throughout the day provides students with ownership of their decision-making and communicates that they have choices in the classroom environment. Teachers should allow students to **fail without criticism** and should promote self-reflection in order to build students' confidence. Teachers should promote self-management and organizational skills like instructing students on how to **break down tasks**.

Promoting Critical Thinking Skills

Critical thinking is a self-directed thinking process that helps people make logical, reasonable judgments. This is an especially challenging skill for students with **developmental disabilities**, who often demonstrate deficits in logical thinking and reasoning abilities. In order to teach these students **critical thinking skills**, the focus should be on encouraging critical thinking across **home and school environments** and providing opportunities for students to practice this type of thinking. Teachers and parents can encourage critical thinking by implementing teaching strategies focused on fostering **creativity** in students. Instead of providing outlines or templates for lesson concepts, students can use their prior knowledge to figure out the boundaries of the lessons independently and explore new concepts. Parents and teachers should not always be quick to jump in and help students who are struggling. Sometimes the best way to help is by facilitating ways for students to solve problems without doing things for them. Opportunities for brainstorming, classifying and categorizing information, comparing and contrasting information, and making connections between topics are teaching strategies that also facilitate critical thinking skills.

Career-Based Education

During their schooling years, students with disabilities have the additional challenge of determining possible **career options** for life after high school. Fortunately, instruction can be provided during the school day or within after-school programs that address career-based skills. Effective **career-based programs** for students with disabilities should work collaboratively with community and school resources. Students should receive information on career options, be exposed to a range of experiences, and learn how to self-advocate. Information regarding career options can be gathered via **career assessments** that explore students' possible career interests. Students should receive exposure to **postsecondary education** to determine if it is an option that aligns with their career interests. They should also learn about basic job requirements, such as entry requirements for different types of jobs and what it means to earn a living wage. Students should be given opportunities for job training, job shadowing, and community service. It is helpful to provide students with opportunities to learn and practice **work and occupational skills** that pertain to specific job interests. Students need to learn **self-advocacy skills**, such as communicating the implications of their disabilities to employers, in order to maintain success in postsecondary work environments.

Learning Across the Curriculum

Teaching Multiple Subjects in Special Education Settings

Special education classrooms, whether inclusive, self-contained, or resource room settings, often need to deliver instruction in **multiple subject areas**. Students in these settings also represent many **levels of learning**. Therefore, one instructional strategy is not always the most effective way to teach students in these settings. In order to provide quality instruction, special educators can place students with similar skill levels into **small groups** during instruction in the content areas. This way, small groups of students can be working on skills that cater to their specific needs. **Classroom centers** are another way to group students. Classroom centers often feature self-guided instruction in skill or content areas where students can work at their own pace. **Rotating centers** allows teachers to instruct groups of students while the other groups work independently on previously learned skills. **Thematic instruction** is a teaching strategy where multiple subject areas are connected and taught within one lesson unit. Themes are effective in special education classrooms because they tie multiple content areas together. Special educators should also provide **multiple levels** of materials and books for student learning to target different learning levels.

Developmentally Appropriate Math Skills for Young Children

Starting in pre-kindergarten and first grade, children should be able to count to 100, learn how to write numbers, and demonstrate basic addition and subtraction skills. Older students can demonstrate skills associated with counting money and telling time, and they can also understand decimal, place value, and word problem concepts. Students with disabilities may or may not develop what are considered to be **developmentally appropriate mathematics skills** by certain ages or grades. In inclusive special education settings, the needs of these students can be addressed with a number of strategies. **Scaffolding** is the process of breaking down concepts into chunks. Scaffolding addresses the issues that arise when some students are well behind others by allowing students to work at their own pace and helping them connect prior knowledge to new information. This ensures that students have solidified knowledge of concepts before moving on to new concepts.

Teaching Mathematics

Students whose disabilities affect their performances in mathematics require specialized instruction. Eligible students will have Individualized Education Program goals to address their specific needs but are also expected to learn content connected to **state standards**. Additionally, **accommodations and modifications** are available for qualifying students to assist with mathematics instruction. Strategies that can be effective for math instruction for students with disabilities include:

- Using the same instructional strategies in all settings, including the home environment and all school environments
- Using concrete objects to teach math concepts, such as using manipulatives to count out number values
- Providing assistive materials, such as calculators and scrap paper
- Explaining and modeling objectives clearly
- Allowing time for students to check their work
- Activating prior knowledge to assist students with learning new concepts
- Providing opportunities for extra tutoring or one-on-one instruction
- Assisting students with self-monitoring their progress
- Encouraging math games to engage learning and interest in math concepts

Implications of a Mathematics Disability

Disabilities like **dyscalculia** are specific learning disabilities associated with mathematics. Students that have specific learning disabilities in mathematics have trouble with number-related concepts and using symbols or functions. Symptoms of **math disorders** include difficulties with counting numbers, solving math word problems, sequencing events or information, recognizing patterns when adding, subtracting, multiplying or dividing, and understanding concepts associated with time, like days, weeks, seasons, etc. Recalling math facts is also difficult for students with math disabilities. The severity of the disability is impacted when it **coexists** with dyslexia, attention-deficit/hyperactivity disorder, anxiety, or other disabilities. Special educators, math tutors, or other professionals can help students with math deficits by providing multimodal instruction to engage multiple senses and enhance the chances of the students learning the concepts. They may also receive supports according to 504 Plans or Individualized Education Programs that level the educational playing field, such as use of a calculator. Use of concrete examples, visual aids, graph paper, or scratch paper can also assist students with math disabilities.

Components of Direct Reading Instruction

The purpose of direct learning instruction is to specifically target the needs of students with learning disabilities. **Direct learning instruction** can be provided in many educational settings. Direct instruction breaks concept learning into specific tasks and processes, with focus on mastering one skill before moving onto another skill. With **direct reading instruction**, the key components are teaching phonemic awareness, phonics, fluency, vocabulary development, and comprehension. Effective reading programs address all five areas of reading instruction. **Phonemic awareness** focuses on breaking words into sound units (phonemes). **Phonics** focuses on connecting these sound units with letters (graphemes). Phonics instruction allows students to approach decoding by sounding words out instead of attempting to read the whole words. **Fluency** instruction focuses on teaching students to read unfamiliar words and texts quickly and accurately. **Vocabulary development** helps increase familiarity with frequently occurring words in texts. **Comprehension** instruction focuses on helping students to understand what they have read. In comprehension instruction, learners connect prior knowledge to the texts.

Benefits of the Direct Reading Process

Direct reading instruction is an approach to teaching reading which focuses on specific skill development for early readers. Students frequently enter their schooling years with deficits in reading skills, especially when they are identified as having disabilities. Effective **direct reading programs** include the teaching of phonemic awareness, phonics, fluency, vocabulary development, and comprehension. Teachers are generally trained to implement direct reading programs instead of creating direct instruction curriculum. Specific programs ensure that teachers use the same curriculum and methods in order to effectively implement direct reading instruction. Direct reading instruction and programs are especially helpful for **skill remediation** for at-risk students. Efficient direct reading instruction communicates high standards for learning, is replicable or able to be implemented across a variety of settings, and offers support materials, professional development, and implementation guidance. Direct reading instruction is also proven to be effective for the improvement of reading abilities in at-risk students.

Teaching Comprehension with Research-Based Reading Intervention Strategies

Comprehension refers to a person's understanding of something. As it pertains to reading, **comprehension** is the understanding of content that has been read. Students with disabilities often struggle with comprehension, which makes teaching comprehension strategies essential to their learning. Special educators should teach students to **monitor** their comprehension by being aware of what they have read, identifying what they do not understand, and implementing problem-solving strategies to address what they do not understand. Special educators can also teach students to demonstrate **metacognitive strategies**, such as identifying specifically what they do not understand in texts (e.g., identifying the page numbers or chapters where they are struggling), looking back through the texts to find answers to comprehension questions, rereading sentences or sections they do not understand, and putting sentences they do not understand into their own words. **Graphic organizers**, like story maps and Venn diagrams, also allow students to map out the information they have read by laying out important concepts.

Helping Students with Disabilities Become Solid Emergent Readers

Emergent reading refers to the reading and writing abilities of young readers. They precede **conventional literacy**, which refers to older children's reading and writing behaviors, such as decoding, reading comprehension, oral reading fluency, spelling, and writing. Children with learning disabilities may demonstrate discrepancies between emergent literacy behaviors and conventional literacy behaviors. They may flip-flop between the two stages, showing progress one moment or day and then seeming to forget the next. Educators can foster skills in emergent and conventional reading by teaching **phonological awareness** and **written letter/sound recognition**. These are both baseline skills that affect students' future phonological awareness development. Additionally, educators can provide engaging, age-appropriate activities that facilitate connections between emergent literacy and conventional literacy skills. Activities that promote students' print awareness and knowledge of book conventions also help build solid emergent reader skills.

Modifying the Stages of Writing to Assist Students with Learning Disabilities

The **writing process** can be challenging for new learners but especially for students with disabilities. The writing process can be facilitated by special educators and general educators in order to build adequate writing skills. Teachers must first address the needs of their classes before engaging in the pre-writing stage. Getting to know students provides insight into their prior knowledge and abilities. In the **pre-writing (brainstorming) stage**, teachers help students prepare for the writing process by establishing good content or thinking of things that interest them to write about. In the **writing stage**, students should be taught to write their content using graphic organizers or diagrams that assist with using appropriate formatting, grammar, and punctuation. The **rewriting/revising stage** can be facilitated by providing checklists of errors and having students self-check and revise their own work. In the **editing/proofreading stage**, students can self-check their work or exchange their final written projects with other students or their teachers. This can also be facilitated using formatting checklists and/or grammar and punctuation checklists to monitor the writing process.

Teaching Social Studies

Depending on their special education classroom placements, students with **disabilities** receive varying degrees of instruction in other core content areas like social studies and science. Students with mild disabilities, such as learning disabilities, likely participate in inclusive classroom settings or general education classroom settings. Depending on a student's grade level, the student may attend a classroom setting with one or two teachers or switch classes and attend settings with many different teachers. Across all settings, students with mild disabilities receive any **accommodations or modifications** explicitly written in their Individualized Education Programs. Students with mild to moderate disabilities may receive instruction in special education classrooms for part or most of the day. In these instances, general education social studies or science classes may not be the most appropriate educational settings. Special educators then teach the content in the special education classrooms, sometimes connecting it with related tasks or skills. Students with moderate disabilities may receive **indirect instruction** in these content areas that is loosely based on content standards and more appropriate for the ways they acquire knowledge.

Learning Environments for Students with Disabilities

Determining the Special Education Setting Placement

Special education setting placement is determined in a student's Individualized Education Program (IEP), as specified by the Individuals with Disabilities Education Act (IDEA). IDEA requires that students be placed in **general education classrooms** to the maximum extent possible. Students should be placed in environments that are most appropriate for them, known as the **least restrictive environment**. If students can be educated in general education classrooms (**inclusion**) when provided with appropriate accommodations, they can be placed in general education classrooms. When students with disabilities need modifications to curriculum that are significantly below grade level or different than their peers, the students may be placed in **resource rooms** for remedial instruction. However, the students may also participate in the general education curriculum with modified work that meets their current abilities. For example, a student who struggles in math can use a calculator accommodation in the inclusion setting. A student whose math skills are two grade levels below the skills of same-aged peers may be placed in an inclusion setting with modifications or receive instruction in a resource room.

Full or Partial Inclusion Settings vs. Self-Contained Classrooms

Students with mild to moderate disabilities are often placed in **inclusion** or **partial inclusion classrooms**. The responsibilities of the special educator include assisting and collaborating with the general education teacher to create a curriculum with **modifications** that meets the learning styles and needs of the students with disabilities. The special educator may circulate during lessons or classwork to help students when needed and provide modifications to the general education curriculum to best meet the individual needs of each student.

The role of a special educator in a **self-contained classroom** is much different. Students in a self-contained classroom typically have disabilities that significantly limit their ability to receive quality education in inclusion or partial inclusion settings. Students with moderate disabilities in self-contained classrooms receive **modified instruction** with accommodations. The special educator is usually assisted by teaching assistants or paraprofessionals who help the educator meet the needs of individual students.

Special educators in inclusion, partial inclusion, and self-contained classrooms share some similar **responsibilities**. These responsibilities include monitoring IEP data on annual goals for each student, giving standardized pre-tests and post-tests, facilitating parent-teacher conferences, completing annual IEP reviews, and developing curriculum.

Structured Learning Environments

A structured learning environment is an important component of good **classroom management**. Teachers that create environments that are conducive for teaching and learning create environments where students feel safe. In **effective structured learning environments**, teachers create solid relationships with students by getting to know them and their interests. Often, this information can be used to implement learning activities based on students' interests. Another way to promote effective structured learning environments is to consistently follow implemented rules and maintain **consistency** in procedures in order to communicate what to expect to students. Transitioning students appropriately between activities increases time spent learning. Additionally, teachers create solid environments for their students by spending time designing effective lesson plans that anticipate student behaviors. Teachers can also establish good learning environments by promoting target behaviors. This means promoting standards of behavior and clear consequences for breaking rules. Students that have clear expectations learn in effective structured learning environments.

Non-Traditional Classroom Seating Arrangements

Seating arrangements are part of good classroom management strategies, especially for students with disabilities. Special education settings and inclusion settings often require flexibility with instruction and versatility with **seating arrangements**. The traditional setting includes rows of desks facing the area where the teacher conducts instruction. More **student-centered arrangements** include a horseshoe seating arrangement, a group pod arrangement, or a paired arrangement. A **horseshoe seating arrangement** is conducive to student-centered instruction because it allows the students to face each other and the instructor to move around the classroom easily. This setup facilitates classroom discussions and encourages interactions between instructors and students and among peers. The **group pod** or **paired-pod arrangement** is useful for student-centered instruction like small group work. This arrangement is also helpful when students need to rotate through lesson stages or work in small groups on projects. Effective teachers do not use one seating arrangement for the entire year. Best practices indicate that seating arrangements should change and be tied to the intent of lesson objectives.

Inclusive Learning Environments That Meet Unique Needs

Effective inclusive environments abide by the **universal design for learning (UDL) framework**. Special educators and general educators can work together to create learning environments that are accessible to students with unique language or physical needs. This can be done by providing **multiple ways** for students to access lesson concepts, express learned concepts, and engage in the learning process. For students with language barriers, signs, symbols, pictures, and learning concepts may have different meanings than they do for students without language barriers. Keeping this in mind, teachers can address UDL guidelines for students with **language barriers** by providing diverse ways to activate prior knowledge, emphasizing key learning elements, and using visuals to guide the learning process. For students with **physical barriers**, teachers can level the learning process by making their physical classroom environments accessible and providing different ways for students to express what they have learned. In general, teachers abiding by the UDL framework would have these supports in place in order to ensure that the needs of diverse learners are met.

Positive and Inclusive Learning Environments

Whether in the general education classroom or special education classroom, the UDL model should foster **positive and inclusive learning environments**. General education and special education teachers can take measures to ensure the UDL concept is implemented to address the unique needs of students with **cognitive or behavioral needs**. Since each student presents different needs, a one-size-fits-all approach to learning is not suitable or UDL compliant for these students. Special educators and general educators should openly communicate about students' unique learning or cognitive needs. General strategies include receiving regular **input from special educators** on how to best meet the needs of the students in the classroom. This includes sharing information with any **paraprofessionals and aides** regarding how to assist the students in the general education classroom. UDL-based strategies include the general educators providing multiple means by which students can complete the assignments. Students with cognitive disabilities may also benefit from the use of concrete examples and instruction, especially when addressing abstract concepts.

Learning Environments that Support Students with Behavioral Needs

The **UDL concepts** can be implemented to reduce challenging behavior in the classroom. They can also be used to help students with behavioral needs find success in the general education classroom. **Lack of student engagement** is compatible with the presentation of **challenging behaviors**. When UDL concepts are demonstrated appropriately, engagement can improve. Providing **multiple means of representation** is one UDL strategy for improving engagement and challenging behavior. This means the classroom teacher provides multiple ways of presenting the teaching material in order to engage as many students as possible. Teachers that provide multiple means of representation look to activate prior knowledge and help students make sense of the current content. UDL-compliant strategies also include providing **multiple means of expression**. Teachers applying UDL principles recognize that differentiating activities and assignments addresses a variety of abilities and learning styles. UDL-compliant teachers should also provide **multiple means of engagement**. Successful engagement in learning can often offset challenging behaviors by helping students focus on lesson material. Offering both challenging and simplistic work options and making engaging, solid connections to past and/or future lesson content can minimize the possibility of problems arising in the classroom.

Classroom Strategies Promoting Social-Emotional Development and Growth

Classroom environments should emanate **positivity** and **growth**. Classrooms that promote **social-emotional development and growth** provide security for students and create environments where learning takes place. Teachers can promote social-emotional development and growth by creating predictable classroom routines with visual reminders, keeping classrooms free of dangerous objects and materials, and arranging for learning to take place in large and small groups. They can also rotate activities and materials to keep students engaged, provide appropriate materials for learning centers, and create opportunities for children to engage socially. Teachers can act as nurturing adults by encouraging social interactions and problem solving, modeling appropriate language and social skills, encouraging and validating children's thoughts and feelings, and using clear signals to indicate transitions between activities. Teachers should build community environments in their classrooms, build appropriate relationships with students by getting to know their strengths and weaknesses, and demonstrate good conflict resolution and problem-solving abilities.

Effect of Emotional and Psychological Needs of Students with Disabilities

When a child is diagnosed with a disability, educators often primarily focus on the educational implications. However, students with disabilities also have **emotional needs** associated with their disabilities. These needs vary by student and disability. Generally, students with disabilities struggle emotionally. Symptoms may include low self-esteem, anxiety, acting out, reduced intrinsic motivation, and physical effects, like headaches. Educators, parents, and other professionals can manage the emotional needs of students with disabilities by talking with them about the disability diagnoses and educational implications. Educators can increase their **awareness** of how students might be feeling about the diagnoses and identify situations that may cause anxiety or acting out. Educators can also help by praising students consistently, even for small actions, which can help with confidence. Parents, educators, and other professionals can also work together to ensure that the students receive instruction in the most appropriate educational environments for their disabilities.

Lifting Guidelines for Students Who Require Physical Lifting

Teachers and paraprofessionals may encounter students with physical disabilities who require **assisted transfers**. In some circumstances, students must be **lift-assisted** from their wheelchairs in order to participate in physical therapy or floor activities. While this practice is more common in low-incidence classrooms and not always a job requirement, it is important to know school guidelines for **lifting techniques** to keep staff and students safe. Knowing school guidelines for lifting can also help prevent back injuries from occurring. Physical therapists working with the students should be consulted before attempting student lifts. They are trained professionals who know specific procedures for lifting students in order to keep the students and staff members safe. Every school district has policies for lift-assisted student transfers. Each student should be evaluated to determine if a one-person lift or two-person lift is needed. Two-person lifts are for heavier students, and some school districts do not allow two-person lifts for safety reasons.

Managing Distractions That May Affect Learning and Development

Managing distractions is a part of good teaching practices. Special educators demonstrate good **classroom management strategies** when they do the following:

- Create positive learning environments by getting to know students' individual emotional, intellectual, social, and physical needs.
- Remove or accommodate environmental triggers specific to students.
- Remove or accommodate behavioral triggers.
- Encourage students to help with classroom jobs and small tasks.
- Create lesson plans with anticipated behaviors in mind.
- Attempt verbal de-escalation first when behavioral issues arise.
- Set clear, consistent rules.
- Set and follow through with consequences for breaking the rules.
- Take time to get to know students and their triggers.
- Create seating arrangements that minimize distractions, such as placing distractible students closer to the teacher.
- Teach social, thinking, test-taking, problem-solving, and self-regulation skills alongside academic content.
- Use visual aids in lessons.
- Utilize peer-instruction opportunities.
- Provide opportunities for breaks.
- Incorporate computer-based programs, which can hold the attention of students with disabilities like autism.

Effect of Home Life Factors on Learning and Development

Students' home lives are interconnected with their school lives. **Home life factors**, especially negative ones, are difficult for students to avoid generalizing to the school environment. **Home stressors** can often develop into dysfunction at school. Factors that affect the learning and development of students with disabilities include academic, environmental, intellectual, language, medical, perceptual, and psychological factors. **Academic factors** include developmental delays in core content areas, lack of basic skills, and apparent inconsistency of learning in certain stages of development. **Environmental factors** occur when children are exposed to home life trauma, such as divorce, drug abuse, alcoholism, parental fighting, or family illness. **Intellectual factors** include limited intellectual abilities or unnoticed gifted abilities. **Language factors** include issues with language barriers or language acquisition, such as aphasia, bilingualism, expressive language disorder, and pragmatic language disorder. **Medical factors** include attention-deficit/hyperactivity disorder, muscular problems, and hearing problems. **Perceptual factors** include any factors that affect or slow down students' processing of information. **Psychological factors** include depression, anxiety, and conduct disorders.

Team Teaching Models

Components of a Successful Team-Teaching Model

A successful team-teaching model is one where the teachers involved set clear, effective, specific **goals** for performance. These goals must demonstrate clarity. All team-teaching members must be clear on the components of the goals and their potential outcomes. Clear goals allow team members and students to know what they are working towards as a classroom. Goals should be specific and measurable. **Goal criteria** should be qualified in percentages or quantities. This provides hard evidence for how effectively the team-teaching classroom is meeting the goals. Challenging goals set high expectations for what the team needs to work towards. Challenging goals ensure that team members and classroom students are working to achieve goals right outside their ability levels. Goals that are too challenging can be frustrating for all team members and students. A successful team-teaching model also reflects **commitment** from team members and any other professionals involved in the classroom.

Function of a Multidisciplinary Team-Teaching Model

The three disciplinary team models include a multidisciplinary team, an interdisciplinary team, and a transdisciplinary team. The **multidisciplinary team** is usually composed of the special educator, general education teacher, parents, paraprofessionals, principal, and school psychologist. As a whole, this team presents a comprehensive group of expertise, qualifications, and skills. In the multidisciplinary team model, these professionals do not collaborate but instead work alongside each other to pursue a **common goal** for the individual student with special needs. The multidisciplinary team model is effective for evaluating a student for referral for special education, completing pre-referral testing, and completing an Individualized Education Program or Evaluation Team Report. Sometimes this team is referred to as the child study team or student support team. In this model, professionals usually pull out students to work with them individually. Parents and legal guardians are a part of this process. Professionals working with the student should openly communicate their processes and the results of any evaluations or informal observations.

Interdisciplinary Team Model

An interdisciplinary team model features the **general education teacher** providing all curriculum and accommodations for a student with an Individualized Education Program (IEP). In this model, the special educator and other professionals relevant to the education of the student collaborate to ensure that the curriculum meets the needs of the student and the accommodations are appropriate. This model is not a team-teaching model. Advantages of this model include the collaboration of all IEP team members towards a common goal and the student's needs being addressed by one teacher instead of several different teachers or professionals. The disadvantages of this model include difficulties with collaboration between professionals and issues with delivering related services to students who need them. Related service provision sometimes includes one-on-one instruction, which requires the student to be pulled out for a certain amount of time during general education instruction. This model may also not be appropriate for students with intense needs, as they often require **individualized education** in order to meet IEP goals. They may also require specific accommodations and modifications not suitable for the general education classroom.

Transdisciplinary Team-Teaching Model

In this model, professionals working with the student work together collaboratively to ensure the individual needs of the student are met. The **special educator** may teach in the general education classroom, delivering instruction to both students with and without disabilities. This model features a team-teaching experience for classroom students, where the special educator and general educator may take turns teaching. The presence of the special educator in the general education setting means the special educator can offer advice for **accommodating** the students with special needs in the classroom. Additionally, this model provides opportunities for teachers and other professionals to communicate consistently about students' progress, share ideas, and work collaboratively to solve any issues that arise. The effectiveness of this model relies heavily on the collaboration of the special educator and the general educator in addressing the major features of this team-teaching model.

Advantages and Disadvantages of Team-Teaching Models

Students with and without disabilities present a variety of **learning abilities** in the general education classroom. One advantage of team-teaching models in this setting is being able to target the unique abilities, learning methods, and skills that each student brings to the classroom. Another advantage is effective classroom management. In an **effective team-teaching model**, one teacher provides the instruction, while the other practices classroom management skills to minimize disruptions and promote a safe learning environment. This model encourages class participation, facilitates group activities, and provides multiple means of engagement for learning content. One disadvantage is there may be an offset between the teachers sharing a class. When one teacher is not open to multiple methods of delivering instruction, the team-teaching approach is ineffective. Planning and making group decisions regarding curriculum can be time consuming and stressful in a team-teaching environment.

Chapter Quiz

Ready to see how well you retained what you just read? Scan the QR code to go directly to the chapter quiz interface for this study guide. If you're using a computer, simply visit the online resources page at **mometrix.com/resources719/texesspedsupp** and click the Chapter Quizzes link.

Foundations and Professional Roles and Responsibilities

Transform passive reading into active learning! After immersing yourself in this chapter, put your comprehension to the test by taking a quiz. The insights you gained will stay with you longer this way. Scan the QR code to go directly to the chapter quiz interface for this study guide. If you're using a computer, simply visit the online resources page at **mometrix.com/resources719/texesspedsupp** and click the Chapter Quizzes link.

Disability Education Laws

Individuals with Disabilities Education Act

The Individuals with Disabilities Education Act (**IDEA**) includes six major principles that focus on students' rights and the responsibilities public schools have for educating children with **disabilities**. One of the main principles of IDEA is to provide a **free and appropriate public education** suited to the individual needs of a child with a disability. This requires schools to provide special education and related services to students identified as having disabilities. Another purpose of IDEA is to require schools to provide an appropriate **evaluation** of a child with a suspected disability and an **Individualized Education Program (IEP)** for a child with a disability who qualifies under IDEA. Students with IEPs are guaranteed **least restrictive environment**, or a guarantee that they are educated in the general education classroom as much as possible. IDEA also ensures **parent participation**, providing a role for parents as equal participants and decision makers. Lastly, **procedural safeguards** also serve to protect parents' rights to advocate for their children with disabilities.

Review Video: Development of the Individuals with Disabilities Education Act
Visit mometrix.com/academy and enter code: 100350

People Protected by Parts B and C of IDEA

Early intervention services are provided to children with special needs from birth to age three under **IDEA Part C**. Children from birth to age 3 who are identified as having disabilities and qualify under IDEA receive **Individualized Family Service Plans (IFSPs)**.

Special education and related services are provided to children with disabilities from ages 3 to 21 under **IDEA Part B**. Children ages 3 to 21 who are identified as having disabilities and qualify under IDEA receive educational documents **IEPs**.

Individualized Education Programs vs. Individualized Family Service Plans

IFSPs and IEPs are both educational documents provided under the Individuals with Disabilities Education Act to service the rights of children with disabilities and their families. The major differences between IEPs and IFSPs, aside from the ages they service, is that **IFSPs** cover **broader services** for children with disabilities and their families. IFSP services are often provided in the children's homes. **IEPs** focus on special education and related services within the children's **school settings**.

Purpose of IEPs and Function of the PLOPs

An IEP is a written statement for a child with a disability. Its primary purposes are to establish **measurable annual goals** and to list the **services** needed to help the child with a disability meet the annual goals.

The Individuals with Disabilities Education Act mandates that a statement of the child's academic achievement and functional performance be included within the IEP. This statement is called **Present Levels of Performance**. It provides a snapshot of the student's current performance in school. Present Levels of Performance should also report how a student's disability is affecting, or not affecting, progress in school.

IDEA mandates that an **Annual Goals section** be provided within the IEP. Annual goals outline what a student is expected to learn within a 12-month period. These goals are influenced by the student's PLOPs and are developed using objective, measurable data based on the student's previous academic performance.

Review Video: 504 Plans and IEPs
Visit mometrix.com/academy and enter code: 881103

Child Find Law

Child Find is part of the Individuals with Disabilities Education Act and states that schools are legally required to find children who have **disabilities** and need **special education** or other services. According to the **Child Find law**, all school districts must have processes for identifying students who need special education and related services. Children with disabilities from birth to age 21, children who are homeschooled, and children in private schools are all covered by the Child Find law. Infants and toddlers can be identified and provided with services so that parents have the right tools in place to meet their children's needs before they enter grade school. The Child Find law does not mean that public schools need to agree to evaluate students when evaluations are requested. Schools may still refuse evaluation if school professionals do not suspect the children of having disabilities.

Steps to Implementing IEPs

The five most important steps in the IEP process are the identification via "Child Find" or the referral for special education services; evaluation; determination of eligibility; the first IEP meeting at which the IEP is written; and the ongoing provision of services during which progress is measured and reported. The referral can be initiated by a teacher, a special team in the school district, the student's parent, or another professional. The evaluation provides a snapshot of a student's background history, strengths, weaknesses, and academic, behavioral, or social needs. An IEP team of professionals as well as the student's parents/guardians use the evaluation and any other reports regarding a student's progress to determine if the student is eligible for special education services. Once a student has been found eligible for special education, the first IEP meeting is held during which an IEP is written by a special education teacher or other specialist familiar with the student. The IEP meeting, either initial or annual, is held before the new IEP is implemented. Once the IEP meeting has occurred, services will be provided as detailed in the written IEP, during which the student's progress will continually be measured and reported. The IEP team includes the student, parents/guardians, special education teacher, general education teacher, school psychologist, school administrator, appropriate related service professionals, and any other professionals or members that can comment on the student's strengths.

Manifestation Determination

Manifestation determination is a process defined by IDEA. The **manifestation determination process** is put into effect when a student receiving special education needs to be removed from the educational setting due to a suspension, expulsion, or alternative placement. Manifestation determination is the process that determines if the **disciplinary action** resulted from a **manifestation of the student's disability**. This is important because if the action was a manifestation of the disability, the outcome of the disciplinary action may change. During the initial part of this process, relevant data is collected about the student and the circumstances of the offending behavior. The student's Individualized Education Program team determines whether or not the student's behavior was related to the disability. If they determine that the behavior was not related to the disability, the disciplinary action is carried out. If the behavior is determined to be related to the disability, the student is placed back into the original educational setting.

Provision of Title III of the Americans with Disabilities Act

Title III of the Americans with Disabilities Act (ADA) prohibits discrimination against people with disabilities in **public accommodations**. Title III seeks to level the playing field of access for people with disabilities participating in public activities. Businesses open to the public, such as schools, restaurants, movie theaters, day care facilities, recreation facilities, doctor's offices, and restaurants, are required to comply with **ADA standards**. Additionally, commercial facilities, such as privately-owned businesses, factories, warehouses, and office buildings, are required to provide access per ADA standards. Title III of the ADA outlines the general requirements of the **reasonable modifications** that businesses must provide. Title III also provides detailed, specific requirements for reasonable modifications within businesses and requires new construction and building alterations to abide by ADA regulations. Title III also outlines rules regarding **enforcement of ADA regulations**, such as the consequences for a person or persons participating in discrimination of a person with a disability. Title III provides for **certification of state laws or local building codes**. This means that a state's Assistant Attorney General may issue certification to a place of public accommodation or commercial facility that meets or exceeds the minimum requirements of Title III.

Larry P. v. Riles

The *Larry P. v. Riles* (1977) court case examined possible **cultural discrimination** against African-American students. The court case questioned whether an intelligence quotient (IQ) test was an accurate measurement of a student's true intelligence. The case argued that a disproportionate number of African-American students identified as needing special education services; the term at the time was "educable mentally retarded" (EMR) program services. The court plaintiff, Larry P., argued that IQ tests were **biased** against African-American students, which resulted in their placements in limiting educational settings. The defendant, Riles, argued that the prevalence of African-American students in the EMR classes was due to genetics and social and environmental factors. The court ultimately ruled that the IQ tests were discriminatory and resulted in the disproportionate placement of African-American students in the EMR setting. It was determined that these particular assessments were **culturally biased**, and the students' performances would be more accurately measured using adaptive behavior assessments, diagnostic tests, observations, and other assessments.

Diana v. State Board of Education

Diana v. State Board of Education (1970) was a court case involving a student who was placed in special education after results of the Stanford-Binet intelligence test indicated she had a mild case of "mental retardation." This class-action lawsuit was developed on behalf of nine **Mexican-American children**, arguing that IQ scores were not an adequate measurement to determine special education placement. The case argued that Mexican-American children might be at a disadvantage because the IQ tests were written and administered in English. This might possibly constitute **discrimination**. The plaintiffs in the case argued that IQ scores were not a valid measurement because the children might have been unable to comprehend the test written in English. In the conclusive results of this case, the court ordered children to be tested in their primary language, if it was not English. As a result of this case, IQ tests were no longer used as the sole assessments for determining **special education placement**. There was also increased focus on **cultural and linguistic diversity** in students.

Winkelman v. Parma City School District

This court case began as an argument against a **free and appropriate public education** (FAPE) as required by IDEA. The parents of Jacob Winkelman believed their son was not provided with a FAPE in his special education setting in Parma City Schools. The disagreement became about whether or not children can be **represented by their parents** per IDEA in federal court. The U.S Court of Appeals for the Sixth Circuit argued that IDEA protected the rights of the children and not the parents. In the end, the District Court ruled that parents could represent their children within disputes over a free and appropriate public education as constituted by IDEA. Ultimately, this settled the question of whether or not **parents have rights under IDEA**, in addition to their children. The court case determined that parents play a significant role in the education of their children on IEPs and are IEP team members. Therefore, parents are entitled to litigate *pro se* for their children.

Honig v. Doe

Honig v. Doe (1988) was a Supreme Court case examining the violation of the **Education for All Handicapped Children Act** (EAHCA, an earlier version of the Individuals with Disabilities Education Act) by the California School Board. The offense occurred when a child was suspended for a violent behavior outburst that was related to his disability. The court case centered on two plaintiffs. Both were diagnosed with an emotional disturbance and qualified for special education under EAHCA. Following the violent incident, the school suspended the students and recommended them for expulsion. The plaintiff's case argued that the suspension/expulsion went against the **stay-put provision of the EAHCA**, which states that children with disabilities must remain in their current educational placements during review proceedings unless otherwise agreed upon by both parents and educational representatives. The defendant argued that the violence of the situation marked an exception to the law. The court determined that schools are able to justify the placement removal of a student when maintaining a **safe learning environment** outweighs a student's right to a free and appropriate public education.

Pennsylvania Association for Retarded Children v. Commonwealth of Pennsylvania

The Commonwealth of Pennsylvania was accused by the Pennsylvania Association for Retarded Children (PARC 1971), now known as the Arc of Pennsylvania, of denying a **free and appropriate public education** to students with disabilities. The Commonwealth of Pennsylvania was accused of refusing to educate students who had not reached the "mental age of 5." The groups argued before the District Court of the Eastern District of Pennsylvania. This case was significant because PARC was one of the first institutions in the country to challenge the **placement of students with special needs**. The plaintiffs argued that all children should and would benefit from some sort of educational instruction and training. Ultimately, this was the beginning of instituting the state requirement of a free and appropriate public education (**FAPE**) for all children in public education from ages 6–21. The Commonwealth of Pennsylvania was tasked with providing a FAPE and sufficient education and training for all eligible children receiving special education. They could no longer deny students based on their mental ages. This triggered other state institutions to make similar decisions and led to the creation of similar federal policies in the **Education for All Handicapped Children Act** (1974).

1990 Amendments to IDEA

The Individuals with Disabilities Education Act (IDEA) replaced the Education for All Handicapped Children Act in 1990. IDEA amendments changed the **age range** for children to receive special education services to ages 3–21. IDEA also changed the language of the law, changing the focus onto the **individuals with disabilities** rather than the **handicapped children**. Therefore, the focus shifted from the conditions or disabilities to the individual children and their needs. IDEA amendments also **categorized** different disabilities. IDEA 1997 increased the emphasis on IEPs for students with disabilities and increased parents' roles in the educational decision-making processes for their children with disabilities. Part B of the 1997 amendment provided services to children ages 3–5, mandating that their learning needs be outlined in **IEPs** or **Individualized Family Service Plans**. Part C of IDEA provided **financial assistance** to the families of infants and toddlers with disabilities. Part C states that educational agencies must provide **early intervention services** that focus on children's developmental and medical needs, as well as the needs of their families. Part C also gives states the option to provide services to children who are at risk for developmental disabilities.

Disabilities Education Improvement Act of 2004

In 2004, the Individuals with Disabilities Education Act (IDEA) implemented the **Individuals with Disabilities Education Improvement Act**; IDEA was reauthorized to better meet the needs of children in special education programs and children with special needs. As a result of these changes:

- Special educators are required to achieve **Highly Qualified Teacher status** and be **certified in special education**.
- Individualized Education Programs must contain measurable **annual goals** and descriptions of how progress toward the goals will be **measured and reported**.
- Schools or agencies must provide science or research-based **interventions** as part of the evaluation process to determine if children have specific learning disabilities. This may be done in addition to assessments that measure achievement or intelligence.

The changes made to require science or research-based interventions resulted in many districts implementing **Response to Intervention procedures**. These procedures meet IDEA 2004 requirement of providing interventions in addition to achievement reports or intelligence tests on the Individualized Education Programs for children with disabilities.

Development of Educational Laws Like Goals 2000 and No Child Left Behind

President Bill Clinton signed the **National Educational Goals Act**, also known as Goals 2000: Educate America Act, into effect in the 1990s to trigger standardized educational reform. The act focused on **outcomes-based education** and was intended to be completed by the year 2000. The goals of this act included ensuring that children are ready to learn by the time they start school; increasing high school graduation rates; demonstration of competency by students in grades 4, 8, and 12 in core content areas; and positioning the United States as first in the world in mathematics and science achievement. Goals 2000 was withdrawn when President George W. Bush implemented the **No Child Left Behind Act (NCLB)** in 2001. The NCLB also supported standards-based reform, and it mandated that states develop more **skills-based assessments**. The act emphasized state testing, annual academic progress, report cards, and increased teacher qualification standards. It also outlined changes in state funding. The NCLB required schools to meet **Adequate Yearly Progress (AYP)**. AYP was measured by results of achievement tests taken by students in each school district, and consequences were implemented for school districts that missed AYP during consecutive years.

Every Student Succeeds Act of 2015

The NCLB was replaced in 2015 by the Every Student Succeeds Act (**ESSA**). The ESSA built upon the foundations of NCLB and emphasized **equal opportunity** for students. The ESSA currently serves as the main K–12 educational law in the United States. The ESSA affects students in public education, including students with disabilities. The purpose of the ESSA is to ensure a **quality education** for all students. It also aims to address the achievement of **disadvantaged students**, including students living in poverty, minority groups, students receiving special education services, and students with limited English language skills. The ESSA determined that states may decide educational plans as long as they follow the government's framework. The ESSA also allows states to develop their own educational standards and mandates that the curriculum focus on preparing students for postsecondary educations or careers. The act requires students to be tested annually in math and reading during grades 3–8 and once in high school. Students must also be tested in science once in elementary school, middle school, and high school. **School accountability** was also mandated by the ESSA. The act requires states to have plans in place for any schools that are underperforming.

ESL Rights for Students and Parents

As public schools experience an influx of English as a Second Language (ESL) students, knowledge of their **rights** becomes increasingly important. The **Every Student Succeeds Act (ESSA)** of 2015 addresses funding discrepancies for ESL students and families. The ESSA allocates funds to schools and districts where low-income families comprise 40 percent or more of the enrollment. This is intended to assist with ESL students who are underperforming or at risk for underperforming. The ESSA also provides funding for ESL students to become English proficient and find academic success. However, in order for schools and districts to receive this funding, they must avoid discrimination, track ESL student progress, assess ESL student English proficiency, and notify parents of their children's ESL status. Avoiding discrimination includes preventing the over-identification of ESL students for special education services. The referral and evaluation process must be carried out with caution to ensure that students' perceived disabilities are actual deficits and not related to their English language learning abilities.

Rehabilitation Act of 1973

The Rehabilitation Act of 1973 was the law that preceded the Individuals with Disabilities Education Act of 1975. The Rehabilitation Act protects the rights of people with disabilities in several ways.

- It protects people with disabilities against discrimination relating to **employment**.
- It provides students with disabilities equal access to the **general education curriculum** (Section 504).

Americans with Disabilities Act of 1990 (ADA)

The Americans with Disabilities Act (1990) also protects the rights of people with disabilities.

- The ADA provides **equal employment** for people with disabilities. This means employers must provide reasonable accommodations for people with disabilities in their job and work environments.

- It provides **access** for people with disabilities to both public and private places open to the public (e.g., access ramps and automatic doors).
- It provides **telecommunications access** to people with disabilities. This ensures people with hearing and speech disabilities can communicate over the telephone and Internet.

Elementary and Secondary Education Act (ESEA)

The Elementary and Secondary Education Act (ESEA) also protects the rights of people with disabilities.

- Passed by President Johnson in 1965, the ESEA was part of the president's "War on Poverty." The law sought to allow **equal access to a quality education**.
- The ESEA extended more funding to secondary and primary schools and emphasized high **standards and accountability**.
- This law was authorized as the **No Child Left Behind** (2001) under President Bush, then reauthorized as the **Every Student Succeeds Act** under President Obama.

Section 504

A Section 504 Plan comes from the civil rights law, Section 504 of the Rehabilitation Act of 1973, and protects the rights of individuals with disabilities. A 504 Plan is a formal plan or blueprint for how the school will provide services to a student with a disability. This essentially removes barriers for individuals with disabilities by ensuring that **appropriate services** are provided to meet their special needs. A 504 Plan includes:

- **Accommodations**: A 504 Plan includes accommodations a student with a disability may need to be successful in a regular education classroom. For example, a student with ADHD may need to sit near the front of the room to limit distractions.
- **Related Services**: A 504 Plan includes related services, such as speech therapy or occupational therapy, a student may need to be successful in the general education classroom.
- **Modifications**: Although it is rare for a 504 Plan to include modifications, sometimes they are included. Modifications change what the student is expected to do, such as being given fewer homework assignments.

504 Plans vs. Individualized Education Programs

- A 504 Plan and an IEP are similar in that they serve as a blueprint for a student with a disability. However, a 504 Plan serves as a blueprint for how the student will have **access to school**, whereas the IEP serves as a blueprint for a student's **special education experience**.
- A 504 Plan helps level the playing field for a student with a disability by providing services and changes to the **learning environment**. An IEP provides individualized special education and related services to meet the **unique needs of a student with a disability**. Both IEPs and 504 Plans are provided at no cost to parents.
- The 504 Plan was established under the **Rehabilitation Act of 1973** as a civil rights law. The Individualized Education Program was established under the **Individuals with Disabilities Education Act** (1975 and amended in 2004).
- Unlike an IEP, a 504 Plan does **not** have to be a planned, written document. An IEP is a **planned, written document** that includes unique annual learning goals and describes related services for the student with a disability.

Informed Parental Consent

IDEA requires that parents be **informed** before a student is evaluated for special education services. IDEA mandates that a school district receive **parental consent** to initiate an evaluation of a student for special education services. Consent means the school district has fully informed the parent of their intentions or potential reasons for evaluation of the student. Legally, the request must be written in the parent's native language. This consent does not mean the parent gives consent for a student's placement in special education. In order for a student to be initially placed in special education or receive special education services, parental consent must be given for this issue separately. At any time, parents can withdraw consent for special education placement or special education services. Schools are able to file **due process** if they disagree with the parental withdrawal of consent. Parents also have a right to consent to parts of a student's IEP, but not necessarily all of the IEP. Once parental consent is granted for all parts of the IEP, it can be implemented.

Tiers of the Response to Intervention Model

- **Tier 1: High Quality Classroom Instruction, Screening, and Group Interventions**: In Tier 1, **all students** are screened using universal screening and/or the results of statewide assessments. Students identified as at risk receive supplemental instruction. Students who make adequate progress are returned to their regular instruction. Students who do not make adequate progress move to Tier 2.
- **Tier 2: Targeted Interventions**: These interventions are designed to improve the progress of the students who did not make adequate progress in Tier 1. Targeted instruction is usually in the areas of reading and math and does not last longer than one grading period. This is applied generally to smaller groups and not the full classroom as in Tier 1.
- **Tier 3: Intensive Interventions and Comprehensive Evaluation**: Students who are not successful in Tier 2 move on to Tier 3. They receive intensive interventions that target their specific deficits. Students who do not meet progress goals during intensive interventions are referred to receive comprehensive evaluations and are considered to be eligible for special education under the Individuals with Disabilities Education Act.

Stakeholders in Special Education

Stakeholders that play roles in educating students with disabilities include the students, parents, general educators, administrators, and community members. Students should receive an educational **curriculum** based on strict standards, such as the Common Core Content Standards. This ensures that they receive good educational foundations from which to grow and expand upon during their school careers. Parents, legal guardians, and sometimes agencies act in the best interests of their children. If they do not think the IEPs suit the needs of their children, they can request **due process hearings** in court. Requirements for a free and appropriate public education and least restrictive environment ensure that students are educated alongside peers in general education classrooms by general educators. General educators collaborate with special educators to create **successful inclusion classrooms**. When inclusion is done successfully, the students with disabilities meet their IEP goals.

Multi-Factored Evaluations or Evaluation Team Reports

Multi-Factored Evaluations (MFEs) are processes required by the Individuals with Disabilities Education Act to determine if a student is eligible for special education. When a student is suspected of having a disability, the parent or school district can initiate the evaluation process. **Student information** that is evaluated in an MFE includes background information, health information, vision testing, hearing testing, social and emotional development, general intelligence, past and current academic performance, communication needs, gross and fine motor abilities, results of aptitude or achievement tests, academic skills, and current progress toward IEP goals. Progress reporting on IEP goals is only appropriate during an annual MFE when a student has already qualified for special education services. The purpose of an MFE is to provide **comprehensive information** about a student for professionals working with the student. An MFE also helps determine what academic or behavioral **goals** or related services might be appropriate for a student with disabilities.

Free and Appropriate Public Education Components

IDEA defines free and appropriate public education (FAPE) as an educational right for children with disabilities in the United States. FAPE stands for:

- **Free**: All students found eligible for special education services must receive free services, expensed to the public instead of the parents.
- **Appropriate**: Students are eligible for educations that are appropriate for their specific needs, as stated in their IEPs.
- **Public**: Students with disabilities have the right to be educated in public schools.
- **Education**: An education must be provided to any school-aged child with a disability. Education and services are defined in a student's IEP.

Ideally, FAPE components are put in place in order to guarantee the best education possible that also suits the individual needs of a student with a disability. FAPE should take place in the least restrictive environment, or the environment with the fewest barriers to learning for the individual student with a disability.

Review Video: Legal and Ethical Issues in Special Education
Visit mometrix.com/academy and enter code: 934372

Multi-Factored Evaluation or Evaluation Team Report

A Multi-Factored Evaluation (**MFE**), sometimes referred to as an Evaluation Team Report (**ETR**), serves as a snapshot of a child's abilities, strengths, and weaknesses. An MFE is conducted to determine a student's eligibility for special education. Once a student with a disability qualifies for special education, an MFE is conducted at least every three years after the initial MFE date. MFEs are conducted for students ages 3 to 21 who are on IEPs. The purpose of the MFE is to influence a student's IEP. An MFE reports on a student's **current abilities** and how the disability may affect **educational performance**. MFEs can also determine if a student qualifies for related services, such as occupational therapy or speech-language therapy. An MFE can be requested by a parent or school district when a child is suspected of having a disability. The school district typically has 30 days or less to respond to a parental request to evaluate a student, giving consent or refusal for an evaluation. While initial MFEs are conducted as a means to determine special education qualification, annual MFEs are conducted to address any changes in the needs or services of a student already receiving special education services.

Least Restrictive Environments to Deliver Special Education Services

Special education services are delivered to students that qualify with a **disability** defined by IDEA. IDEA also requires that students who qualify for special education must receive special education services in **least restrictive environments** that provide the fewest barriers to their learning. A student's most appropriate instructional setting is written out in the **IEP**. Some special education instructional settings include:

- No instructional setting
- Mainstream setting
- Resource room
- Self-contained classroom
- Homebound instruction

With **no instructional setting**, students participate in the general education curriculum but may receive related services, such as speech-language therapy or occupational therapy. In the **mainstream setting**, students are instructed in the general education classroom for most or part of the day and provided with special education supports, accommodations, modifications, and related services. A **resource room** is an environment where students receive remedial instruction when they cannot participate in the general curriculum for one or more subject areas. A **self-contained classroom** is a setting for students who need special education and related services for more than 50 percent of the day. **Homebound instruction** is for students who are homebound or hospitalized for more than four consecutive weeks.

Due Process Rights Available to Parents and Legal Guardians

When parents or legal guardians and school districts cannot agree on components of IEPs for students with disabilities, parents and legal guardians have a right to **due process**. Due process is a legal right under IDEA that usually involves the school district violating a legal rule. Examples of these violations include a school district not running an IEP meeting, failing to conduct a triannual evaluation, or failing to implement a student's IEP. Disputes often involve a student's instructional placement, appropriate accommodations or modifications, related services, or changes to IEPs. School districts' due process policies vary depending on the district. IDEA, however, mandates that a **due process legal form** be completed by the parent or legal guardian in order to move forward. This form must be completed within two years of a dispute. **Mediation**, or the process of coming to an agreement before filing due process, can be a solution to the dispute. IEP meetings, even when it is not time for an annual review, are also appropriate options for resolving a dispute before filing due process.

Purpose of Mediation in Lieu of a Parent or Legal Guardian Filing for Due Process

Mediation is a process used to address a dispute prior to a parent or legal guardian filing for due process. The purpose of mediation is to **resolve a dispute** between the parent or legal guardian of a student with a disability and the school district. Disputes occur when the parent or legal guardian does not agree with an IEP component, such as what related services are provided or the way a student's IEP is being implemented. Mediation is not a parent or legal guardian's legal right, but school districts often support mediation to offset a **due process filing**. Mediation involves the attempt to resolve a dispute and includes a meeting between the parent or legal guardian, school district member, and a neutral third party, such as a mediator provided by the state. States have lists of **mediators** available for these situations. Agreements that come out of the mediation process are put into writing and, if appropriate, put into a student's IEP. Disagreements can continue to be mediated, or the decision may be made to file due process. Prior to mediation, parents or legal guardians and school districts have the option of holding IEP meetings (outside of annual meetings) to resolve disputes.

MAINTAINING CONFIDENTIALITY AND PRIVACY OF STUDENT RECORDS

Similar to the Health Insurance Portability and Accountability Act of 1996 (HIPAA), the **Family Educational Rights and Privacy Act (FERPA)** is a law that protects privacy. However, the FERPA is specific to the privacy of students. The FERPA law applies to any school or agency that receives funds from the US Department of Education. This ensures that schools or agencies cannot share any confidential information about a student without a parent or student's written consent. **Student educational records** can be defined as records, files, documents, or other materials which contain a student's personal information. **IEPs** and **ETRs** are examples of private documents under the FERPA law. The responsibility of a school covered by the FERPA is to maintain confidentiality and privacy. The members of an IEP team, such as special educators, related service professionals, general educators, or other professionals, cannot share any identifying, private information about a student. Information addressing the needs of individual students found on an IEP, ETR, or other identifying document must remain confidential unless express written consent is given by the parent or legal guardian.

PRE-REFERRAL/REFERRAL PROCESS FOR A STUDENT WITH A DISABILITY

The purpose of a pre-referral process for a child with a suspected disability is to attempt **reasonable modifications and accommodations** before the child is referred for special education services. Schools often have **pre-referral teams** whose purpose is to identify the strengths and needs of a child, put reasonable strategies into action, and evaluate the results of this pre-referral intervention. If the results do not show any change, another intervention can be attempted, or the student can be referred for a special education evaluation.

If a child is suspected of having a disability and did not succeed with pre-referral interventions, the school or parent can request an **evaluation**. During the evaluation process, the school compiles information to see if the student needs special education or related services. This information is used to determine if the student's disability is affecting school performance and if the student qualifies for special education. The evaluation lists and examines the student's strengths, weaknesses, and development and determines what supports the student needs in order to learn. An evaluation must be completed before special education services can be provided.

ROLE OF A SCHOOL PSYCHOLOGIST IN SPECIAL EDUCATION

School psychologists are certified members of school teams that **support the needs of students and teachers**. They help students with overall academic, social, behavioral, and emotional success. School psychologists are trained in data collection and analysis, assessments, progress monitoring, risk factors, consultation and collaboration, and special education services. In special education, school psychologists may work directly with students and collaborate with teachers, administrators, parents, and other professionals working with particular students. They may also counsel students' parents, participate in the Response to Intervention process, and perform initial evaluations of students who are referred for special education services. School psychologists also work to improve academic achievement, promote positive behavior and health by implementing school-wide programs, support learning needs of diverse learners, maintain safe school environments, and strengthen and maintain good school-parent relationships.

OVERREPRESENTATION OF STUDENTS FROM DIVERSE BACKGROUNDS

Disproportionate representation occurs when there is not an equal representation of students from different **cultural and linguistic backgrounds** identified for special education services. Students from different cultural and linguistic groups should be identified for special education services in similar proportions. This ensures that no one group is **overrepresented** and **overidentified as having special needs** due to their cultural or linguistic differences.

Disproportionality can occur based on a child's sex, language proficiency, receipt of free and reduced lunch, or race and ethnicity. Historically, most disproportionality has been a civil rights issue and due to a child's cultural or linguistic background. Recently, the focus has been on the disproportionate number of students who spend time in special education classrooms instead of being educated alongside regularly educated peers.

The referral process, **Response to Intervention (RTI)**, provides safeguards against disproportionality. The RTI process requires instruction and intervention catered to the unique, specific needs of the individual student. The purpose of RTI is not the identification of a disability or entitlement to services. Instead, it focuses on data used to make educational decisions about individuals, classrooms, schools, or districts. Models like RTI address disproportionate representation, but they are not perfect.

Special Education Models

Purpose of Special Education

Special education is specially designed instruction delivered to meet the individual needs of children with disabilities. Special education includes a free and appropriate education in the least restrictive environment. In the past, a special education model might consist of a self-contained classroom of students with special needs whose needs were addressed in that setting. Today, students who qualify for special education must receive instruction in **free and appropriate settings**. This means they receive special education services in settings that provide the **fewest barriers** to their learning. The most appropriate setting varies, depending on the student and the disability. The purpose of special education is to ensure that the unique needs of children with disabilities are addressed. In the public-school setting, the Individuals with Disabilities Education Act mandates that students with disabilities receive free and appropriate public educations. The goal of special education is to create **fair environments** for students with special needs to learn. Ideally, the settings should enable students to learn to their fullest potential.

Co-Teaching Models

Co-teaching models are utilized in collaborative, inclusive teaching settings that include students with and without disabilities. General educators teach alongside special educators and hold all students to the same educational standards. In the **one teach/one support model**, one instructor teaches a lesson while the other instructor supports students who have questions or need assistance. A **parallel teaching model** involves a class being split into two groups, with one instructor teaching each group. The **alternative teaching model** may be appropriate in situations where it is necessary to instruct small groups of students. In this model, one instructor teaches a large group of students while the other provides instruction to a smaller group of students. In **station teaching**, students are split into small groups and work in several teaching centers while both instructors provide support. Teachers participating in **team teaching** collaboratively plan and implement lesson content, facilitate classroom discussions, and manage discipline. Successful co-teaching uses all of these models as appropriate to meet the needs of diverse groups of learners in the inclusive classroom setting.

Remedial Instruction vs. Special Education

Though the terms are sometimes used interchangeably, remedial instruction does not always equal special education. The difference between remedial instruction and special education has a lot to do with the intellectual levels of the students. In **remedial instruction**, a student has average or better-than-average intellectual abilities but may struggle with **skills** in one or more content areas. Remedial instruction provides one-on-one instruction to students who are falling behind. Remedial programs are often mainstreamed into general education classrooms to address the varying learning abilities of students. Remedial instruction can be delivered by general education teachers. **Special education** programs address the needs of students who may have lower intellectual abilities and require individualized instruction. Students in special education have **disabilities** specified by the Individuals with Disabilities Education Act and use Individualized Education Programs. Unlike remedial instruction, special education requires qualified and credentialed special educators to decide how to best provide interventions in classroom settings for students with disabilities.

Remedial Instruction vs. Compensatory Approaches to Intervention

Compensatory interventions can be offered in the form of programs or services that help students with special needs or students who are at risk. The compensatory approach is different from remedial instruction because remedial instruction involves the breaking of concepts or tasks into smaller chunks and reteaching information. The **remedial approach** focuses on repetition and developing or reinforcing certain skills. The **compensatory approach** is implemented when a remedial approach is not working. It focuses on building upon students' strengths and working with or around their weaknesses. Tools such as audiobooks, text-to-speech software, speech recognition software, and other types of assistive technology are compensatory accommodations that help provide a free and appropriate education for students with disabilities who might otherwise continue to demonstrate skill deficits without these tools. Compensatory approaches and remedial instruction can and should be delivered at the same time to help ensure that students with disabilities are meeting their potential.

Collaborating with IEP Team Members

It is important for Individualized Education Program (IEP) team members to **collaborate** with each other in order to ensure that students are receiving educational plans that are suitable to their needs in the least restrictive environments. **IEP team members** include special education teachers, general education teachers, parents or legal guardians, students, school district representatives, and others knowledgeable about the students' performances. Each member brings a valuable piece of information about the students for instructional planning and IEP planning meetings. It is important for special educators to establish good relationships and collaborate with the students and parents or legal guardians in order to gauge the students' strengths and weaknesses. Collaboration is essential between the general and special educators in order to ensure that students' IEP goals and needs are being met in the appropriate settings. Collaboration with district team members or others like school psychologists is helpful for gaining insight on special education procedures or assessment results.

Review Video: Collaborating with Other Professionals
Visit mometrix.com/academy and enter code: 100351

Communicating with Service Members Across All Special Education Settings

In order to provide the best educations possible for students with disabilities, it is important for special educators and related service members to **communicate** effectively. Communication is important due to the degree of collaboration required between the special educators and the related service members. Related service members are often IEP team members and help students meet their IEP goals and objectives. **Related service members**, like speech pathologists and occupational therapists, also work on a consultation basis with special educators. They may also consult with general education teachers to ensure that students receive required related services in the general education or inclusive classroom settings. Special educators and related service members must collaborate in order to ensure the needs of the students are met, especially when IEP goals or objectives are out of the scope of the special educators' knowledge bases. For example, a speech pathologist might help a teacher address a student's fluency goal.

Communicating with Parents of Students with Disabilities

It is good practice to communicate with parents outside of progress reporting times and Individualized Education Program meetings. This is especially important for students with **communication deficits** who may not be able to communicate with their parents or legal guardians. Communication also helps prevent potential crises or problem behaviors and alerts parents or legal guardians before any major issues arise. Special educators should find methods of communication that work best for parents or legal guardians, such as phone calls, emails, or writing in daily communication logs. Email is beneficial for creating paper trails, especially for any discussions about educating students. However, email lacks tone and body language and can sometimes be misunderstood. Phone calls fulfill an immediate need to speak with a parent or legal guardian. However, there are no paper trails with phone calls, and they can also lead to misunderstanding. Phone calls may be time consuming, but they can be conducted on special occasions or when behavioral issues need to be discussed. Written communication logs are useful for writing brief summaries about students' days. With any mode of communication, it is essential to **document** what is communicated between the parents or legal guardians and the educators.

The Roles and Rights Families have in the Education of Children with Disabilities

Under the Individuals with Disabilities Education Act, parents and legal guardians of children with disabilities have **procedural safeguards** that protect their rights. The safeguards also provide parents and legal guardians with the means to resolve any disputes with school systems. **Parents and legal guardians** may underestimate their importance to IEP teams. However, they are important members of IEP teams and integral parts of the decision-making processes for their children's educational journeys. Parents and legal guardians often work more closely with their children than other adults. Therefore, as part of IEP teams, they serve as **advocates** and can often provide insight regarding the children's backgrounds, educational and developmental histories, strengths, and weaknesses. Parents and legal guardians are also important decision-makers in transition meetings, when students with disabilities move from one level of school to another. Their input in transition meetings helps ensure that appropriate services and supports are in place at the next levels of school so that students can succeed.

Roles of Parents/Legal Guardians and the School District During Evaluation

If parents or legal guardians suspect their children have disabilities, they can request that the school districts **evaluate** the children for special education. A parent or legal guardian can send a **written evaluation request** to the child's school, principal, and the school district's director or director of special education services. In some states, parents and legal guardians may be required to sign a school district form requesting the evaluation. Parents should follow up on the request and/or set a time frame for the school district to respond. The school district may choose to implement the **Response to Intervention (RTI) pre-referral process**. RTI is a process by which the school gives the student special academic support before determining whether or not to move forward with the evaluation process. Not all states or school districts have the same method for applying RTI. Under the Individuals with Disabilities Education Act, the time frame for completion of RTI is 60 days. However, some states can set their own timelines. RTI should not be the only means by which the school district collects data on the student and should be part of a comprehensive evaluation conducted by the student's school.

Speech Language Pathologist

Speech language pathologists (**SLPs**) provide interventions for children with communication disorders. They can assist, evaluate, prevent, and diagnose a variety of **speech issues**, from fluency to voice disorders. Before children reach grade school age, it is important that they receive early interventions for suspected communication disorders. SLPs are helpful with targeting speech or language issues, identifying at-risk students, or providing interventions for children and adults. SLPs also play a role in helping children develop good reading and writing skills, especially when deficits are evident. SLPs work collaboratively with special educators to deliver **interventions** to children with speech and language disorders in grade school. In schools, SLPs play a role in prevention, assessment, intervention, program design, data collection and analysis, and Individualized Education Program compliance. SLPs work with special educators, parents, students, reading specialists, occupational therapists, school psychologists, and others in order to provide effective services to students who require them.

Occupational Therapist

Students with special needs may need **occupational therapy services**. The number of services students receive is defined on their IEPs. **Occupational therapists (OTs)** may help students on IEPs refine their fine motor skills, improve sensory processing deficits, improve visual skills, and improve self-care skills. OTs can also assist with behavior management, social skills, and improving attention and focus. When a student is identified as possibly needing occupational therapy, the OT spends time observing the student in a variety of settings where the skill or skill deficit will be demonstrated. Prior to the student's IEP meeting, the OT typically meets with the student's teachers, parents, and other professionals in order to discuss observations, assessment results, and determinations. **Determinations** are then put into the IEP and implemented as related services. Fine motor skill instruction begins with the OT instructing the student on a particular skill. OTs can set up regimens for teachers and parents to generalize using the fine motor skills in the classroom and home environments.

Paraprofessional

The US Department of Education requires paraprofessionals to have high school diplomas or the equivalent under Title I law. Paraprofessionals (paras), sometimes called **paraeducators**, assist classroom teachers with classroom activities and help students with special needs. In a special education setting, a para works with a certified teacher to help deliver **instruction** and help students meet **Individualized Education Program goals and objectives**. Paras are not responsible for teaching new skills or introducing new goals and objectives to students. In this respect, special educators generally work alongside the paras and students to introduce new skills, goals, or objectives. At times, paras may be responsible for helping students maintain behavior plans, working with students who may be aggressive or violent, and providing physical assistance if necessary. Training is usually provided by the school district for situations when physical assistance is a possible necessity. Paras can also help take notes on students' progress toward meeting their goals or objectives. They can also discuss how students are progressing with behavior plans.

Behavioral Issues for Students with Disabilities

Behavioral Issues and Intervention Strategies

Behavior issues occur with students with and without disabilities. However, they may occur more frequently or to a higher degree for some students with disabilities. Behavior issues are often a **manifestation** of a child's disability. For example, students with attention-deficit/hyperactivity disorder may present with attention and focus issues and impulsivity. **Common behavior issues** include the following:

- Emotional outbursts
- Inattention and inability to focus
- Impulsivity
- Aggression
- Abusive language
- Oppositional defiance
- Lying or stealing
- Threatening adults or peers

Other behavior issues may include inappropriate sexual behavior, inability to control sexual behavior, self-harm, or self-harm attempts. Behavior issues can be **avoided** or **remediated** with classroom management skills like setting clear and consistent classroom goals, setting time limits, and providing visuals to assist with transitions or concepts. When a student is in an aggressive state, it is important for the teacher to remain calm, provide choices for the student, and restate the consequences of any aggressive outbursts.

Review Video: Student Behavior Management Approaches
Visit mometrix.com/academy and enter code: 843846

Review Video: Promoting Appropriate Behavior
Visit mometrix.com/academy and enter code: 321015

Managing Students with Emotional Disorders

Managing a classroom of students with emotional disorders can be challenging and unpredictable. Students with emotional disorders have Individualized Education Program (IEP) goals that focus on **controlling** or **monitoring** their daily behavior choices. However, this does not always mean they will engage in meeting these goals. It is important for educators to know how to **manage** issues that students with emotional disorders may bring to the classroom. When creating resources and lesson plans, an educator should do the following:

- Establish a **safety plan**, which includes knowing how to implement a **crisis prevention plan**.
- Maintain an environment that reduces **stimulation** and provides **visual cues** for expected behavior.
- Implement **intervention-based strategies** for managing student behavior.
- Collect and use **data** to identify triggers, track behaviors, and recognize strategies that produce positive outcomes.
- Practice open **communication** about classroom expectations to students, parents, and other teachers.

Special education teachers can be helpful in implementing these guidelines, especially when students with emotional disorders are in inclusive settings.

Supporting Students with Mental Health Issues

Students with disabilities may also have mental health issues. These students may not necessarily be diagnosed with emotional disturbances, as mental health issues can occur concurrently with other disabilities. Students' mental health symptoms may fluctuate on an hourly, daily, or weekly basis. Intervention techniques and supports must be determined by the individual needs of each student. General and special educators across all special education settings can **support** these students by learning how to **recognize mental health issues** in schools. Teachers can use observations and research-based strategies for identifying issues. Training in working with students who have certain mental health disorders may also be useful. Occasionally, training in crisis prevention plans is required of teachers working with students who may become aggressive due to their disorders.

Behavior Assessment and Intervention

Cognitive Behavioral Theory

The cognitive behavioral theory states that people form their own negative or positive concepts that affect their behaviors. The cognitive behavioral theory involves a **cognitive triad** of thoughts and behaviors. This triad refers to thoughts about the **self**, the **world and environment**, and the **future**. In times of stress, people's thoughts can become distressed or dysfunctional. Sometimes cognitive behavioral therapy, based on the cognitive behavioral theory model, is used to help people address and manage their thoughts. This process involves people examining their thoughts more closely in order to bring them back to more realistic, grounded ways of thinking. People's thoughts and perceptions can often affect their lives negatively and lead to unhealthy emotions and behaviors. **Cognitive behavioral therapy** helps people to adjust their thinking, learn ways to access healthy thoughts, and learn healthier or safer behaviors.

Antecedents, Behavior, and Consequences as Stimuli Used in Behavior Analysis

Antecedents and consequences play a role in behavioral analysis, which is important for evaluating the behaviors of students. The purpose of behavior analysis is to gather information about a specific behavior demonstrated by a student. **Antecedents** are the actions or events that occur before the behavior occurs. It is important to recognize antecedents for behaviors to better understand under what circumstances the behavior is occurring. The **behavior** is the undesirable action that occurs as a result of the antecedent. **Consequences** are what happens immediately after the behavior occurs. These can be natural or enforced. A student might desire a certain consequence when engaging in the behavior. Understanding the relationships between antecedents, behavior, and consequences allows a professional to determine how to minimize or eliminate the behavior. In some circumstances, antecedents and consequences can be manipulated, changed, or removed in order to avoid reinforcing the undesired behavior.

Behavior Rating Scale Assessments

Behavior rating scales address the needs of students with emotional disorders who are referred to special education. Problems with behavior are often the reason a student has been referred for special education. These scales are used in determining a student's **eligibility** for special education, and in addressing **undesirable behaviors** demonstrated by students already in special education for reasons other than behavior problems. They are similar to adaptive behavior scales in that teachers or other professionals can administer the scales with little training as long as they are familiar with the students. Behavior rating scales help measure the frequency and intensity of the behaviors for a particular student often by assigning numbered ratings. They serve as a starting point for learning more about a student's behavior so that behavior interventions and management can take place. These scales are **norm-referenced**, so the outcomes of the behavior rating scales are compared to the behaviors of others.

Negative and Positive Reinforcement Related to Applied Behavior Analysis

Part of applied behavior analysis (**ABA**) is applying negative and positive reinforcement strategies, which are forms of conditioning strategies. In behavioral conditioning, the term **reinforcement** refers to trying to increase the frequency of a desired behavior, whereas the term **punishment** refers to trying to decrease the frequency of an undesired behavior. Similarly, when discussing behavioral conditioning methods, the word **positive** refers to the *addition* of a stimulus, whereas the word **negative** refers to the *removal* of a stimulus. These four terms tend to be confused but are very specifically used to denote particular types of behavioral conditioning.

Positive reinforcement works by providing a desired **reward** for a desired behavior. For example, parents may give a child an allowance (the positive reinforcement) for doing chores (the behavior). In contrast, **negative reinforcement** removes an aversive stimulus to encourage a desired behavior. An example of this might be that a parent rewards a child's behavior by taking away some of his chores. Negative reinforcement is different from a punishment because the goal of punishment is to *discourage* an unwanted behavior while the goal of negative reinforcement is to *encourage* a desirable behavior. Although it is not commonly discussed, positive and negative stimuli may be used at the same time in conditioning to effect a greater change.

Term:	Example:
Positive Reinforcement	A teacher *gives* the high-scorers on a test a sticker.
Negative Reinforcement	A teacher *takes away* an assignment if the class performs well on a test.
Positive Punishment	A police officer *gives* a driver a speeding ticket.
Negative Punishment	A parent grounds a student, *taking away* video games for two weeks.
Combination Reinforcement	A physical education teacher *replaces* a workout (negative) with a game (positive) because the class was well-behaved.
Combination Punishment	A student gets low grades and is required to complete extra schoolwork (positive) and is not allowed to participate in sports for a week (negative).

Developing Positive Behavioral Interventions and Supports

Positive behavioral intervention and support (**PBIS**) plans can be implemented in classrooms or schoolwide to encourage specific, positive outcomes in groups of students with and without disabilities. A PBIS plan, such as an anti-bullying campaign, is put in place to encourage **good behavior** and **school safety** and to remove **environmental triggers** of undesirable behavior. The goal of a PBIS plan is for students to learn appropriate behavior just as they would learn an academic subject. Effective PBIS plans are based on research and analysis of data collected on targeted, large-scale behaviors. As with any behavioral plan, the success of PBIS plans is determined by monitoring student progress. PBIS plans should change if they do not work or if they stop working.

Developing a Functional Behavior Assessment

A functional behavior assessment (**FBA**) is a formal process used to examine student behavior. The goal of an FBA is to identify what is causing a specific behavior and evaluate how the behavior is affecting the student's educational performance. Once these factors are determined, the FBA is useful in implementing **interventions** for the behavior. When an FBA is developed, a student's behavior must be specifically defined; then the teacher or other professional devises a plan for collecting data on the behavior. These points of data are helpful in determining possible causes of the behavior, such as environmental triggers. The teacher or other professional can then implement the most appropriate plan for addressing the student's behavior. Often, this means implementing a **behavior intervention plan**, which includes introducing the student to actions or processes that are incompatible with the problem behavior. It is important to monitor the plan to ensure its effectiveness or remediate certain steps.

> **Review Video: Functional Behavior Assessments**
> Visit mometrix.com/academy and enter code: 783262

Developing Behavior Intervention Plans

A behavior intervention plan (**BIP**) is based on a functional behavior assessment. The purpose of the BIP is to teach the student actions, behaviors, or processes that are incompatible with the problem behavior. The BIP may be included in an Individualized Education Program (IEP) or 504 Plan, or components of the BIP may be written out as IEP goals. Once an FBA is conducted, a BIP is put in place that describes the target behavior, lists factors that trigger the behavior, and lists any interventions that help the student avoid the behavior. The interventions include problem-solving skills for the student to use instead of demonstrating the target behavior. If the interventions fail to target the problem behavior or are no longer effective for targeting the behavior, then the FBA must be revisited and a new BIP developed.

Positive Classroom Discipline Strategies

A core element of effective classroom management, positive classroom discipline is a means of holding students accountable for their actions, and it starts with establishing clear and consistent **consequences** for poor choices. Students learn to predict consequences and self-correct their behaviors. It is helpful to give students **reminders** about behavior and rules instead of immediately resorting to consequences. **Pre-reminders** about expectations can be given before starting a lesson. **Nonverbal reminders** such as looks, touches, silence, or removal are possible ways to discourage students from engaging in poor choices. Removal as a consequence involves sending the student out of the classroom either to protect the other students from harm or to prevent a student from impeding the course of instruction. Removal laws vary between states and local districts, but removal is generally mandatory whenever a student is being violent. **Spoken reminders** can be used to further encourage self-management skills and should be used as precursors for reminding students about expectations instead of delivering immediate consequences.

Promoting Appropriate Behavior in Inclusive Learning Environments

Effective classrooms have good management strategies in place that promote good learning environments and minimize disruptions. Teachers with effective classroom management strategies demonstrate good leadership and organization skills. They also promote positive classroom experiences, establish clear expectations for behavior, and reinforce positive behaviors. In **inclusive learning environments**, it is important for teachers to keep all students on track with their learning. When it comes to students with disabilities, planning classroom management strategies presents different challenges. Effective teachers understand how students' special needs come into play with expected classroom behaviors. General and special educators can demonstrate effective classroom management strategies by figuring out what is causing students to act out or misbehave. They should collaborate with other professionals and students' parents to ensure the success of students with special needs in their classrooms. Lastly, effective classroom management includes setting goals for inclusive classrooms to achieve. Clear goals help establish good rapport with students with special needs because they know what is expected of them.

Crisis Prevention and Management

Crises and Crisis Prevention and Management Plans

Crises

A **crisis** is generally defined as a situation that is so emotionally impactful that an individual is not able to cope with the situation by normal means and is at risk of harming themselves or others. Crises can arise from either developmental changes that happen throughout life, such as going through puberty or graduating from school, or they can be situational and arise at any time. Examples of situational crises include sickness, losses, family deaths, and any other kind of unpredictable situation that comes up throughout life. Students with disabilities often have particular difficulty coping with stressful life situations and may need the help of a **crisis prevention plan** as a result. Crisis prevention and management goals generally focus on coping mechanisms and healthy anticipation of unavoidable situations to help the individual understand and safely navigate their way through a crisis.

Crisis Prevention Plans

Crisis prevention plans essentially serve to help with early identification of a crisis and to provide the necessary support to help the individual through a crisis to an effective resolution. These plans are often put together with the help of various members of an individual's support team, taking into account past behaviors, health, and other factors of his or her life. Some organizations, such as the Crisis Prevention Institute, specialize in crisis prevention and intervention training for professionals. Crisis prevention plans should take into account principles of least restrictive environment to support individuals in their normal environments, while also removing or being aware of any known **behavioral triggers** that may be problematic. In the event that the individual in crisis becomes physically violent or harmful to themselves, stronger emergent response may be warranted. The ultimate goal is to keep the individual and others safe until his or her emotional state has been normalized. There is no specific duration of time for a crisis, but any intervention should be treated as short-term to prevent restricting the individual's rights through unnecessary intervention. It is important to provide the individual with clear structures and expectations to help understand direct consequences for undesired choices prior to entering a crisis. Crisis prevention plans should also provide clear processes that professionals and family members can use when students do enter a crisis in order to de-escalate the situations.

> **Review Video: Crisis Management and Prevention**
> Visit mometrix.com/academy and enter code: 351872

Chapter Quiz

Ready to see how well you retained what you just read? Scan the QR code to go directly to the chapter quiz interface for this study guide. If you're using a computer, simply visit the online resources page at **mometrix.com/resources719/texesspedsupp** and click the Chapter Quizzes link.

TExES Practice Test

Want to take this practice test in an online interactive format?
Check out the online resources page, which includes interactive practice questions and much more: **mometrix.com/resources719/texesspedsupp**

1. What type of assertiveness is a teacher displaying when she clearly states her concerns and works to correct negative behaviors?

a. Hostile assertiveness
b. Constructive assertiveness
c. Empathic assertiveness
d. Inflexible assertiveness

2. According to IDEA, which one of the following areas is not considered when determining eligibility for the developmental delay category?

a. Fine motor development
b. Cognitive development
c. Language development
d. Personal development

3. When working as a case manager for students with Individualized Education Programs (IEPs), which role must be taken on as part of that duty?

a. Ensuring students on the caseload do not fail.
b. Ensuring students on the caseload attend class.
c. Ensuring students on the caseload meet IEP goals.
d. Ensuring students on the caseload access accommodations.

4. Mr. Harley previously worked in a mental health program with students who had no physical disabilities but had major mental illnesses. As such, they often had violent behavior and were also very strong. He is now a new teacher with a different population. Most of these students have multiple physical disabilities, as well as intellectual disabilities and in some cases mental illness. Mr. Harley was trained at his previous job in techniques for controlling violent behavior. His new employers require him to undergo their training in behavior control. What is the reason for this?

a. The techniques for working with physically fragile individuals are different.
b. Mr. Harley's certification at his previous place of employment is no longer current.
c. The law mandates that he receive training specific to the given workplace.
d. The training is a formality and is given to all new employees during orientation.

5. Christopher is an eight-year-old boy with multiple disabilities, including profound intellectual disabilities, spastic quadriplegia, and right-sided vision and hearing impairments. Though wheelchair-bound, he is very active, traveling through the halls, visiting different classrooms, and moving on to other places. If he is not closely monitored, he will take off for parts unknown, and staff need to supervise him constantly to keep up with his activities. When not watched, he has chewed on countertops to the point of damaging them (as well as possibly his teeth). He is also quite capable of getting into dangerous or toxic substances, such as cleaning supplies. Staff members disagree: Some teachers and even one nurse believe that he has attention-deficit hyperactivity disorder (ADHD) and should be prescribed medication to reduce his peripatetic and sometimes destructive behaviors. Another nurse, the doctor, and the psychologist are not convinced of this. What is another likely explanation for Christopher's behavior?

a. His developmental level
b. A lack of proper training
c. An impulse control disorder
d. A non-stimulating environment

6. For which group of students would it be most appropriate to implement a functional curriculum at the elementary school level?

a. Students with intellectual disabilities
b. Students with specific learning disabilities
c. Students with speech or language impairments
d. Students with developmental delays

7. A student displays a slight learning disability, which mostly effects reading and writing development. He is removed from the general student body to receive special education. While this student's disability has put him behind in his English class, he is not behind in any other class. What has the school violated in removing this student from the general student body?

a. Individual Education Plan
b. Human Rights Act
c. Americans with Disabilities Act
d. Least Restrictive Environment (LRE)

8. Samantha easily becomes lost, even in places where she has been before. She gets mixed up about left and right and has trouble judging distances. Even when she is given directions, she has difficulty following them correctly. Samantha's LD is characterized by:

a. Motor coordination deficits
b. Spatial perception problems
c. Executive functioning deficit
d. Difficulties with sequencing

9. A student with a disability takes online courses and struggles with communication and seeking help in social situations. Which of the following instructional strategies would be most effective in supporting the student in online instruction?

a. Supplementing online instruction with face-to-face instruction
b. Assisting the student in seeking support from the online teacher
c. Providing opportunities to demonstrate the knowledge learned online
d. Ensuring the student's accommodations are documented in the student's IEP

10. Kim is in a general education classroom and receives special education sessions for a mild disability. She wants to talk to her special education teacher about her college applications. Which of the following is the correct scenario for such a conversation?

a. They discuss the subject in the hallway with students, faculty, and staff passing by.
b. They discuss the subject in the teacher's office during a small group therapy session.
c. They discuss the subject alone together in the teacher's office during a free period.
d. They discuss the subject in Kim's general education classroom before class begins.

11. Samuel is a student with a specific learning disability in the area of oral expression. What kind of assessment would be most appropriate in order to evaluate his continued eligibility?

a. Expressive language
b. Receptive language
c. Auditory discrimination
d. Verbal intelligence

12. Ms. Loomis is a teacher of LD (Learning Disabilities) students in Texas. This term she has had a new group of students referred to her for reading difficulties. She realizes that all of these students are English language learners (ELLs). Which statement about these referrals is most likely to be true?

a. These students will have reading problems regardless of which language they are reading.
b. The language acquisition process may well be the cause of these students' reading problems.
c. These students' reading problems are most likely the result of their learning disabilities.
d. These students' reading problems and their ESL status are most likely a coincidence.

13. Susie and Stevie are kindergarten students receiving special education services. Stevie is blind and Susie is not. Both students' IEPs have nearly identical learning objectives for listening, speaking, and communication, but Susie's IEP has learning objectives for reading and print awareness, which Stevie's IEP does not. Relative to the Texas Essential Knowledge and Skills (TEKS), which of the following best characterizes both children's IEP objectives?

a. Both children's IEP objectives are separate from the TEKS because they receive special education.
b. Susie's IEP objectives are very similar to the TEKS, but Stevie's are not because he is blind.
c. Both children's IEP objectives are similar to the TEKS only because both reflect important basic skills.
d. Both children's IEP objectives are deliberately designed to reflect the TEKS as closely as possible.

14. Patrick is a third-grade student with Individual Education Program goals in math problem-solving and math calculations. What is the best instructional strategy to provide a spiraling curriculum?

a. Reviewing class material using similar instructional methods
b. Completing upcoming homework assignments in advance
c. Implementing both visual and auditory explanations of math content he learns in school
d. Increasing the complexity of the math work and problems gradually as he gains mastery

15. Corey is a second-grade student who receives special education services due to a specific learning disability in the area of reading fluency. Which of the following is the best strategy for ensuring success for Corey if he is severely impacted by his reading fluency deficiencies?

a. Providing additional support in the classroom
b. Pulling Corey for small-group reading fluency intervention
c. Modifying the material that Corey is to complete
d. Pulling Corey for one-to-one reading fluency intervention

16. When teaching a new group of students, which one of the following strategies is most productive in creating a supportive classroom environment?

a. Including community-building activities
b. Allowing the students to negotiate
c. Posting student work in the room
d. Establishing authority as the teacher

17. Response to Intervention (RTI) is:

a. Parents, classroom teacher, special education teacher and other caring persons stage an intervention to express how a student's socially unacceptable behavior upsets them
b. An opportunity for a student to openly and freely respond to specific interventions without fear of reprimand
c. A strategy for diagnosing learning disabilities in which a student receives research-supported interventions to correct an academic delay. If the interventions do not result in considerable improvement, the failure to respond suggests causal learning disabilities
d. A formal complaint lodged by a parent or guardian in response to what they consider an intrusion by a teacher into private matters

18. Which of the following is true about discipline and students who receive special education services according to IDEA?

a. Manifestation determinations are required for students with disabilities who have been suspended for 10 consecutive days.
b. Students with disabilities cannot be suspended more than 10 days.
c. Discipline for special education students is the same as general education.
d. Special education services are not provided for expelled students.

19. Tina is a student with a seizure disorder. Despite medication, she has sustained head injuries during past seizures. She now wears a helmet to protect her against further injuries. Other students, general education teachers, and various people in the community do not know why she wears the helmet and have a lot of misconceptions about it. How can her special education teacher help?

a. Recommend that Tina not wear the helmet in public anymore because it is too stigmatizing.
b. Recommend that Tina not wear the helmet in public and have someone accompany her at all times to prevent head injuries if she has a seizure.
c. Educate general education teachers and other school and community personnel about the helmet and enlist their aid to educate others about it.
d. Advise Tina that it is her sole responsibility to explain to everybody she encounters daily about her helmet and about why she needs to wear it.

20. Sixth graders Alfie and Honesty ride the same bus. Honesty constantly teases Alfie. Alfie is embarrassed because he believes she is berating him. The bus driver told their teacher it was possible that Honesty is actually interested in Alfie, but doesn't express it well. The best form of conflict resolution would be for the teacher to:

a. Take Honesty aside and explain boys don't like overly aggressive girls.
b. Take Honesty aside and teach her less embarrassing methods of getting a boy's attention.
c. Explain to Alfie that Honesty probably teases him because she likes him and he should take it as a compliment.
d. Suggest to Alfie that if he is disturbed by Honesty's teasing, he have a calm, assertive conversation with her and tell her he doesn't like it and insist she stop.

21. Which one of the following instructional strategies allows students to move around the room while still learning?

a. Embodied learning
b. Inquiry-based learning
c. Blended learning
d. Service learning

22. In an IEP meeting, who is the best choice to interpret a student's evaluation results?

a. Whoever can best explain the educational implications of those results
b. The student's special education teacher on the IEP team
c. The school psychologist who may or may not be an IEP team member
d. Another professional who is not a part of the student's IEP team

23. When holding an Individualized Education Program (IEP) meeting with stakeholders, which method would be least effective in establishing rapport?

a. Facilitated meetings
b. Slide show meetings
c. Student-led meetings
d. Scripted meetings

24. Greg is a student with intellectual disabilities who qualified for group home placement in the community and has been living there successfully for a while. His late mother provided all of his personal care when he was growing up. Greg has a poor sense of balance and recently slipped in the shower, fell, and broke his hip. His father still approves of the placement but is currently very anxious about his son being injured again. What might be appropriate for his teacher to do?

a. Recommend a different placement with more direct personal care to avoid more falls.
b. Counsel Greg's father that the injury was unfortunate but that these things happen in life.
c. Initiate an investigation of the group home staff to determine if they were negligent.
d. Work with residential services on installing non-slip flooring and grab bars in the tub.

25. Which of the following is true about the Family Educational Rights and Privacy Act and students with disabilities?

a. Each teacher in the school has access to the student's IEP.
b. Schools are not required to allow parents to inspect previous IEPs.
c. Previous IEPs can be amended at any time.
d. Parents have the right to access testing protocols.

26. What statement is true regarding literacy?

a. The same literacy skills in students apply across subjects
b. The literacy demands of society have changed over time
c. Literacy required of pupils stays constant across grades
d. Literacy is best taught in the schools in a separate lesson

27. Chad is a fifth-grade student with ADHD who needs active involvement to stay focused, but he enjoys being away from people. How can the use of a workspace in the corner of the class be best implemented in the classroom to be beneficial for Chad?

a. Chad can be sent to the corner when he becomes disruptive.
b. Chad can go to the corner when he has an assignment to work on.
c. Chad can go to the corner to reward good behavior after he finishes his work.
d. Chad can go to the corner when he needs a break.

28. A kindergarten teacher has a new student who will not make eye contact with anyone, so she doesn't appear to be listening. She often rocks back and forth and does not stop when asked or give any indication she has heard. She avoids physical contact. Sometimes the teacher must take her arm to guide her from one place to another. Occasionally the student erupts, howling in terror and fury. The most likely diagnosis is:

a. Conduct Disorder
b. Obsessive-Compulsive Disorder
c. Autism
d. Oppositional Defiant Disorder

29. A third grade boy is new to the school. His teacher has noticed he happily plays with other children, redirects his attention without upset when another child rejects his offer to play and doesn't mind playing on his own. However, the boy doesn't pay attention when academic instruction is given. He continues to speak with other children, draws, or distracts himself. The teacher reminds him repeatedly to listen and follow instruction. When he does not, she moves him to a quiet desk away from the others. When isolated, the boy puts his head on the desk and weeps uncontrollably, or stares at a fixed spot and repeats to himself, "I hate myself, I hate myself. I should be dead." During these episodes, the teacher cannot break through to the student; his disconnection seems complete. The teacher has requested a conference with his parents, but they do not speak English and have not responded to her offer of a translator. The teacher should:

a. Establish a consistent set of expectations for the child. He needs to understand there are appropriate times for play and for learning
b. Isolate the boy first thing. His behavior suggests manipulation. By third grade children fully understand they are expected to pay attention when the teacher is speaking. The boy is punishing the teacher with tears and repetitive self-hate, consciously or unconsciously attempting to make the teacher feel guilty
c. Immediately refer him to the counselor. The boy is exhibiting serious emotional distress suggesting abuse or neglect at home or outside of school
d. Recognize the child's highly sensitive nature; offer comfort when he acts out self-loathing. Carefully explain why he must learn to pay attention so he will use reason instead of emotion when making future choices

30. Researchers have found that students with arithmetic disabilities:

a. Have the same general working memory deficits as students with reading disabilities
b. Have specific deficits in working memory for processing both numbers and language
c. Have specific deficits in numerical processing, but these are not for working memory
d. Have working memory deficits specifically for processing numerical information only

31. Ross is a third-grade student who receives special education services as a student with another health impairment due to ADHD. Which of the following strategies would likely be LEAST effective for Ross?

a. Providing extra thinking time when asking a question
b. Providing one-on-one math instruction
c. Providing a setting with fewer distractions
d. Providing a model to demonstrate the task

32. What type of classroom model do schools utilize if they also utilize an IEP and limit the use of special education classrooms?

a. Inclusion
b. Exclusion
c. Diversion
d. Transition

33. Which of the following best describes the purpose of the present levels of academic achievement section of the IEP?

a. To describe how the child is performing educationally
b. To determine the accommodations that the school accesses
c. To identify which disability category is appropriate
d. To compare a student's performance to peers

34. Which of the following is not one of the benefits of using curriculum-based assessments?

a. To measure short-term student growth
b. To match all of the standards in the classroom curriculum
c. To inform a teacher's instruction
d. To motivate students to improve

35. What is NOT an environmental factor that could lead to positive student development?

a. Relationships with teachers
b. Structure in daily routine
c. Getting enough sleep
d. Genetic predisposition for high IQ

36. Bruce is a student who periodically has behavioral crises when his level of tension rises too high. His behavior assessment does not indicate that his episodes are attention-seeking. His behavior can become violent if it is not de-escalated, but he responds well to intervention and has only rarely ever hurt himself or others. Based on this information, what would be the most appropriate form of *early* crisis intervention for him?

a. Physical restraint
b. Mechanical restraint
c. Verbal de-escalation
d. Extinction (ignoring)

37. Which of the following pieces of special education legislation implemented the child find process for students who are suspected of having disabilities?

a. Education for All Handicapped Children Act of 1975
b. Individuals with Disabilities Education Act of 1990
c. Individuals with Disabilities Education Act of 2004
d. Elementary and Secondary Act of 2001

38. Positive behavioral interventions are most likely to...

a. Control the problem behavior
b. Suppress the problem behavior
c. Replace the problem behavior
d. Analyze the problem behavior

39. Which of the following is most likely to be true about students with learning disabilities and their families?

a. Families that have children with disabilities typically bond closer.
b. Parents can sometimes be the cause of a learning disability.
c. Parents will often suspect a disability before the school does.
d. Families often seek out information about disabilities.

40. Which of the following best describes how often at minimum a behavior intervention plan should be updated?

a. Once a year at the annual IEP meeting
b. Each time the student has a new teacher
c. On every progress report date
d. As the IEP team deems it necessary

41. Which of the following best describes how daily learning objectives can be implemented to assist students who are working on adaptive skills?

a. To teach students to learn how to complete a new task
b. To teach students to improve reading ability
c. To teach students to learn about organization
d. To teach students to improve basic math skills

42. Of the following criteria for defining intellectual disabilities, which was NOT used before 1961?

a. IQ score
b. Social incompetence
c. Impaired adaptive behavior
d. Essentially incurable

43. Of the following criteria for defining intellectual disabilities, which one was widely used only from 1961 on?

a. Mental deficiency/incomplete development
b. Originates during the developmental period
c. Associated with impaired adaptive behavior
d. A condition manifested at maturity

44. Which of the following models used in planning instruction for students with disabilities is described as an example of student-directed planning?

a. The model and process of Group Action Planning (GAP)
b. The Choosing Outcomes and Accommodations for Children (COACH) model
c. The model and process of Making Action Plans (MAPs)
d. The Planning Alternative Tomorrows with Hope (PATH) model

45. Which of the following is the most common disability in children aged 5-21 according to the IDEA annual reports to Congress?

a. Specific learning disability
b. Speech or language impairment
c. Intellectual disability
d. Emotional disturbance

46. Which of the following best describes the role of the special education teacher in the multitiered system of supports (MTSS) process?

a. To provide input on students with disabilities
b. To discuss students who may need to be evaluated
c. To provide interventions for students
d. To discuss students who exit special education

47. Which of the following best describes the purpose of the standard score when interpreting assessment data?

a. To determine how spread out the numbers are
b. To determine how far a score is from the average
c. To determine the rank of the score compared to others
d. To determine the hypothetical range of scores

48. Bobby is a 4-year old who was born with Down syndrome, congenital cataracts, and profound intellectual disabilities. Because of his disabilities, his parents wanted nothing to do with him after his birth. The State Department of Family Services took his case when the family waived parental rights at the hospital. His caseworker got him a placement in a state-funded group home and day habilitation training program. What documents would be written on Bobby's behalf?

a. An Individual Education Program (IEP)
b. An Individualized Family Services Plan (IFSP)
c. It would depend on the state where he lives.
d. Both an IFSP and an IEP should be written.

49. Zachary is a 10th-grade student who receives special education services as a student with an other health impairment due to his ADHD, and he struggles to sit still for long periods of time. Which of the following strategies would be most effective in providing opportunities for Zachary to move around?

a. Giving Zachary a pass to move around when he needs to
b. Giving Zachary a timer to get up and stretch every 10 minutes
c. Organizing the classroom so that Zachary has his own area
d. Incorporating movement activities for the entire class

50. Which of the following best describes alternate assessments and students that receive special education services?

a. Most students who receive special education services take alternate assessments.
b. Students who take alternate assessments do not receive high school diplomas.
c. Parents have the option to choose whether students take alternate assessments.
d. Alternate assessments must be based on grade-level standards.

51. Which of the following is a disadvantage to having special education teachers support classrooms rather than co-teach?

a. Special education teachers do not have as much time to plan.
b. Special education teachers are not as familiar with the content.
c. Special education teachers cannot differentiate instruction.
d. Special education teachers must collaborate with classroom teachers.

52. Brittany is a four-year-old preschool student who is administered a developmental assessment as part of her special education evaluation. Which of the following disability categories would least likely be considered as a result of these assessments?

a. Development delay
b. Speech or language impairment
c. Specific learning disability
d. Autism spectrum disorder

53. A major review of an exceptional student's IEP is required...

a. Once every year
b. Once every three years
c. In one or three years by state
d. In varying periods by each state

54. Which of the following activities would be considered atypical cognitive development for a four-year-old?

a. Making up words and stories
b. Drawing pictures of objects
c. Pretending to read and write
d. Pointing to objects they want instead of using words

55. Joseph has Down syndrome. He can communicate with short, simple verbal phrases. He can read only a few words that he learned over a long time. He lives just a few blocks from his school. His area is not served by the school bus system. His teacher has a goal for Joseph to learn the directions to and from school so his mother will no longer need to accompany him. Which of these would be a good way for the teacher to work with him on this goal?

a. Send Joseph out first with a map, monitoring him remotely.
b. Send Joseph out first with written directions and shadow him from a distance.
c. Walk with Joseph, prompting him to verbalize the route until he learns it.
d. Gradually decrease the number of days his mother walks with him

56. Which of the following strategies can a special education teacher implement to best ensure that inclusion is successful in their school?

a. Articulating the need for inclusion to the school administrators
b. Collaborating with general education teachers
c. Developing new assessments to measure student growth
d. Providing professional development to staff

57. Which of the following instructional strategies is most appropriate in supporting the immediate transition of eighth-grade students into high school?

a. Researching professions that they may be interested in
b. Researching colleges that they may want to attend
c. Researching classes that the high school offers
d. Researching independent skills that they may need

58. Which of the following strategies most directly promotes generalization of learning?

a. Having a student practice a new skill in a variety of different settings/contexts
b. Having a student practice a new skill regularly and periodically testing that skill
c. Having a student practice a complex skill one step at a time, then adding steps
d. Having a student practice a new skill in class before applying it in real-life tasks

59. When co-teaching a high school English class, which one of the following instructional strategies is likely to be least effective in ensuring that all students are achieving in the class?

a. Both teachers teaching as a team
b. Teaching the students in stations
c. One teacher instructing while the other supports
d. Teachers working together but without clearly defined objectives

60. Which of the following strategies would likely be most beneficial in preparing a student with a specific learning disability for adulthood?

a. Incorporating a postsecondary goal in the student's IEP
b. Incorporating money management skills in the student's class
c. Incorporating transition services into the student's IEP
d. Incorporating job application writing in the student's class

61. Which of the following is the most accurate statement about teaching across the curriculum?

a. This is a method of planning a lesson so general that it can apply to any content area.
b. Career planning for students is better addressed by other, more specific methods.
c. Application of school subjects to life is best served by different methods.
d. A single lesson plan includes math, English, reading, social studies, art, science, etc.

62. Johnny's IQ score places him in the 97th percentile rank of the population. This means that:

a. 3 percent of the population has an IQ score higher than Johnny's.
b. 97 percent of the population has an IQ score higher than Johnny's.
c. 96 percent of the population has an IQ score higher than Johnny's.
d. 3 percent of the population has an IQ score lower than Johnny's.

63. Anna is a fourth-grade student with a disability who is struggling with reading comprehension in her social studies class. Which of the following would be the best option for ensuring that Anna can appropriately access the general education curriculum?

a. Moving Anna to the third-grade social studies class
b. Reteaching the concepts in her special education class
c. Placing a paraprofessional in her social studies class
d. Modifying the content in her social studies class

64. In order for students to make progress on their IEP goals, which of the following makes the most sense when grouping students for a math intervention group?

a. Grouping students based on their ability level
b. Grouping students based on their grade level
c. Grouping students based on their teachers
d. Grouping students based on their maturity level

65. The emotional balance of a classroom can be upset by conflict. Appropriate methods for a teacher to use in handling conflict do not include:

a. Gathering information and re-capping the situation
b. Allowing children to come up with a solution themselves
c. Letting the issue drop once a solution has been agreed upon
d. Dealing with the conflict calmly and with a quiet voice

66. Which of the following is an independent federal agency that makes recommendations to both the President and Congress regarding issues related to disabilities?

a. Federation for Children with Special Needs (FCSN)
b. Center for Personal Assistance Services (CPAS)
c. National Disability Rights Network (NDRN)
d. The National Council on Disability (NCD)

67. What recent legislation has placed additional accountability on schools?

a. No Child Left Behind Act
b. Americans with Disabilities Act
c. Family Education Rights and Privacy Act
d. Human Equity Act

68. What is the *primary* purpose of universal newborn hearing screenings?

a. Educational planning
b. Disability diagnosis
c. Early identification
d. IDEA eligibility

69. When teaching a classroom with students with disabilities, which of the following would be most effective in building self-esteem?

a. Giving them work that does not challenge them
b. Being patient with their learning needs
c. Allowing students to work in groups
d. Using positive nonverbal communication

70. When developing a lesson plan for a small group of students to specifically address IEP goals in writing, which one of the following should be the primary focus of the lesson?

a. Ensuring that the students are accessing their accommodations
b. Ensuring that the students are working on their IEP goals
c. Ensuring that the students have access to the general education curriculum
d. Ensuring that the students have access to an alternate curriculum

71. A classroom teacher has a student with learning disabilities that affect her ability to do math. The teacher consults with the special education teacher and decides she will modify the work the child is given by reducing the number of problems, letting her have extra time to finish, and providing her with a multiplication chart. Which of the following statements on the teacher's actions is accurate?

a. The teacher is giving the student an unfair advantage. Letting her have extra time should be sufficient.
b. The teacher is giving the student an unfair advantage. Providing a multiplication chart should be sufficient. With that, she should get her work done on time.
c. The teacher is making appropriate modifications. Each child is different. In this case, she consulted with the special education teacher and concluded the child needs multiple supports.
d. The teacher is modifying the student's work because it makes it easier on the teacher. There is less to explain and less to grade.

72. Parker is a sixth-grade student who receives special education services as a student with a specific learning disability. Which of the following responsibilities would the special education teacher most likely perform in assisting Parker?

a. Monitoring the progress of his IEP goals
b. Providing mental health support
c. Ensuring he has access to modifications
d. Providing executive functioning interventions

73. Richard is blind, has profound intellectual disabilities, and uses a wheelchair. He displays behaviors of constant head weaving and frequent hand clapping. What are some programs you might recommend for him?

a. Apply soft restraints to his head and hands to minimize or control these behaviors until he gets used to not doing them and stops.
b. Place noise-making objects like rattles, jingle bells, or tambourines in his hands to replace the clapping behavior.
c. Have the doctor examine him for a possible neurological problem that could explain the head weaving.
d. Give him a variety of sensory stimulation using sound, touch, taste, and smell, and do nothing about the head weaving.

74. Courtney is an eighth-grade student with a specific learning disability who is at risk due to her use of drugs and alcohol in her home. Which of the following initial interventions would likely be most beneficial in helping Courtney focus on school?

a. Offering to meet with her and her parents
b. Offering to take her to rehabilitation
c. Offering to refer her to a counselor
d. Offering to keep her secret safe

75. Which of the following is typically not required during the pre-referral process for special education?

a. Parental consent
b. Data
c. Monitoring
d. Strategy discussion

76. Tran is a student who recently arrived in the USA from Vietnam. According to federal regulations mandated by IDEA, which can be done if a learning disability is suspected?

a. Give Tran an IQ test to determine whether he has any specific learning disability.
b. Give Tran a reading evaluation test and a writing evaluation test, both in English.
c. Give Tran special education, depending on tests, with written parental consent.
d. Give Tran a written IEP for a learning disability regardless of the results of tests.

77. Mr. Law wants to facilitate his high school students' ability to expand their vocabulary. He seizes the opportunity when a student comes in perplexed at having seen the word "antidisestablishmentarianism." He asks the class, "What parts of this word have you seen before in other words?" One student volunteers that he recognizes "anti-" from "antibiotic;" another says "Anti-Trust Law." A third student then identifies "dis-" from "disability" and a fourth says "dislike." Most of the class then sees the next parts as "establish" or "establishment." He then asks them if they have seen other words ending in "-ary" and, following their responses, "-ism." What technique is Mr. Law using?

a. Multiple exposures to a word
b. Choosing appropriate words
c. Making a contextual analysis
d. Teaching them word analysis

78. When teaching an eighth-grade class, which one of the following strategies in communicating with parents best promotes a safe classroom environment?

a. Sending home the list of class rules to the parents
b. Getting to know the background and interests of the parents
c. Ensuring that behavior issues are communicated to parents
d. Reporting positive student behavior to the parents

79. Which of the following is not true about the referral process for special education eligibility?

a. Parental consent is required to start the evaluation.
b. The evaluation must be completed in 30 days.
c. The evaluation must be conducted by a multidisciplinary team.
d. The referral may be initiated by a parent.

80. Which of the following statements is most true about adaptations teachers may need to use in testing, teaching, and materials to address the needs of individual students?

a. Some students use communication modes unfamiliar to the teacher
b. Differentiation of instruction is unnecessary between boys and girls
c. Teachers are unlikely to encounter age differences in the same class
d. Students speaking other languages must quickly adapt to using English

81. The development of an IEP is a(n) __________ process.

a. indirect
b. collaborative
c. mathematical
d. single

82. Mr. Price has a multicultural class. Michael's family is Jehovah's Witness, so he abstains from saying the pledge of allegiance. Ellen's family is Christian Scientist, so her parents object to her being sent to the school nurse. Both Mai's family and River's family object to school competitions and do not view students helping one another as cheating. Fatima's family and Nobu's family both believe in a tradition of arranged marriages at early ages for their children. Mr. Price is perplexed. What can he do?

a. Ask the school psychologist to help explain abnormal psychology to him.
b. Ask the school social worker to help him arrange family counseling for his students.
c. Ask the school librarian for sources to educate himself on cultural variations.
d. Ask the school principal to reassign him to a more culturally homogenous class.

83. Clyde is 16 years old, has visual impairment, and reads on a first-grade level. What would be a good choice of materials for his teacher to provide him?

a. Large-print books on subjects relevant to teens
b. Children's books, which have large print and simple text
c. Regular library books with a magnifying glass
d. Large-print books with subjects geared to teens but with simplified text

Refer to the following for question 84:

Bobby is a fifth-grade student who struggles with reading comprehension and writing. For an English unit, students will be reading a story independently and then participating in classroom activities based on the story for the next few weeks.

84. What is an instructional strategy that would be the least effective for Bobby's ability to learn the subject matter?

a. Grouping the students based on their abilities
b. Including hands-on activities
c. Offering choices for learning
d. Using technology

85. Which of the following classroom arrangements would be most appropriate for active teaching and learning?

a. Traditional rows and columns
b. Horseshoe shape
c. Clusters
d. Runway seating

86. David is a fourth-grade student who has been struggling with some of his behaviors. Which of the following frequent behaviors would be most concerning when observing David?

a. Using swear words with peers
b. Bragging to gain attention
c. Telling lies and being dishonest
d. Having disagreements with friends

87. Which of the following is true about learned helplessness and students with disabilities?

a. Students with disabilities typically do not suffer from learned helplessness.
b. Students with disabilities often learn to control situations.
c. Students with disabilities tend to reach out for help before they get to learned helplessness.
d. Students with disabilities often feel like they have no control.

88. Which of the following statements is true of professional development?

a. Professional development is not site-specific, since some principles of teaching are universal.
b. Professional development is about strategies rather than content.
c. Professional development is not necessarily job-embedded, because it is an opportunity to explore other educational roles.
d. Professional development is designed by experts and teachers.

89. Why might it be difficult to incorporate different kinds of activities each day when teaching a class with students of varying disabilities?

a. Some students require structure in their daily routine.
b. Some students may not have the knowledge required for each activity.
c. Some students may not be comfortable working with other students.
d. Some students require specific activities in their IEPs.

90. Jeffrey is an eighth-grade student with a deficiency in reading fluency. Which of the following assistive technology devices would be least appropriate in supporting his needs?

a. Text-to-speech device
b. Speech-to-text device
c. Audiobooks
d. Graphic organizers

91. Jason is a second-grade student with an intellectual disability. Which of the following characteristics would you most expect to impact his educational performance?

a. Significantly subaverage general intellectual functioning
b. Concomitant impairments that cause severe educational needs
c. Disorder in one or more of the basic psychological processes
d. An injury to the brain caused by an external force

92. Which of the following are children born with rubella NOT more likely to have?

a. Deafness
b. Paralysis
c. Blindness
d. Cataracts

93. Which of the following is least likely to be the responsibility of an elementary school special education teacher?

a. Communicating accommodations to general education teachers
b. Managing the schedules of paraprofessionals
c. Team-teach lessons in the classroom setting
d. Facilitation of 504 plans and meetings

94. Ms. Hutchinson is supervising her small class at lunch. Ann, who has Down syndrome, displays some rude behaviors at times. On this day, she deliberately breaks wind at the table, which offends and "grosses out" the others, who complain about it. Ann does not seem concerned and does not apologize. Later, the other students are still upset with her, and Ann does not understand why. In a 1:1 conversation with Ann, Ms. Hutchinson asks her, "What if one of the other students passed gas at the table while you were eating?" Ann looks surprised and then disgusted as she imagines this. "Oh!" she responds, "that would be awful!" "Yes," Ms. Hutchinson agrees, "so now do you see why they were upset when you did it?" "Yes," says Ann, and she apologizes to the others, promising not to do this again. What is the best description of what Ms. Hutchinson did here?

a. She enforced more proper manners by inducing guilt in Ann for her inappropriate behavior.
b. She modeled some more appropriate behavior for Ann by demonstrating a better example.
c. She aided self-awareness, self-control, and self-management by enabling perspective-taking.
d. She increased self-reliance and self-confidence in Ann by treating her as a respected equal.

95. When writing a behavior intervention plan, what is the purpose of preventive strategies?

a. Identifying the behaviors targeted for reduction or increase
b. Finding behaviors that serve the same purpose as the unwanted behaviors
c. Eliminating the triggers or providing access to events
d. Teaching the individual skills needed to use tools

96. An intellectually disabled teen has been offered a job by an elderly neighbor. The neighbor wants the teen to work alongside her in the garden twice a week. They will plant seeds, transplant larger plants, weed, lay mulch, water, and fertilize. Later in the season, they will cut flowers and arrange bouquets, pick produce, and sell them at the neighbor's roadside stand. The neighbor, the teen's mother, and special education teacher meet to discuss the proposal. The plan is:

a. Tentatively accepted. Because the teen is excited about having a job, her mother and teacher reluctantly agree. They both know the girl is likely to lose interest quickly and caution the neighbor that if she truly needs help, she may want to look elsewhere. However, no one wants to disappoint the girl, and all decide the experience will be good for her.
b. Rejected. Despite the teen's insistence she can manage these tasks, her mother and teacher believe she cannot. They fear trying will set her up for failure.
c. Rejected. The teacher and her mother are very uncomfortable with the neighbor's offer. They suspect the elderly woman is simply lonely or may be a predator who has selected an intellectually disabled victim because such children are particularly vulnerable.
d. Enthusiastically accepted. The adults discuss a background check and the possibility the teen might discover gardening is not for her and may want to quit. However, this is most likely to happen early in her employment, giving the neighbor sufficient time to find another helper.

97. Relative to public schools, the basic legal and ethical principles on which both FERPA and the student record Privacy Rule of HIPAA were founded…

a. Are completely unrelated
b. Overlap in some areas
c. Are the same principles
d. Differ in important ways

98. Lee, a student in a residential facility, has severe physical disabilities including cerebral palsy with spastic quadriplegia and severe scoliosis. He is unable to sit up, and due to his scoliosis he cannot lie straight. He is accommodated with a large, very wide, bedlike reclining wheelchair with high wooden sides, which was built by Kim, the occupational therapist. Lee is a very good-natured and cooperative individual who enjoys performing any activity his physical limitations will allow. Gigi, the behavior specialist, needs to give Lee an IQ test. Ordinarily she would take an individual student into her office for private testing. But when they arrive, they discover that Lee's chair is too wide to fit through the doorway. Also, some tasks in the test include marking on paper with a pen and pointing to things on the paper. Lee can grasp a pen put into his hand and can manipulate it. He can also point to things. But the only position possible for Lee is lying on his back, making it difficult for him to mark on the paper. The office area is empty and quiet at this time of day. The school's funds are limited at present, and Kim is the only OT for a large group of students. Tom, the chief of psychological services, is helping Gigi with the logistics of administering the test. He suggests solutions to both of these problems. What does he suggest?

a. Give Lee the test in the classroom with the teacher and other students engaged in many different activities around them, and omit the pointing and marking tasks.
b. Ask Kim to come up with some temporary seating device that is narrow enough to fit through the doorway, with an adaptive paper holder attached to it.
c. Give Lee the test in the hallway outside Gigi's office, and put the papers on a clipboard that Tom will hold above Lee for him to do the marking and pointing items.
d. Come up with a different IQ test that does not include marking and pointing tasks, and administer it in the hall outside the classroom.

99. In the IEP process, which of the following takes place first?

a. Referral
b. Eligibility
c. Identification
d. Development

100. Which assistive technology is most appropriate for a student with a voice disorder that interferes with audible speech production?

a. Speech-to-text computer software
b. Text-to-speech computer software
c. Voice recognition computer software
d. Voice synthesizer computer software

Answer Key and Explanations

1. B: Constructive assertiveness is used when a teacher is able to identify a problem, state his or her concerns in a clear and concise manner, and strive to correct the behaviors as soon as possible. Using these methods, the teacher does not make a direct attack on the student, but rather works with the student to correct problems. However, teachers must be cautious, because assertiveness is a continuum, which can range from hostile to constructive. The words a teacher uses, as well as his or her body language, will send signals to the students and determine their response to the teacher.

2. D: Personal development is not one of the categories or subcategories that are considered when determining students' eligibility for services as a student with a developmental delay. Personal development could potentially fall into one of the other categories, but it is not specific enough to evaluate. When considering the developmental delay category, it is important to look at each of the specific types of development. Answer a is incorrect because fine motor skills are important to consider as part of physical development. Answer b is incorrect because it is important to consider cognitive abilities or intellectual development. Answer c is incorrect because language and speech are also considered to be part of communication development.

3. D: It is the responsibility of the special education case manager to ensure that each student on his or her caseload is accessing accommodations and that general education teachers know how to implement them. Answer A is incorrect because it is not the responsibility of the case manager to make sure students do not fail. Answer B is incorrect because it is also not the responsibility of the case manager to make sure students are attending school. Answer C is incorrect because although the case manager will track the progress of students on their IEP goals, it is not their job to make sure they meet the goal.

4. A: When dealing with able-bodied, strong individuals who are psychotic and who may become very violent, there are techniques that can be used to stop them from injuring or killing care staff. However, these techniques have the potential to easily injure or kill physically disabled individuals who may also be physically fragile. Techniques are adapted for this population to avoid harming either party involved. Therefore option A is correct.

The given information does not reveal whether Mr. Harley's previous training is current or not. He would have been required to update it regularly at his previous job. If he has just changed positions without interruption, his previous training may still be current. This is not the reason for requiring him to take different training. Therefore option B is incorrect.

No law universally mandates that behavior management training be specific to each institution. The individual school or facility's charter or policies would dictate this. If the state government runs the facility, training would be legally required, but its specifics would be stipulated by the facility's bylaws. Therefore option C is incorrect.

Training in techniques to manage maladaptive behavior without harming the parties involved is required in any institution that serves individuals with disabilities. Such training is never merely a formality of new employee orientation but a necessity to prevent injuries. Therefore option D is incorrect.

5. A: An eight-year-old child with profound intellectual disabilities is at a developmental level similar to that of a baby or toddler. As such, he is very busy exploring and learning about his environment by roaming around and interacting with it. Chewing on countertops reflects a baby's tendency to explore objects orally. Piaget would describe this as assimilating other activities into the child's early sucking schema established during nursing. Individuals whose cognitive development has only reached the level of a baby but whose physical development is farther along, and who thus have teeth, often have different results from mouthing objects than do toothless infants or toddlers with few teeth. Developmental level is the most likely reason for Christopher's behavior, so option A is correct.

There is no reason to assume Christopher lacks training. An eight-year-old with a profound level of intellectual disabilities could be receiving excellent training, but considering his level of disability, progress may nevertheless be very slow. Christopher's energy level is high, as evidenced by his activity level. A particular training program might modify his behavior, but it cannot be assumed that what he does is a result of a lack of training. His behaviors are developmentally typical of a younger child, congruent with his cognitive level, so option B is incorrect.

This child has multiple disabilities, but an impulse control disorder is not one of them. At the chronological age of eight years, it is quite normal for a boy to be physically very active. At Christopher's much lower cognitive age, it is normal to explore his environment and to mouth objects. Also, his behaviors do not include any specific symptoms of an impulse control disorder such as screaming, grabbing, hitting, uncontrolled eating/drinking, or other behaviors that could indicate this disorder in a child of his chronological and mental ages, so option C is incorrect.

No information is given about the school environment here. While it is possible Christopher is searching for additional stimulation, it is equally possible that this school is a stimulus-rich environment that motivates him to move around and explore the various stimuli. His high activity level would not necessarily accompany boredom or lack of stimulation. With no information about the environment, it is impossible to assume he does not find it stimulating enough, so option D is incorrect.

6. A: Although functional curriculum can be implemented for students of any age or disability, it is most often taught to students with intellectual disabilities. Functional curriculum focuses on life skills and other daily living skills that students will need after high school. It may be appropriate for certain students to start working on some of these skills as early as the elementary school level. Answer B is incorrect because students with specific learning disabilities likely would not access this curriculum until high school. Answer C is incorrect because students with speech or language impairments are not likely to need this curriculum to supplement their knowledge. Answer D is incorrect because students with developmental delays may or may not access this curriculum later on, but the elementary school age tends to be early for most students.

7. D: Under IDEA, students with disabilities must be educated in the least restrictive environment, meaning they should be placed with nondisabled peers to the maximum extent appropriate. Removing this student from the general education setting for all classes when he only struggles in English violates LRE, because he could remain with his peers for subjects in which he is performing adequately while receiving targeted support for reading and writing.

8. B: Samantha's LD is characterized by (B) spatial perception problems. Spatial perception allows us to orient ourselves in space, tell left from right, judge how far something is, follow directional instructions, etc. Motor coordination deficits (A) cause clumsiness, such as bumping into things or people, when they affect gross motor coordination, and difficulty manipulating small objects, including writing implements, when they affect fine motor coordination. Executive functioning deficits (C) cause difficulties with planning, organizing, managing time, making decisions, solving problems, using self-regulation, and other tasks involving management and coordination of various cognitive processes. Difficulties with sequencing (D) are likely to cause trouble with the correct order of letters in spelling, of numbers in math, and of class notes in general; with prioritizing; with following step-by-step directions; with the structure of readings or lectures; or with relationships of concepts within a hierarchy.

9. B: Assisting the student in seeking support from the online teacher would likely be the most helpful for the student out of the options listed. Students who take online classes often struggle to understand how to seek help or who to contact if they need it. The question notes that the student often has trouble seeking help, so this would be a good first step.

The question also notes that the student struggles with communication in social situations, so face-to-face instruction likely would not be helpful. Option C focuses on assessment instead of instructional access. Option D focuses on administrative responsibility, which would not directly help the student access online instruction.

10. C: Kim and her teacher should not discuss Kim's college applications in the hallway since they would be surrounded by other students, faculty, and staff. This disregards Kim's right to privacy. Therefore, option A is incorrect.

Discussing Kim's college applications in a small group session would expose the conversation to a few other students. This also does not respect her privacy. Therefore, option B is incorrect.

Discussing the subject alone in the teacher's office during a free period would ensure the confidentiality of the conversation. Therefore, option C is correct.

Discussing the subject in the general education classroom is not appropriate. Even though class has not yet begun, there are likely to be many other students already in the room. This would not be respecting Kim's privacy. Therefore, option D is incorrect.

11. A: In order to assess a student for oral expression abilities, a test to measure their expressive language abilities is most appropriate. Students who struggle with oral expression tend to struggle expressing themselves orally due to many factors. This kind of assessment can guide the data collection needed for classroom instruction and skills to work on. Answer B is incorrect because receptive language assessments are more appropriate for students who struggle with language input rather than output. Answer C is incorrect because auditory discrimination tests are used for students who struggle with different sounds. Answer D is incorrect because this kind of assessment would be more appropriate in measuring a student's cognitive abilities.

12. B: The only way to identify a true learning disability with reading would be to test these students in reading both English and their native language. Without ruling out English as a second language being the source of their reading difficulties, it is impossible to assume they all have learning disabilities regardless of language. Therefore, option A is incorrect.

Because these students are all English language learners, it is more likely that this is the true source of their reading difficulties rather than learning disabilities. Therefore, option B is correct.

Since English is a second language for these students, it cannot be assumed that the first or most likely cause of their reading difficulties is a learning disability. Therefore, option C is incorrect.

It is so common for ELLs to perform less well in reading English than native English speakers that it is highly unlikely for reading problems and ESL status to be a complete coincidence with every student in the group. Therefore, option D is incorrect.

13. D: Any child receiving special education must have an IEP. Any IEP should reflect the TEKS as closely as possible. Because they both receive special education, neither child's IEP is separate from the TEKS. Therefore option A is incorrect.

Blindness is only one of many disabilities entitling a student to special education services. Since both receive special education, Susie and Stevie both have some kind of disability. Each IEP is adjusted for that particular student's needs. Stevie's IEP reflects the TEKS as closely as possible, allowing for the fact that print awareness is not an attainable objective for a blind student. Both students' IEPs reflect the TEKS as closely as possible while keeping their individual needs in mind. Therefore option B is incorrect.

Option C implies that any resemblance of the IEP objectives to the TEKS is a coincidence and is only because both cover important basic skills. This is not the case. The IEP objectives should be written to reflect the TEKS. Therefore option C is incorrect.

Both students' IEP objectives have been deliberately written by their educators to reflect the TEKS as closely as possible. Therefore option D is correct.

14. D: A spiraling curriculum involves revisiting key concepts throughout instruction in increasing complexity and depth, building upon previous learning. Reviewing material in the same way as it was initially taught doesn't involve progression. Completing homework in advance does not involve revisiting content with increased complexity. While implementing visual and auditory explanations might be useful, it is not an example of spiraling curriculum.

15. D: Although all of these choices may benefit Corey to a certain extent, providing one-to-one intervention in reading fluency is most likely to improve his reading fluency. One-to-one instruction allows Corey to move at his own pace and move on to the next skill when he has mastered the previous skill. This allows the teacher to truly meet Corey's needs in reading fluency and give him complete attention during the intervention time. Answer A is incorrect because a student with a severe deficiency in reading fluency likely needs additional intervention outside the classroom. Answer B is incorrect because a small group would not allow Corey to work at his own pace and provide the individual instruction that he may need. Answer C is incorrect because modifying the material will not allow Corey to build his reading fluency skills.

16. A: Although all of these choices may have their own benefits in helping students feel welcome, community building is likely the best long-term strategy in ensuring that the students feel supported. When students have opportunities to get to know each other and the teacher, they will be more likely to feel welcome and needed. If students do not feel welcome in the class, they may not feel safe and may start to distance themselves from the rest of the class. Answer B is incorrect because if there is too much room to negotiate, the students will not clearly understand the rules. Answer C is incorrect because although posting work in the room can make some students feel welcome and important, other students may be embarrassed. Answer D is incorrect because although it is important to establish authority, it is also important that the students feel like they are involved in the process as well.

17. C: A strategy for diagnosing learning disabilities in which a student with an academic delay receives research-supported interventions to correct the delay. If the interventions do not result in considerable academic improvement, the failure to respond suggests causal learning disabilities.

18. A: It is a requirement to hold a manifestation determination meeting whenever students with disabilities are suspended for 10 or more consecutive days. These meetings are also required if the student is suspended for 10 nonconsecutive days if the suspensions happened for similar reasons.

This is to ensure that the student is not being disciplined simply because they have a disability. If the behavior is not a manifestation of the student's disability, then they will receive the same punishment as any other general education students. Answer b is incorrect because these students can be suspended for more than 10 days if it is not a manifestation of their disability. Answer c is incorrect because discipline may be different depending on the manifestation results. Answer d is incorrect because services can still be provided to students who get expelled from school.

19. C: Recommending that Tina not wear the helmet would result in endangering her, which would be irresponsible. Therefore option A is incorrect.

To recommend that another person constantly accompany Tina rather than have her wear a helmet would be impractical or impossible. It would also be more restrictive. Wearing a helmet may look unusual, but it affords Tina more independence than would having a constant companion, even if this could be arranged. Therefore option B is incorrect.

Educating general education teachers and other school and community personnel about why Tina wears a helmet would clear up their misconceptions. Additionally, asking them to relay what they have learned to others would further dispel ignorance and discrimination. Therefore option C is correct. (Note: We are assuming here that this would be done using ethical practices for confidential communication.)

If Tina has the ability, it is a good idea for her to know how to explain to others, if she chooses, why she wears a helmet. However, telling her that it is her sole responsibility is an unfair burden. She is only one student dealing with the entire school and community. Since teachers and other personnel assist students with disabilities as needed, she can benefit from their assistance in this regard. Therefore option D is incorrect.

20. D: Suggest to Alfie that if he is disturbed by Honesty's teasing, he might have a calm, assertive conversation with her in which he tells her he doesn't like it and insist she stop. By encouraging Alfie to act on his own, it shows him he has primary responsibility for taking care of himself. By offering social strategies, he learns a set of skills that will serve him throughout life. If Honesty continues to tease him, he can ask a teacher to step in, but doing so without his invitation is inappropriate.

21. A: Embodied learning allows students to participate in activities that get the whole body involved. It allows students to move while still learning the content. Many students struggle to sit and learn all day, so this kind of instruction allows them to get up and move. It is important to provide a variety of learning activities in order to meet the needs of all of the students in the class. Answer B is incorrect because inquiry-based learning involves having students ask questions in order to learn. Answer C is incorrect because blended learning involves a combination of online and traditional learning. Answer D is incorrect because service learning typically involves students going out into the community to learn.

22. A: Whichever professional is best able to explain what the student's test results imply for the student's education should interpret those results for the IEP team members. Which professional varies: it could be the student's special education teacher, who will be an IEP team member (A); it could be the school psychologist, who may or may not be on the student's IEP team (C); or it could be another professional who is not on the IEP team (D), because being a member of the IEP team is not required for this function. The important factor is the ability to relate assessment results to educational planning and programming that will address needs and strengths identified in those results.

23. D: If the IEP meeting is already scripted, it does not provide each of the stakeholders with an opportunity to provide input and share their side of the story. Answer A is incorrect because facilitated meetings are a great way to make everyone feel included and have a say. Answer B is incorrect because a slide show presentation can be more entertaining than simply reading from the IEP. Answer C is incorrect because a student-led meeting heavily includes the student and allows him or her to truly be the center of the meeting.

24. D: Advising a more restrictive placement is a step backward. Greg is young, and since his father approves his current placement, he should be allowed as much independence as possible. Therefore option A is incorrect.

Counseling Greg's father to accept the injury is irresponsible. Though it is true that accidents do happen in life, in this case Greg's disabilities include a poor sense of balance. Thus the odds of his falling are greater than those of a person with a normal sense of balance, and some precautions should be taken. Therefore option B is incorrect.

In this kind of placement it has already been determined that Greg is capable of taking a shower without group home staff directly supervising him. They were following his IEP objectives for personal care, so an investigation is unnecessary and inappropriate since they were not negligent. Therefore option C is incorrect.

It is part of the teacher's role to collaborate with community personnel in implementing Greg's IEP. Suggesting to the residential services program running Greg's group home that they install non-slip material on the tub floor and grab bars on the walls is a good idea. As he has showered many times before without falling, with these safeguards in place Greg could continue to shower independently, but with less risk of slipping and falling again. This would be safer for Greg's wellbeing and would also probably relieve a lot of his father's anxiety. Therefore option D is correct.

25. D: According to the Family Educational Rights and Privacy Act, parents have the right to access testing protocols that are used to evaluate students for special education services. These protocols are considered educational records and part of the student's file. Because of this, the Family Educational Rights and Privacy Act requires that school personnel make these available to parents upon request. Answer a is incorrect because only teachers and staff that work directly with the student have access to that student's IEP. Answer b is incorrect because parents have the right to review and inspect previous IEPs that they may not have copies of. Answer c is incorrect because once an IEP from a prior year is finalized and becomes part of the student's educational record, it cannot be amended. Only the current IEP may be amended through appropriate procedures.

26. B: Modern society demands greater literacy today than in the past. For example, as cited by Dr. Rebecca C. Faulkner, the Air Force manual for repairing fighter planes was seven pages long in World War II and 7,000 pages long in 2008. The same literacy skills in students do not apply across all subjects (A) because different literacy skills are needed for different content areas. Literacy required of school pupils also does not stay constant across grades (C) because literacy requirements advance along with each advance in grade level. Finally, literacy is not best taught in schools as a separate lesson (D) because that would be insufficient; in order to meet the changing demands of society, literacy must be taught and incorporated throughout the school day.

27. C: Offering the corner workspace to reward good behavior, such as active participation in class, is the best way to use a corner workspace. Teachers should be very consistent with implementation of incentives, as reinforcement can backfire if a reward is used incorrectly. Chad usually requires active involvement from the teacher to stay on task, so giving Chad extra space to do work is not likely to be a successful solution. It is important to have a consistent plan for the corner to only be used when Chad is finished with his assignments for the day. Since Chad likely perceives the corner workspace as a reward, it is not a good idea to use it when Chad is disruptive, as it may help to reinforce disruptive behaviors. Similarly, Chad should not be allowed to use the corner whenever he thinks he needs a break, as Chad may try to take advantage of the incentive to avoid doing work.

28. C: The most likely diagnosis is autism. Autistic children are typically very withdrawn, avoid eye contact, and are not responsive to verbal or physical attempts to connect. Some autistic children fall into repetitive behaviors that are very difficult to arrest or prevent. These behaviors include rocking, spinning and handshaking.

29. C: Immediately refer him to the counselor. The boy is exhibiting serious emotional distress suggesting either abuse or neglect at home or elsewhere. While his behavior may seem manipulative, the fact that the boy is unreachable once he's in the highly charged emotional state in which he repeats, "I hate myself" suggests emotional trauma. The fact the child is socialized with peers, playing with them when invited and not taking rejection personally, suggests his emotional distress may be caused by an adult who has convinced him he is unworthy. A trained counselor is the best choice.

30. D: Researchers have found that students with arithmetic disabilities (d) have working memory deficits specifically for processing numerical information only. They have not found that these students (a) have the same general working memory deficits as students with reading disabilities. Students with RDs seem to have such general deficits in working memory which affect their processing of both language and numbers, while students with arithmetic disabilities have not been found to (b) have specific deficits in working memory for processing both numbers and language. They were found to have neither general nor specific WM deficits for both areas, but specific WM deficits for numbers only. These specific deficits in numerical processing were for working memory (c).

31. B: Although individualized instruction is helpful for many students, including students with a disability such as ADHD, it is the least effective of those listed for targeting the specific educational needs of students with ADHD. Many students with ADHD will simply need support in the classroom or in a separate setting that reduces opportunities for distraction. Strategies such as small-group instruction or separation from the rest of the class are more restrictive than the other options, so they should only be used when the IEP determines they are necessary. Instead, a teacher should seek to provide support within the student's primary class if possible. Answer A is incorrect because extra think time can allow students to collect their thoughts before they speak. Answer C is incorrect because settings with fewer distractions allow these students to concentrate. Answer D is incorrect because providing a model to demonstrate can allow the student to see how something is done before doing it.

32. A: Inclusion programs allow students to stay in a regular classroom for all or most of the day. This promotes diversity in the classroom and gives all students equal educational opportunities. Typically, students with special needs and their parents will meet with school staff to develop an Individualized Education Plan, which outlines issues, goals (both long-term and short-term), objectives, and rewards. The student will then be monitored in the regular classroom and be assessed on a regular basis. If necessary, the student's IEP will be revised to reflect progress and new goals.

33. A: The present levels of academic achievement determine the current academic and social functioning in the academic environment. The present levels are crucial in establishing the foundation for the rest of the IEP based on how the student is currently functioning. This may include progress on goals, strengths, needs, and how the student is performing with regard to grades and other scores. Answer b is incorrect because the accommodations are typically determined in the accommodations section of the IEP. Answer c is incorrect because the disability category is determined before the IEP is written. Answer d is incorrect because the present levels section does not compare a student to peers and instead states how the student is currently performing.

34. B: Although there are many benefits to using curriculum-based assessments (CBAs), they do not always correlate perfectly to the classroom curriculum. Curriculum-based assessments are designed to monitor the progress of student understanding throughout instructional units to help quickly adjust instruction to meet student needs. CBAs are commonly used in conjunction with IEPs as a means of ensuring students with learning disabilities are making progress toward their particular goals. CBAs do not comprehensively measure curriculum mastery, but only serve as samples of student comprehension. Answer A is incorrect because curriculum-based assessments can measure the progress of students over a short period of time such as one week. Answer C is incorrect because a teacher's instruction can be informed based on the needs of the student and what they may need to work on. Answer D is incorrect because students can chart their scores and work toward improving them.

35. D: Environmental factors that lead to positive development include the influences from the outside world that shape who we are or who we become. Having intelligent parents is a biological factor that may shape who we are. Answers A, B, and C are incorrect because each of these involve environmental factors and influences that come from the outside world. Although they may each have a positive impact, they would be considered environmental factors.

36. C: Bruce responds well to de-escalation and rarely becomes violent with early intervention. Physical restraint would thus be an entirely inappropriate form of early intervention, so option A is incorrect.

Mechanical restraint is even more restrictive than physical restraint. Since Bruce responds well to de-escalation techniques, mechanical (or any) restraint is not indicated as an early intervention, and option B is incorrect.

Verbal de-escalation is a way of reducing tension early in the behavior—before it becomes violent—without resorting to physical means. This would be most appropriate given the information on Bruce's behavior, so option C is correct.

Bruce's behavior assessment shows that his behavior is not attention-seeking. Extinction, or planned ignoring, addresses behaviors that seek attention. Without attention, such behaviors eventually stop, as they are not producing the desired effect. Since Bruce's behavior is not attention-seeking and may become violent if ignored, ignoring would likely be both ineffective and dangerous in his case, so option D is incorrect.

37. C: The Individuals with Disabilities Act of 2004 established the child find process in order to identify students with disabilities starting from an early age. This process required schools to locate and evaluate students suspected of having a disability, no matter how severe or impactful it may be. This legislation was important in establishing a process to identify these students and provide the support they may need access to. Answer a is incorrect because the Education for All Handicapped Children Act of 1975 ensured that services were provided to students who already had disabilities. Answer b is incorrect because the Individuals with Disabilities Act of 1990 was implemented to provide the same opportunities for students with disabilities as those without. Answer d is incorrect because the Elementary and Secondary Act of 2001 was implemented to close student achievement gaps for all students.

38. C: Positive behavioral interventions are more effective by teaching a more appropriate behavior to replace the problem behavior. Because all behaviors have some function, a problem behavior cannot simply be eliminated; some other behavior will arise to fulfill the same purpose. Interventions to control problem behaviors (A) or to suppress them (B) are not considered positive. These tend not to be maintained over time or generalized to other situations as there is no positive replacement for the undesirable behavior. It is not the interventions that analyze the behavior (D), but the prior analysis on which the subsequent intervention is based.

39. C: Although some of these choices may be true in certain situations, parents of students with disabilities will typically see some of the signs before the child is evaluated at school. The parents likely spend a good deal of time with these children, so they are aware of what they can and can't do. They may not know for certain whether or not a student has a disability, but they can determine what they struggle with at home. Answer A is incorrect because families of children with disabilities are more likely to experience issues than they are to come together. Answer B is incorrect because parents are not the cause of the learning disability and also cannot be the cure. Answer D is incorrect because while some families do often seek out information to learn more about disabilities, this is not as consistently seen as families suspecting a disability is present in a child before the school does.

40. A: A behavior intervention plan is required to be updated at least once a year at the annual IEP meeting. Although there is no timeframe for when the behavior intervention plan must be implemented other than the annual IEP meeting, it is important to monitor. When students exhibit new behaviors or change behavior patterns, it might be time to make an update. Other students may not need updates more than once per year. Each student has different needs, and it is vital that each member of the team takes part in monitoring the student and their plan.

41. A: Adaptive skills are skills that people use every day in order to function at home, school, or work. There are many skills in caring for oneself and accessing the community that are important to practice and complete in order to demonstrate understanding. When teaching these skills, it is important to provide opportunities to practice these tasks to determine what students have mastered and what skills need additional work. Answer B is incorrect because although improving reading ability is important, it would not likely help students in learning everyday skills to function. It is more of an academic skill. Answer C is incorrect because learning about organization is not typically a skill that is practiced in isolation when considering adaptive skills. Answer D is incorrect because although basic math skills are also important skills, they would not be the most effective skill to teach when working on a student's adaptive skills.

42. A: An IQ score one or more standard deviations below the mean, or a score of 85 or lower, is a criterion used in the definition by Heber of the American Association on Mental Deficiency (American Association on Intellectual disabilities) in 1961. Definitions widely used prior to 1961 did not include this criterion. Therefore option A is correct.

Social incompetence was included as one of six criteria for the definition of intellectual disabilities by Edgar A. Doll in 1941. (Doll developed the Vineland Social Maturity Scale, now the Vineland Adaptive Behavior Scales.) Therefore option B is incorrect.

Impaired adaptive behavior was cited in 1937 by Tredgold of Great Britain: "...the individual is incapable of adapting himself to the normal environment..." Therefore option C is incorrect.

Being essentially incurable is another one of Doll's 1941 six criteria for the definition of intellectual disabilities. Therefore option D is incorrect.

43. B: James M. Baldwin used the term "mental deficiency" in 1901. In 1937, Tredgold referred to "a state of incomplete mental development," so option A is incorrect.

The criterion that intellectual disabilities originate during the developmental period, defined as from birth to age 16, was used by Heber for the AAMD's 1961 definition. It does not appear in earlier definitions, so option B is correct.

The association of intellectual disabilities with impaired adaptive behavior appears as early as 1937. In Tredgold's definition, he states "...that the individual is incapable of adapting himself to the normal environment of his fellows..." Therefore, option C is incorrect.

Contrary to Heber's 1961 AAMD definition, which states that intellectual disabilities originate in the developmental period, or Grossman's 1973 AAMD definition, which extends the developmental period to age 18, Edgar A. Doll's 1941 definition includes as one of his six criteria that intellectual disabilities "obtains at maturity." Therefore, option D is incorrect.

44. B: The COACH model (Giangreco, Cloninger and Iverson, 1998) is a collaborative approach described by educational researchers as student-directed planning, which they claim goes "beyond person-centered planning" (Wehmeyer et al, 2002) by making the student central in the process. Person-centered planning typically centers more on family and social support systems. GAP (Turnbull & Turnbull, 2002) (A); MAPs (Pearpoint, Forest, & O'Brien, 1996) (C); and PATH (D), which extends the MAPs process to develop "a more definitive plan of action," are all examples of person-centered planning.

45. A: The IDEA annual reports to Congress consistently show that specific learning disability is the most common disability. The 2024 46th Annual Report to Congress illustrates that the second most common disability was speech or language impairment, followed by other health impairment.

46. B: Although all of these choices may be involved in the MTSS process in some capacity, it is most likely that the special education teacher discusses which students may need to be evaluated for special education services. The MTSS process is designed to provide general education support for students who may be struggling academically, socially, or emotionally. The special education teacher is typically involved in this process to provide input on students who may not be responding appropriately to these interventions and need to be evaluated for special education services. Answer A is incorrect because the MTSS process is not typically designed to provide support for students who are already identified as having disabilities. Answer C is incorrect because the special education teacher typically is not the individual responsible for providing these general education interventions. Answer D is incorrect because although it may be possible that students who exit special education are discussed through the MTSS process, it is more often designed for students who have yet to be evaluated.

47. B: The standard score in an assessment is used to give the student a numbered score in order to compare that number to the average. Many tests will consider 100 to be the average standard score based on the results of the assessments. Students will then be given standard scores that are compared to that average score. Answer A is incorrect because the standard deviation typically determines how spread out the numbers are. Answer C is incorrect because comparing the rank of the score to other students is considered the percentile rank. Answer D is incorrect because the hypothetical range of scores is considered the confidence interval.

48. D: Being a ward of the State Department of Family Services, Bobby should have an IFSP written for him but will also need an IEP to provide training and learning objectives. Therefore option A is incorrect.

Bobby needs an IEP for his daily school attendance and training in his new group home placement. But he should also have an IFSP since his parents have not been his legal guardians since he was born and Family Services is responsible for his care. Therefore option B is incorrect.

It does not depend on which state Bobby lives in. By law, no matter what state he lives in, he should have an IFSP as well as an IEP. Therefore option C is incorrect.

Bobby needs an IFSP because Family Services is responsible for him rather than his parents, and he needs an IEP to provide for his educational and training needs. Therefore option D is correct.

49. D: All students can benefit from movement activities as a method of stimulating their brain, so incorporating this strategy for all students would be the most beneficial. Although it may not always be possible each class period, finding creative ways to get Zachary up and moving with the rest of the class will make him feel less singled out. It is important to develop a plan for when these movement breaks are needed for students like Zachary and how they can be implemented for the entire class. Answer A is incorrect because Zachary may take advantage of the pass system and use it more than he really needs to. Answer B is incorrect because giving him a timer also might become a distraction to Zachary and other students around him. Answer C is incorrect because giving a student his own area might end up making him feel singled out.

50. D: Alternate assessments must be based on grade-level standards for students. Alternate assessments are created for students who are unable to participate in general assessments with accommodations. Answer A is incorrect because most students who receive special education services take the general assessment. Answer B is incorrect because although many students who take the alternate test do not receive a high school diploma, this is not always the case. Answer C is incorrect because the decision about alternate testing is typically up to the IEP team based on the needs of the student.

51. B: Although there are many pros and cons to co-teaching, one of the advantages is that both teachers are familiar with the content and can plan together. When special education teachers are supporting the general education classroom teachers, they do not have this opportunity. This can cause special education teachers to be lost and supporting students in content they are not familiar with or experts in. Answer A is incorrect because special education teachers will likely still have the same amount of time to plan either way. Answer C is incorrect because special education teachers have the opportunity to differentiate instruction in either one of these models. Answer D is incorrect because collaborating with classroom teachers should be used in every method when assisting students with disabilities.

52. C: Developmental delays typically do not include tests that would determine a student eligible for a specific learning disability. Although these developmental assessments are beneficial in determining what a student may struggle with, it is difficult to determine the academic skills of children at such a young age. Specific learning disabilities typically manifest as students have had more instruction in reading, writing, and math. Answer A is incorrect because the developmental delay category is common for preschool students who are struggling in certain developmental areas. Answer B is incorrect because speech or language impairments are also common with preschool students. Answer D is incorrect because students with a diagnosis of autism are often identified in the autism spectrum disorder category as a preschooler.

53. A: By law, a major review of the IEP is required every year (A). In 2004, an IDEA pilot study attempted to save on paperwork and administrative duties and some participating states allowed for reviews once every three years. However, it is standard fare for an annual IEP review meeting to review a student's services and needs and assess the student's progress toward their goals. As a student's social, behavioral, familial, or health-related factors change, an IEP may be necessary to address changes in services or needs. Other aspects of a student's eligibility may follow different cycle times, such as eligibility criteria, which may need to be reviewed once every three years, depending on state law.

54. D: Children at the age of four will no longer just point to the objects that they want in most cases. These children are able to communicate verbally and ask for what they want with words. If a child is still pointing to objects that he or she wants instead of using age-appropriate verbal communication at the age of four, this may indicate some kind of developmental delay. Answer A is incorrect because making up words and stories is considered typical development. Answer B is incorrect because drawing pictures of objects that they see is common with four-year-olds. Answer C is incorrect because pretending is also an activity that comes with the development of a child who is four years old.

55. C: Since Joseph has never walked the route alone, he would get lost if sent out on his own now. Therefore, option A is incorrect.

Sending Joseph out with written directions is not a good idea since he does not have good reading skills. He would likely get lost if he went out alone without prior practice in finding his way. A teacher shadowing him would have to catch up with him to redirect him when he went the wrong way or stopped when he did not know which way to go. Therefore, option B is incorrect.

Since Joseph is used to walking the route with his mother, it would be better to accompany him at first. Doing so would provide a point from which to transition gradually to walking alone. Unlike his mother, the teacher will be prompting him to verbalize the route. Since his expressive language skills are better than his reading skills, this is a more effective modality to help him learn the directions. Therefore, option C is correct.

Gradually decreasing the days his mother goes with him, such as by having her go four days and having him go alone one day, then having her go three days and having him go alone two days, is not a good idea. Joseph's mother has never taught him the route, so he does not know the directions and cannot find his way independently. Since he has always relied on his mother, he would get lost the first time he tried to go on his own. Therefore, option D is incorrect.

56. B: Although all of these choices can be helpful in ensuring that inclusion programs are successful, collaboration between teachers can best help students with disabilities access the general education curriculum. This collaboration can allow teachers to develop lesson plans and strategies to promote student growth. Without this collaboration, students with disabilities may not be as successful in their classes as they otherwise could have been. Answer a is incorrect because just meeting with the administrators may or may not change the inclusion programs at the school. Answer c is incorrect because although new assessments can help to measure growth, these may not always ensure successful inclusion. Answer d is incorrect because professional development in itself likely will not improve the inclusion model.

57. C: Although all of these choices may be appropriate for certain students, researching the high school offerings would be considered the most appropriate in supporting the immediate transition into high school. Answer A is incorrect because while career exploration is valuable, this would not aid in the immediate transition into high school. Answer B is incorrect because researching colleges is less immediately relevant when transitioning into high school. Answer D is incorrect because although independent skills may be important, researching high school class offerings would be more immediately relevant as a transition activity for eighth grade students.

58. A: Generalization of learning is the ability to apply learning across multiple and varied contexts or settings. Regular practice and periodic testing (B) are designed to promote maintenance rather than generalization. Learning one step at a time (C) is a characteristic of task analysis, which breaks complex skills or tasks down into more achievable steps and is related to promoting skill acquisition rather than generalization. Practicing a new skill before applying it to real-life situations (D) is a way to promote both acquisition and maintenance of the skill before its application and generalization.

59. D: While teacher collaboration is a recommended co-teaching practice, effective collaboration requires clearly defined, shared learning objectives. Without this, instruction could become inconsistent and support is less targeted. Both teachers need to be aligned in instructional strategies to increase the chances of student success. Answer A is incorrect because both teachers teaching as a team can be a great way to reach every student in the class. Answer B is incorrect because station teaching can be beneficial in that each teacher can teach to their strengths. Answer C is incorrect because it can be beneficial for one teacher to teach their area of specialty while the other teacher supports the students who are struggling.

60. B: Although all of these choices would be helpful in preparing these students for adulthood, money management skills would be most likely to translate into life after high school. Students will need to be able to manage money throughout their entire lives. It is important to give them the tools to be successful in navigating specific scenarios in which they will need to manage their money. Answer a is incorrect because simply including a goal will not automatically prepare a student for adulthood. Answer c is incorrect because not all students are eligible for transition services after high school. Answer d is incorrect because although applying for jobs is important, managing money is something that adults do on a daily basis.

61. D: In teaching across the curriculum, one lesson plan incorporates many subjects taught but is not so generic as to apply to any subject (A). For example, a spreadsheet that uses visually beautiful graphic design incorporates math and art. Teaching across the curriculum does facilitate career planning (B) because it shows students different ways that subjects learned in school apply to real life (C), including job choices.

62. A: Johnny's IQ score places him in the gifted range. His rank is in the 97th percentile. This means that only 3 percent (the remainder of 100 percent minus 97 percent) of the population has a higher score than Johnny's. Therefore choice A is correct.

Johnny's score is at or above the scores of 97 percent of the population, not above only 96 percent. Only 3 percent, not 97 percent, of the population scored higher than Johnny. Therefore, choices B and C are incorrect.

The percentage of the population with an IQ score lower than or equal to Johnny's is 97 percent, not 3 percent. 3 percent of the population has a score higher than Johnny's, not lower. Therefore choice D is incorrect.

63. D: Out of the options given, modifying the content can help the most with her reading comprehension struggles. Modifying the content to include less reading or fewer questions she has to answer still allows her to learn most, if not all, of what her peers learn. It is important to understand how to provide support in a way that students can still learn what their general education peers are learning whenever possible. Answer A is incorrect because it may alienate Anna to move her down a grade level. Answer B is incorrect because although reteaching concepts may be beneficial, her time with the special education teacher's time may be better spent working on her reading comprehension abilities. Answer C is incorrect because a paraprofessional likely would not be as beneficial as modifying the curriculum.

64. A: Although all of these choices certainly play a factor in how to group students, in order for them to make progress on their IEP goals it is best that they are grouped by ability level. Each student will have different IEP goals and progress toward those goals, so it is important to place students in groups that will allow for this progress. It may be difficult for students to make progress on these goals if they are in small groups in which they are not working at an appropriate instructional level. Answer B is incorrect because grouping students on their grade level may not help them make progress on their IEP goals because students might be at various levels. Answer C is incorrect because simply grouping students based on their teachers also may involve grouping students at various ability levels. Answer D is incorrect because although grouping students based on maturity level might be important, some students with different maturity levels function at different academic levels.

65. C: There should be follow-up to the conflict resolution to make certain that the children are sticking to their agreed-upon solution and to ensure that the conflict does not re-occur. Some teachers might feel that dropping the issue will help everyone forget the conflict, but that usually is not the case. Conflicts are best handled with calmness and a quiet voice as the teacher gathers information about the conflict in order to get a complete and fair picture of the situation. Then the teacher should review the conflict with the children and ask for their ideas for ways the problem could have been prevented and ways to solve the conflict. Involving the children in the resolution of the problem teaches them self-regulation and respect for themselves and others.

66. D: The National Council on Disability is an independent federal agency that makes recommendations to the President and Congress regarding issues related to disabilities. The FCSN (A) is an organization founded in Boston, Massachusetts that informs, helps, and supports parents of children with disabilities, involved professionals, and communities. The CPAS (B), formed by the University of California, San Francisco (UCSF) through a grant from the National Institute on Disability and Rehabilitation Research (NIDRR), supplies research, dissemination, training, and technical help with personal assistance services concerns nationwide. The NRDN (C) represents the needs of its members in Protection and Advocacy (P&A) before federal agencies and Congress, but is not itself a federal agency and does not make recommendations to the president.

67. A: The No Child Left Behind Act, signed in 2001, was created to place additional accountability on schools and school districts for the education of today's children. Additionally, this legislation decreased the restrictions on schools' use of federal funding and placed particular emphasis on reading and math. Schools and teachers nationwide were challenged and encouraged to use innovative teaching activities and methods in order to reach all students. This legislation also required schools and school districts to submit progress reports on an annual basis for inclusion in national education databases.

68. C: The primary purpose of universal newborn hearing screenings is early identification of hearing loss, which affords early intervention. Professional organizations such as ASHA advocate universal screening because not all infants are screened even though hearing loss is the most common congenital disability. Educational planning (A) is a purpose of later educational testing of a child, not of newborn hearing screening. Disability diagnosis (B) requires a complete audiological evaluation defining type, degree, and configuration of hearing loss instead of just a screening, because that only identifies presence or absence of hearing loss. Eligibility for special education services under the IDEA (D) is a purpose of later, comprehensive assessments of preschool- and school-aged students, not infants.

69. B: Although all of these choices may help in building a student's confidence, being patient and sticking with them can be valuable. Students with disabilities will often struggle with self-esteem and need someone to believe in them and that they can do it. Being patient with them and their needs allows them to make progress at their own pace without any pressure. Answer a is incorrect because if the material is too easy for students, they might not give their best effort. Answer c is incorrect because although working in groups can support confidence and social belonging when structured well, it is not universally successful and not the single most effective strategy given. Answer d is incorrect because although positive nonverbal communication can support a positive classroom environment, it is less impactful than patience.

70. B: When working with students in small-group pull-outs, it is important that the instruction is targeted to their IEP goals. Although each student may have a different goal, the teacher must plan the lesson in a way that fits in parts of each student's goal. Students may or may not have access to the special education teacher throughout the day, so it is vital to monitor and develop these goals when working with students in small groups. Answer A is incorrect because although it is important for students to access their accommodations, they would likely access these in the general education setting. Answer C is not the best answer because, in this particular small-group setting, the most important focus is intensive instruction on students' IEP writing goals; however, these goals and lessons should still be aligned with the general education curriculum so that students can make progress in it. Answer D is incorrect because students do not need to access an alternate curriculum to work on IEP goals.

71. C: The teacher is making appropriate modifications. Each child is different. In this case, she has consulted with the special education teacher and concluded the child needs multiple supports.

72. A: Although all of these choices may be the responsibility for students like Parker some of the time, monitoring the progress of his goals will always be the responsibility of the special education teacher. Students with learning disabilities will have academic goals that require the special education teacher to monitor them frequently. It is important for the special education teacher to monitor the goals of students to ensure that progress is being made and decide if new interventions need to be put into place. Answer b is incorrect because providing mental health support is not likely to be the responsibility of the special education teacher. Answer c is incorrect because students with learning disabilities do not always have modifications due to the impact of their disability. Answer d is incorrect because students learn learning disabilities may or may not need to access executive functioning support.

73. D: Restraints should not be used except in extreme cases to prevent injury to oneself or others. Richard's behaviors do not harm anybody. Research shows that restraining movements does not eventually stop them. Therefore, option A is incorrect.

Noise-making instruments would provide auditory stimuli for Richard but would be disruptive to others. Additionally, this option would only serve as a replacement for the self-stimulatory behavior and would not serve to further enrich his learning environment. Therefore, option B is incorrect.

Head weaving is common in blind individuals. It is often a means of getting sensory feedback in the absence of visual stimuli and can also provide proprioceptive and kinesthetic orientation. Regardless, Richard will have a neurological assessment as part of his physician's examination, but there is no special indication to look for problems on account of head weaving. This behavior can be normal in some blind individuals. Therefore, option C is incorrect.

Because he is blind and has profound intellectual disabilities, a program of sensory stimulation using his other senses would benefit Richard as it would enrich his environment and enhance his learning ability. A need for additional sensory stimulation may also be indicated by Richard's hand clapping. Therefore, option D is correct.

74. C: Students can be at risk for many reasons, and drug and alcohol abuse can be one of them. It is important to seek out help for these students while also providing them support at the same time. These kinds of issues must be reported in order to get the students the help they need because of the impact it has on their life and the future. By working with a counselor to address her substance use and related stressors, Courtney will be able to focus better on her schoolwork. Answer A is not the best first step because the teacher should begin by referring Courtney to the school counselor or other support staff, who are trained to assess risk and coordinate appropriate service, including parent involvement when appropriate. Answer B is incorrect because taking her to a rehabilitation facility may be overstepping the boundaries of a teacher. Answer D is incorrect because students who have reported or are suspected of using drugs and alcohol must be reported in order to get them the help they need.

75. A: During the pre-referral process, parents are not typically required to give their consent. This process typically consists of identifying areas in which the student struggles and developing strategies to assist this student. This may consist of interventions inside or outside of the classroom in addition to accommodations or modifications. Answer B is incorrect because it is important to collect data to determine whether a student is making sufficient progress. Answer C is incorrect because monitoring is important, as it determines whether or not new strategies need to be implemented to better meet student needs. Answer D is incorrect because constantly evaluating the strategies and discussing them as a team is a necessary component of the pre-referral process in meeting student needs.

76. C: An IQ test alone cannot be given because no one test can be used to identify a disability. All areas of any suspected disability must be evaluated. Therefore option A is incorrect.

IDEA 2004 stipulates that tests must be given in the child's native language, that such tests measure a disability rather than limited English language skills, and that they not discriminate on a racial or cultural basis. A reading test and writing test, both in English, would violate these rules. Therefore option B is incorrect.

Following evaluation, if a learning disability is identified, the school can only give Tran special education services with the written permission of his parents. Therefore option C is correct.

The school cannot write an IEP for Tran regardless of his test results. IDEA specifies that, to benefit from the educational program, he must be found to have a specific learning disability as well as a need for special education services. Following Tran's evaluation, a multidisciplinary team meeting should be held, which would include Tran's parents and whose objective is to develop an IEP. Therefore option D is incorrect.

77. D: In this example, Mr. Law is teaching his students word analysis by showing them how to break a complex word down into its prefixes, root words, and suffixes. Knowing these facilitates deducing the meaning of a word by knowing the meanings of each or some of the word's parts. Multiple exposures (A) would involve his presenting this same word to the class in repeated instances and a variety of contexts. Choosing appropriate words (B) would involve his making deliberate word choices that are congruent with his subject and level of instruction. Making a contextual analysis (C) would involve his asking the students to deduce the meaning of a word by finding clues in the sentence and/or the paragraph surrounding it.

78. C: Although all of these choices can help in making sure the classroom is a safe environment, reporting student behavior to the parents immediately can be most effective. When students misbehave, this must be communicated to the parents so further action can potentially be taken. If it is not reported home, students may continue with these poor behaviors and put other students at risk. Answer A is incorrect because simply sending home the class rules may not work for every parent and they may not always keep track of them. Answer B is incorrect because although getting to know the background of the parents might be helpful, this may not benefit the safety of the class. Answer D is incorrect because only reporting the positive behavior can help to build a safe classroom, but it is more important to report negative behavior that might be a safety concern.

79. B: Special education evaluations are required to be completed within 60 days or parent consent, not 30. Districts are required to comply with the 60-day limit in order to determine eligibility for special education services. It is important to understand that although the evaluation needs to consider all of the needs of the student and be in-depth, it must also occur in a timely manner. Answer a is incorrect because parental consent is required before the evaluation process can begin. Answer c is incorrect because a multidisciplinary team, including special services providers, special education teachers, general education teachers, parents, and the student, must be involved. Answer d is incorrect because a parent can request that their child be evaluated for special education services.

80. A: Teachers will not always know a student's preferred communication mode. For example, deaf students often use sign language rather than speech. This is also true of learning modalities, such as blind students reading in Braille. Many teachers do not know either of these systems, but must be able to provide adaptations to meet these students' special needs. They can procure Braille texts without learning Braille, and they can obtain live, online, or video sign language interpreters without learning sign language. Teachers may also need to differentiate instruction based on gender because learning is not always the same for boys as it is for girls (B). Teachers are likely, especially with disability and diversity populations, to encounter age differences in one class (C). Learning English is not the sole responsibility of students (D) because many ESL/ELL programs and methods are available to teachers.

81. B: The creation of an Individualized Education Plan (IEP) is a collaborative process, in that it involves classroom and special education teachers, family members, the student (if appropriate) and other interested parties who collaborate in the student's best interests.

82. C: Mr. Price's students and their families are not displaying psychological aberrations. They come from various cultures and are displaying different beliefs, traditions, and values. Therefore option A is incorrect.

Mr. Price's students and their families are not displaying dysfunctional family dynamics. They are following their own cultural traditions, beliefs, and values. Therefore option B is incorrect.

Mr. Price has students coming from diverse cultural backgrounds with which he has little or no prior experience. The librarian can suggest various research resources whereby Mr. Price can educate himself regarding these families' different practices and beliefs. Therefore option C is correct.

Since Mr. Price has a multicultural class, it is possible that in his school there may not be any other classes with more homogenous demographics. The entire school's population might be similarly diverse. In that case it would not be possible to reassign him. In addition, rather than Mr. Price avoiding the entire situation, educating himself about his students' diverse cultures would add to his knowledge, make him more versatile as a teacher, enable him to meet his students' needs better, and ultimately benefit both Mr. Price and his students. Therefore option D is incorrect.

83. D: Large-print books are a good idea for Clyde's visual impairment and subjects relevant to teens are appropriate for his age, but not for his first-grade reading level. Therefore, option A is incorrect.

Children's books have the large print and simple subject matter Clyde needs but are not appropriate to his age. Therefore, option B is incorrect.

With the availability of large-print textbooks, a magnifying glass is not the easiest way for Clyde to read. Having one would certainly expand the types of media he could see, and it would be beneficial for him to have it if he should want or need to see the small print in everyday media like newspapers and phone books. But for reading, it would not be as easy on his eyes as large print. Also, many books with regular size print will be beyond Clyde's first-grade level of reading comprehension. Therefore, option C is incorrect.

Books in large print and on teen-related topics but with simplified text are the ideal combination for Clyde's visual impairment, age, and reading comprehension level. Therefore, option D is correct.

84. A: Although grouping the students based on their abilities may be the easiest method to teach, it will likely single some students out. It could also make it more difficult for the students to learn if they are all struggling with the content. Answer B is incorrect because having more hands-on learning activities could make it easier for Bobby to learn. Answer C is incorrect because having choices and including each student in the selection process will likely make them more eager to learn. Answer D is incorrect because the use of technology, such as computers, may make the learning easier and more effective.

85. C: Although all of these arrangements may have their benefits for certain students, clusters easily allow students and teachers to work together and move from group to group. Active teaching and learning is a beneficial strategy in that the students get to move around and work with different students. This cluster arrangement allows this movement for all students, including those with disabilities who may need to be accessed quickly and easily. Answer a is incorrect because traditional rows and columns tend to be more teacher-centered and do not allow for much movement throughout the room. Answer b is incorrect because although the horseshoe shape can provide space for the teacher to move, it doesn't provide as much freedom for the students. Answer d is incorrect because runway seating tends to be beneficial for teacher movement, but the students wouldn't be able to move as much.

86. C: Students in fourth grade typically do not display frequent and consistent lying and dishonesty patterns. Although there may be some small lies from time to time, it is concerning if this becomes a pattern for a child of this age. It is important to recognize these kinds of patterns when observing students in order to determine the cause and potentially seek help if necessary. Answer A is incorrect because fourth graders may start to experiment with swear words. Answer B is incorrect because bragging is also considered a normal behavior for a fourth-grade student who is seeking attention. Answer D is incorrect because having disagreements is something that would be considered typical for a fourth grader.

87. D: Students with disabilities often suffer from learned helplessness, or a condition in which they feel like they have no control. These students will often give up because they think that nothing can be done to improve their condition. This is something that impacts individuals with disabilities as they are learning about themselves and what they are able to accomplish. Answer A is incorrect because students with disabilities will often suffer from learned helplessness. Answer B is incorrect because these students with learned helplessness have a difficult time controlling situations. Answer C is incorrect because students with disabilities do not always have the chance to reach out for help before they get to learned helplessness.

88. D: Professional development is not a trickle-down process but rather a collaboration of experts and teachers sharing research and experience. Answer A is not true because, although some principles of teaching are universal, a priority of professional development is to help the teachers where they are in order to help with site-specific needs. Answer B is not true because, although some professional development might be about classroom strategies, other types of professional development are definitely aimed at improving content knowledge. Answer C is not true because, like Answer A, although teachers should be aware of other opportunities in the field of education, a priority of professional development is to help the teacher with the job at hand.

89. A: Although it is typically thought of as a good teaching practice to incorporate different kinds of activities in a lesson, some students struggle with this change. Students with autism or ADHD may have a harder time adjusting to their daily routine being adjusted. Incorporating some elements of the same activity every day might be best for some students' needs. Answer B is incorrect because even if students do not all have the knowledge that is required, the activity might be designed to give them that knowledge. Answer C is incorrect because it is best practice to monitor which students can work together and which students cannot. Answer D is incorrect because though it is important to implement the activities a student can complete according to their IEP, a variety of activities should still be offered so that each student can still feel included in the class.

90. B: Speech-to-text devices are typically designed for students who struggle with writing rather than reading fluency. These speech-to-text devices are valuable in allowing students to speak what they might be thinking, and that is transferred into text. It is important to understand which technology is valuable and works for each student based on their individual needs and interests. Answer A is incorrect because text-to-speech devices can be beneficial in assisting students that may struggle to read the text without making mistakes. Answer C is incorrect because audiobooks provide students like Jeffrey a way to access the text without having to read it. Answer D is incorrect because graphic organizers can be beneficial in organizing the story for students who may struggle to put together what they have read.

91. A: A student with an intellectual disability will have a significantly subaverage general intellectual functioning. This will typically be combined with deficits in adaptive behavior and will be manifested during the developmental period. This is something that likely would be noticed in Jason starting from an early age. Answer B is incorrect because a concomitant, or accompanying, disability would fall under the category of multiple disabilities. Answer C is incorrect because a disorder in basic psychological processes would fall under a specific learning disability. Answer D is incorrect because an injury to the brain by an outside force would be in the "traumatic brain injury" category.

92. B: Children with congenital rubella, or who are exposed in utero to maternal rubella, are NOT more likely to suffer paralysis. Rubella (German measles) causes birth defects related to the sensory systems of vision and hearing. Babies exposed to rubella are more likely to suffer from deafness (A), blindness (C), and/or cataracts (D) of the eyes, which interfere with normal vision.

93. D: Although special education teachers have a variety of roles and responsibilities, facilitating 504 plans is not typically one of them. These plans are often administered by the school counselors or building administrators. Although it is possible that special education teachers are involved in this process in some capacity, it is typically not the expectation. Answer A is incorrect because communicating student accommodations to general education teachers is a crucial responsibility of the special education teacher. Answer B is incorrect because the special education teacher is typically responsible for assisting in developing the schedule for paraprofessionals. Answer C is incorrect because team-teaching lessons with general education teachers is also often a responsibility in ensuring the instruction is differentiated.

94. C: Ms. Hutchinson's technique was not accusatory or scolding. It would not likely induce guilt in someone as unrepentant as Ann. She asked a question that got Ann to consider others' points of view, so option A is incorrect.

Ms. Hutchinson did not model any behavior for Ann. She did not demonstrate anything to provide an example. She simply asked her two questions, so option B is incorrect.

By asking Ann how she would feel if another student had done to her what she did, Ms. Hutchinson helped her overcome her egocentric thinking. Due to her intellectual disabilities, Ann thinks on a concrete operational level, and it will frequently not occur to her on her own to consider another's perspective. She does have the ability to do this, though, with some help. Via this dialogue, Ms. Hutchinson got Ann to realize how the other students felt, so option C is correct.

Though Ms. Hutchinson did treat Ann with respect in this interaction and spoke to her as an equal, self-reliance and self-confidence were not issues that needed to be addressed in this case. Ann's rude behavior at the table did not show a lack of self-confidence. It definitely showed a lack of self-management, and it showed a lack of self-awareness in the sense of not appreciating the impact of her actions on others, so option D is incorrect.

95. C: Preventive strategies typically include what will be done in order to free students from the items or events that typically cause these behaviors. These may include removing a student from distractions or allowing them to run around the gym if they need it. These strategies can be used to help alleviate some of the behaviors once the triggers are determined. Answer A is incorrect because identifying the behaviors typically belongs in the "description of behavior" section of the plan. Answer B is incorrect because behaviors that serve a similar purpose as the unwanted behavior are called replacement behaviors. Answer D is incorrect because teaching the individual skills is considered the teaching strategies.

96. D: Enthusiastically accepted. The adults discuss a background check and the possibility the teen might discover gardening is not for her and may want to quit. However, this is most likely to occur early in her employment, giving the neighbor sufficient time to find another helper. The teacher is pleased because the girl will learn new skills through modeling and repetition. The mother is pleased because the experience will add to the girl's self-esteem as well as show her that she is capable of learning. The elderly neighbor is pleased because she is both compassionate and truly needs help. The girl is delighted the neighbor recognizes her potential and sees her as valuable.

97. C: The Family Education Rights and Privacy Act (FERPA) and the Privacy Rule for student health records of the Health Insurance Portability and Accountability Act (HIPAA) are founded on the same basic legal and ethical principles. FERPA is designed to protect confidential information in students' school records pertaining to education, and HIPAA is designed to protect any confidential health information that is individually identifiable, including student health records in public schools or in any schools covered by FERPA.

98. C: Giving an IQ test in the midst of a busy, noisy classroom would be distracting to Lee, interfering with his ability to give his best responses. It would also violate confidentiality by giving him no privacy during testing. Omitting the marking and pointing items would leave out valuable test results because, despite being a student with many physical limitations, Lee has the ability to do these things. It would also eliminate an opportunity for him to experience success. Therefore option A is incorrect.

Asking Kim to make an alternative seating device is not feasible. She has already built the only kind of device that, because of the severe twisting of his spine, Lee can lie on. . Anything narrower would cause him pain, injure him, or simply be impossible. Even if such a device were not impossible or harmful, the school's limited funding would prohibit it being made. And with Kim being the only OT for many students, the extra work would be an unfair, impractical, and unnecessary burden. Therefore option B is incorrect.

The office area is empty and quiet at the time, so using the hallway outside Gigi's office is a suitable alternative. The test would still be private and extra time would not be used up transporting Lee to another location. Tom's idea to hold the paper on a clipboard involves no building or spending and is a simple and effective solution. Therefore option C is correct.

Finding a different IQ test is unnecessary in this case. Removing tasks Lee can perform gives him less chance to enjoy success. The hall outside the classroom, unlike the office hallway, is noisy. With students inside the classroom, Lee has no privacy during testing. Therefore option D is incorrect.

99. A: After a student is referred to special education services by a teacher, parent, social services, or others, assessments are conducted to identify (C) the student as having a disability or not and, if so, to diagnose the specific disability and establish performance baselines for planning interventions and for comparison in evaluating progress. After identification, the IEP team uses assessment results to determine the student's eligibility (B) for special education and for which specific services. Then the team develops (D) the IEP.

100. D: Computer software with a voice synthesizer produces a digital voice for those who cannot speak. Most of the time, a student who needs this type of assistance will have a device called an augmentative and alternative communication (AAC) device that contains the software and hardware needed to run a voice synthesizer for real-time communications. This differs from text-to-speech software in that AACs contain special programming that allow the user to quickly string together words for real-time communication. Text-to-speech software requires typing and accessible enough to function in real communication for most people. Speech-to-text software (A) allows a person to speak into a computer microphone and the program produces typed text of the spoken language. This helps those who can speak but cannot write or type. Text-to-speech software (B) also produces a synthesized voice to read text, but these programs typically scan the text and read it aloud to assist those with visual impairments and reading difficulties, not to supply a substitute speaking voice. Voice recognition software (C) also transcribes spoken language into typed text, similar to the closed-captioning feature on televisions.

How to Overcome Test Anxiety

Just the thought of taking a test is enough to make most people a little nervous. A test is an important event that can have a long-term impact on your future, so it's important to take it seriously and it's natural to feel anxious about performing well. But just because anxiety is normal, that doesn't mean that it's helpful in test taking, or that you should simply accept it as part of your life. Anxiety can have a variety of effects. These effects can be mild, like making you feel slightly nervous, or severe, like blocking your ability to focus or remember even a simple detail.

If you experience test anxiety—whether severe or mild—it's important to know how to beat it. To discover this, first you need to understand what causes test anxiety.

Causes of Test Anxiety

While we often think of anxiety as an uncontrollable emotional state, it can actually be caused by simple, practical things. One of the most common causes of test anxiety is that a person does not feel adequately prepared for their test. This feeling can be the result of many different issues such as poor study habits or lack of organization, but the most common culprit is time management. Starting to study too late, failing to organize your study time to cover all of the material, or being distracted while you study will mean that you're not well prepared for the test. This may lead to cramming the night before, which will cause you to be physically and mentally exhausted for the test. Poor time management also contributes to feelings of stress, fear, and hopelessness as you realize you are not well prepared but don't know what to do about it.

Other times, test anxiety is not related to your preparation for the test but comes from unresolved fear. This may be a past failure on a test, or poor performance on tests in general. It may come from comparing yourself to others who seem to be performing better or from the stress of living up to expectations. Anxiety may be driven by fears of the future—how failure on this test would affect your educational and career goals. These fears are often completely irrational, but they can still negatively impact your test performance.

Elements of Test Anxiety

As mentioned earlier, test anxiety is considered to be an emotional state, but it has physical and mental components as well. Sometimes you may not even realize that you are suffering from test anxiety until you notice the physical symptoms. These can include trembling hands, rapid heartbeat, sweating, nausea, and tense muscles. Extreme anxiety may lead to fainting or vomiting. Obviously, any of these symptoms can have a negative impact on testing. It is important to recognize them as soon as they begin to occur so that you can address the problem before it damages your performance.

The mental components of test anxiety include trouble focusing and inability to remember learned information. During a test, your mind is on high alert, which can help you recall information and stay focused for an extended period of time. However, anxiety interferes with your mind's natural processes, causing you to blank out, even on the questions you know well. The strain of testing during anxiety makes it difficult to stay focused, especially on a test that may take several hours. Extreme anxiety can take a huge mental toll, making it difficult not only to recall test information but even to understand the test questions or pull your thoughts together.

Effects of Test Anxiety

Test anxiety is like a disease—if left untreated, it will get progressively worse. Anxiety leads to poor performance, and this reinforces the feelings of fear and failure, which in turn lead to poor performances on subsequent tests. It can grow from a mild nervousness to a crippling condition. If allowed to progress, test anxiety can have a big impact on your schooling, and consequently on your future.

Test anxiety can spread to other parts of your life. Anxiety on tests can become anxiety in any stressful situation, and blanking on a test can turn into panicking in a job situation. But fortunately, you don't have to let anxiety rule your testing and determine your grades. There are a number of relatively simple steps you can take to move past anxiety and function normally on a test and in the rest of life.

Physical Steps for Beating Test Anxiety

While test anxiety is a serious problem, the good news is that it can be overcome. It doesn't have to control your ability to think and remember information. While it may take time, you can begin taking steps today to beat anxiety.

Just as your first hint that you may be struggling with anxiety comes from the physical symptoms, the first step to treating it is also physical. Rest is crucial for having a clear, strong mind. If you are tired, it is much easier to give in to anxiety. But if you establish good sleep habits, your body and mind will be ready to perform optimally, without the strain of exhaustion. Additionally, sleeping well helps you to retain information better, so you're more likely to recall the answers when you see the test questions.

Getting good sleep means more than going to bed on time. It's important to allow your brain time to relax. Take study breaks from time to time so it doesn't get overworked, and don't study right before bed. Take time to rest your mind before trying to rest your body, or you may find it difficult to fall asleep.

Along with sleep, other aspects of physical health are important in preparing for a test. Good nutrition is vital for good brain function. Sugary foods and drinks may give a burst of energy but this burst is followed by a crash, both physically and emotionally. Instead, fuel your body with protein and vitamin-rich foods.

Also, drink plenty of water. Dehydration can lead to headaches and exhaustion, especially if your brain is already under stress from the rigors of the test. Particularly if your test is a long one, drink water during the breaks. And if possible, take an energy-boosting snack to eat between sections.

Along with sleep and diet, a third important part of physical health is exercise. Maintaining a steady workout schedule is helpful, but even taking 5-minute study breaks to walk can help get your blood pumping faster and clear your head. Exercise also releases endorphins, which contribute to a positive feeling and can help combat test anxiety.

When you nurture your physical health, you are also contributing to your mental health. If your body is healthy, your mind is much more likely to be healthy as well. So take time to rest, nourish your body with healthy food and water, and get moving as much as possible. Taking these physical steps will make you stronger and more able to take the mental steps necessary to overcome test anxiety.

Mental Steps for Beating Test Anxiety

Working on the mental side of test anxiety can be more challenging, but as with the physical side, there are clear steps you can take to overcome it. As mentioned earlier, test anxiety often stems from lack of preparation, so the obvious solution is to prepare for the test. Effective studying may be the most important weapon you have for beating test anxiety, but you can and should employ several other mental tools to combat fear.

First, boost your confidence by reminding yourself of past success—tests or projects that you aced. If you're putting as much effort into preparing for this test as you did for those, there's no reason you should expect to fail here. Work hard to prepare; then trust your preparation.

Second, surround yourself with encouraging people. It can be helpful to find a study group, but be sure that the people you're around will encourage a positive attitude. If you spend time with others who are anxious or cynical, this will only contribute to your own anxiety. Look for others who are motivated to study hard from a desire to succeed, not from a fear of failure.

Third, reward yourself. A test is physically and mentally tiring, even without anxiety, and it can be helpful to have something to look forward to. Plan an activity following the test, regardless of the outcome, such as going to a movie or getting ice cream.

When you are taking the test, if you find yourself beginning to feel anxious, remind yourself that you know the material. Visualize successfully completing the test. Then take a few deep, relaxing breaths and return to it. Work through the questions carefully but with confidence, knowing that you are capable of succeeding.

Developing a healthy mental approach to test taking will also aid in other areas of life. Test anxiety affects more than just the actual test—it can be damaging to your mental health and even contribute to depression. It's important to beat test anxiety before it becomes a problem for more than testing.

Study Strategy

Being prepared for the test is necessary to combat anxiety, but what does being prepared look like? You may study for hours on end and still not feel prepared. What you need is a strategy for test prep. The next few pages outline our recommended steps to help you plan out and conquer the challenge of preparation.

Step 1: Scope Out the Test

Learn everything you can about the format (multiple choice, essay, etc.) and what will be on the test. Gather any study materials, course outlines, or sample exams that may be available. Not only will this help you to prepare, but knowing what to expect can help to alleviate test anxiety.

Step 2: Map Out the Material

Look through the textbook or study guide and make note of how many chapters or sections it has. Then divide these over the time you have. For example, if a book has 15 chapters and you have five days to study, you need to cover three chapters each day. Even better, if you have the time, leave an extra day at the end for overall review after you have gone through the material in depth.

If time is limited, you may need to prioritize the material. Look through it and make note of which sections you think you already have a good grasp on, and which need review. While you are studying, skim quickly through the familiar sections and take more time on the challenging parts.

Write out your plan so you don't get lost as you go. Having a written plan also helps you feel more in control of the study, so anxiety is less likely to arise from feeling overwhelmed at the amount to cover.

Step 3: Gather Your Tools

Decide what study method works best for you. Do you prefer to highlight in the book as you study and then go back over the highlighted portions? Or do you type out notes of the important information? Or is it helpful to make flashcards that you can carry with you? Assemble the pens, index cards, highlighters, post-it notes, and any other materials you may need so you won't be distracted by getting up to find things while you study.

If you're having a hard time retaining the information or organizing your notes, experiment with different methods. For example, try color-coding by subject with colored pens, highlighters, or post-it notes. If you learn better by hearing, try recording yourself reading your notes so you can listen while in the car, working out, or simply sitting at your desk. Ask a friend to quiz you from your flashcards, or try teaching someone the material to solidify it in your mind.

Step 4: Create Your Environment

It's important to avoid distractions while you study. This includes both the obvious distractions like visitors and the subtle distractions like an uncomfortable chair (or a too-comfortable couch that makes you want to fall asleep). Set up the best study environment possible: good lighting and a comfortable work area. If background music helps you focus, you may want to turn it on, but otherwise keep the room quiet. If you are using a computer to take notes, be sure you don't have any other windows open, especially applications like social media, games, or anything else that could distract you. Silence your phone and turn off notifications. Be sure to keep water close by so you stay hydrated while you study (but avoid unhealthy drinks and snacks).

Also, take into account the best time of day to study. Are you freshest first thing in the morning? Try to set aside some time then to work through the material. Is your mind clearer in the afternoon or evening? Schedule your study session then. Another method is to study at the same time of day that you will take the test, so that your brain gets used to working on the material at that time and will be ready to focus at test time.

Step 5: Study!

Once you have done all the study preparation, it's time to settle into the actual studying. Sit down, take a few moments to settle your mind so you can focus, and begin to follow your study plan. Don't give in to distractions or let yourself procrastinate. This is your time to prepare so you'll be ready to fearlessly approach the test. Make the most of the time and stay focused.

Of course, you don't want to burn out. If you study too long you may find that you're not retaining the information very well. Take regular study breaks. For example, taking five minutes out of every hour to walk briskly, breathing deeply and swinging your arms, can help your mind stay fresh.

As you get to the end of each chapter or section, it's a good idea to do a quick review. Remind yourself of what you learned and work on any difficult parts. When you feel that you've mastered the material, move on to the next part. At the end of your study session, briefly skim through your notes again.

But while review is helpful, cramming last minute is NOT. If at all possible, work ahead so that you won't need to fit all your study into the last day. Cramming overloads your brain with more information than it can process and retain, and your tired mind may struggle to recall even previously learned information when it is overwhelmed with last-minute study. Also, the urgent nature of cramming and the stress placed on your brain contribute to anxiety. You'll be more likely to go to the test feeling unprepared and having trouble thinking clearly.

So don't cram, and don't stay up late before the test, even just to review your notes at a leisurely pace. Your brain needs rest more than it needs to go over the information again. In fact, plan to finish your studies by noon or early afternoon the day before the test. Give your brain the rest of the day to relax or focus on other things, and get a good night's sleep. Then you will be fresh for the test and better able to recall what you've studied.

Step 6: Take a Practice Test

Many courses offer sample tests, either online or in the study materials. This is an excellent resource to check whether you have mastered the material, as well as to prepare for the test format and environment.

Check the test format ahead of time: the number of questions, the type (multiple choice, free response, etc.), and the time limit. Then create a plan for working through them. For example, if you have 30 minutes to take a 60-question test, your limit is 30 seconds per question. Spend less time on the questions you know well so that you can take more time on the difficult ones.

If you have time to take several practice tests, take the first one open book, with no time limit. Work through the questions at your own pace and make sure you fully understand them. Gradually work up to taking a test under test conditions: sit at a desk with all study materials put away and set a timer. Pace yourself to make sure you finish the test with time to spare and go back to check your answers if you have time.

After each test, check your answers. On the questions you missed, be sure you understand why you missed them. Did you misread the question (tests can use tricky wording)? Did you forget the information? Or was it something you hadn't learned? Go back and study any shaky areas that the practice tests reveal.

Taking these tests not only helps with your grade, but also aids in combating test anxiety. If you're already used to the test conditions, you're less likely to worry about it, and working through tests until you're scoring well gives you a confidence boost. Go through the practice tests until you feel comfortable, and then you can go into the test knowing that you're ready for it.

Test Tips

On test day, you should be confident, knowing that you've prepared well and are ready to answer the questions. But aside from preparation, there are several test day strategies you can employ to maximize your performance.

First, as stated before, get a good night's sleep the night before the test (and for several nights before that, if possible). Go into the test with a fresh, alert mind rather than staying up late to study.

Try not to change too much about your normal routine on the day of the test. It's important to eat a nutritious breakfast, but if you normally don't eat breakfast at all, consider eating just a protein bar. If you're a coffee drinker, go ahead and have your normal coffee. Just make sure you time it so that the caffeine doesn't wear off right in the middle of your test. Avoid sugary beverages, and drink enough water to stay hydrated but not so much that you need a restroom break 10 minutes into the test. If your test isn't first thing in the morning, consider going for a walk or doing a light workout before the test to get your blood flowing.

Allow yourself enough time to get ready, and leave for the test with plenty of time to spare so you won't have the anxiety of scrambling to arrive in time. Another reason to be early is to select a good seat. It's helpful to sit away from doors and windows, which can be distracting. Find a good seat, get out your supplies, and settle your mind before the test begins.

When the test begins, start by going over the instructions carefully, even if you already know what to expect. Make sure you avoid any careless mistakes by following the directions.

Then begin working through the questions, pacing yourself as you've practiced. If you're not sure on an answer, don't spend too much time on it, and don't let it shake your confidence. Either skip it and come back later, or eliminate as many wrong answers as possible and guess among the remaining ones. Don't dwell on these questions as you continue—put them out of your mind and focus on what lies ahead.

Be sure to read all of the answer choices, even if you're sure the first one is the right answer. Sometimes you'll find a better one if you keep reading. But don't second-guess yourself if you do immediately know the answer. Your gut instinct is usually right. Don't let test anxiety rob you of the information you know.

If you have time at the end of the test (and if the test format allows), go back and review your answers. Be cautious about changing any, since your first instinct tends to be correct, but make sure you didn't misread any of the questions or accidentally mark the wrong answer choice. Look over any you skipped and make an educated guess.

At the end, leave the test feeling confident. You've done your best, so don't waste time worrying about your performance or wishing you could change anything. Instead, celebrate the successful completion of this test. And finally, use this test to learn how to deal with anxiety even better next time.

Review Video: Test Anxiety
Visit mometrix.com/academy and enter code: 100340

Important Qualification

Not all anxiety is created equal. If your test anxiety is causing major issues in your life beyond the classroom or testing center, or if you are experiencing troubling physical symptoms related to your anxiety, it may be a sign of a serious physiological or psychological condition. If this sounds like your situation, we strongly encourage you to seek professional help.

Online Resources

Due to our efforts to try to keep this book to a manageable length, we've created a link that will give you access to all of your online resources:

mometrix.com/resources719/texesspedsupp

It's Your Moment, Let's Celebrate It!

Share your story @mometrixtestpreparation